the Book of
Psychic Knowledge

By the same author

HOW TO DOUBLE YOUR VOCABULARY (SECOND EDITION)
THOUGHTS OF THE IMITATION OF CHRIST
IN DEFENSE OF GHOSTS
PREMONITIONS: A LEAP INTO THE FUTURE

the Book of Psychic Knowledge
ALL YOUR QUESTIONS ANSWERED

HERBERT B. GREENHOUSE

Taplinger Publishing Company / New York

First published in the United States in 1973 by
TAPLINGER PUBLISHING CO., INC.
New York, New York

Published simultaneously in the Dominion of Canada by
Burns & MacEachern, Ltd., Toronto

Library of Congress Catalog Card Number: 72-6613

ISBN 0-8008-0932-7

To the Parapsychologists,
who have earned their credentials
as scientists

The information in this book has been culled from
the literature—old and new—of psychic phenomena, from
professional papers and journals, from popular
magazines, from experiments in parapsychology laboratories,
and from experiences told to the author by psychics
and others.

Special thanks are due *Psychic* magazine for much
interesting and up-to-date material in the psychic field,
and to the American Society for Psychical Research and
the Parapsychology Foundation for the use of their
libraries.

Contents

lost objects, and missing people; how the divining rod
solves crimes, diagnoses illnesses, locates enemy mines
in wartime, finds breaks in pipes, etc. . . .

the "familiar"; the sabbat and esbat, black and white
magic, the coven, the magic circle; other customs of
witches and warlocks . . .

the Book of
Psychic Knowledge

1 YOUR QUESTIONS ANSWERED ABOUT TELEPATHY AND CLAIRVOYANCE (ESP); WHEN, HOW, WHY, AND TO WHOM ESP HAPPENS; THE DIFFERENCE BETWEEN "SPONTANEOUS" AND LABORATORY ESP; TECHNIQUES IN ESP TESTING; THE DIFFERENCE BETWEEN MEN AND WOMEN IN ESP . . .

What is telepathy?

Psychic awareness—without communication through sight, hearing, and other sensory channels—of what is going on in someone else's mind.

What is clairvoyance?

Mentally "seeing" or having psychic knowledge of events and objects that are out of range of the senses.

What is ESP?

Extrasensory perception, a term coined by Dr. J. B. Rhine of the Parapsychology Laboratory at Duke University. ESP includes telepathy, clairvoyance, and precognition (sensing future events psychically in dreams, visions, hunches, etc. See Chapter 3).

What is parapsychology?

The scientific study of psychic phenomena.

What is "psi"?

A term used by parapsychologists to cover all psychic experiences, but particularly ESP and psychokinesis (mind over matter—see Chapter 4).

Who are the "percipient" and the "agent" in an ESP experience?

The percipient "sees" objects and events clairvoyantly or telepathically picks up the thoughts in the mind of the agent.

In a laboratory ESP test the percipient is also called the "subject" and the agent is the "sender."

What is "spontaneous" telepathy or clairvoyance?

Most ESP experiences are spontaneous, that is, they come unexpectedly while the percipients are going about their usual routine. Laboratory ESP, on the other hand, is induced under controlled conditions.

What state of mind brings on spontaneous ESP?

The percipient is generally relaxed or in a "dissociated" state, somewhat out of touch with his environment. He may be daydreaming, sleeping, in a trance, etc. Writer-psychic Rosalind Heywood speaks of "a more or less inactive brain." Sometimes, however, psychic experience comes when the percipient is in a state of expanded consciousness or hyperawareness. (See Chapter 6 for questions and answers about altered states of consciousness.)

What is the motivation for a telepathic exchange?

The agent is often in trouble or emotionally aroused and communicates this feeling to the percipient. In a celebrated case a child walking home from school suddenly had a vision of her mother lying on the floor in her bedroom, apparently dead. The child immediately ran for the doctor, who hurried to her home and found her mother on the floor with a heart attack. He arrived just in time to save her. All telepathic exchanges are not as dramatic, and sometimes the agent's feeling may be only mild in tone, but there is usually a sympathetic bond between sender and receiver.

What is the relationship between agent and percipient?

Spontaneous ESP occurs most often between members of the same family, lovers, friends, or persons working closely together on the same project. This is also true of laboratory experiments. Thelma Moss, a parapsychologist at the University of California at Los Angeles, believes that for a successful ESP experiment, subject and sender should be intimately related—the subject in a relaxed state and the agent in a highly charged emotional state which increases the electrical activity in his body and may speed up psychic communication.

Do sweethearts send each other mental messages?

Next to mothers and children, lovers probably have the most telepathic rapport. In one test, however, an engaged couple showed no ESP. The man tried mentally to make the girl push the right button on a console. She didn't respond, but this might have been a good test of the love relationship or of psychological factors, such as which of the partners was dominant. Other sweetheart combinations have fared much better in ESP experiments.

Is the telepathic signal sent and received at the same time?

Not always. There may be a "latency" period between the sending and the receiving. What probably happens in such cases is that the percipient holds the message in his or her subconscious until there is a need for it to break into consciousness.

Who starts the telepathic exchange, agent or percipient?

It would seem that the sender does, particularly in laboratory tests when he takes a consciously active role. In recent years, however, a new theory suggests that the generating force in spontaneous cases (and perhaps in the laboratory) sometimes comes from the other direction. In her book *The Infinite Hive* Rosalind Heywood speculates that "a person who is emotionally drawn to another might all the time be 'scanning' . . . for him or her subconsciously." In such cases, instead of the sender beaming the thought or emotion to the percipient, the latter is constantly tuned into the sender with his subliminal radio and actively picks up the telepathic thought rather than passively receives it. Another theory suggests that when there is a close relationship between two persons, neither actively sends nor passively receives the telepathic signal but they share a psychic field in which it arises.

What is a telepathic "impression"?

In "impression" or "intuition" cases there is less extrasensory imagery and more feeling involved. For example, the agent may be ill or in danger some distance away from the percipient, usually a friend or relative. Instead of catching the thought in the mind of the agent or having a mental vision, the percipient reacts with a change of mood, a fit of depression without always knowing the cause, or an urgent need to break off what he is doing and go back home or wherever the friend or loved one is in trouble.

Does the agent always consciously send a thought or impression?

He does in laboratory experiments, since that is the purpose of the experiment, but less often in spontaneous cases. His need to send a message may generate a telepathic signal without his conscious knowledge. In many cases of telepathic impressions, neither agent nor percipient may be aware that a message has been sent or received.

What famous clairvoyant "watched" a fire raging 300 miles away?

Emanuel Swedenborg, a Swedish scientist and mystic of the eighteenth century, was visiting in the city of Goteborg when a vision came to him of Stockholm in flames. He "watched" the city burning for three hours, then sighed with relief and said that the fire had stopped only a few doors from his home. A messenger from Stockholm later verified all the details of Swedenborg's vision.

Does ESP ever come as voices or sounds?

This is known as "clairaudience." The sounds may seem to originate from the outside or may be heard in the mental ear, but their actual source is often out of hearing range. In one case a boy on an ocean trip had fallen into the water and was in danger of drowning. He called out to his mother, who was at home in England, thousands of miles away. When he returned to England, she said she had heard him call her when he was in the water, and she thought he was coming down the street.

Does ESP ever come in the form of pain or a physical blow?

Yes. In one famous case a woman was awakened by a hard blow in the mouth. At that very moment her husband, out sailing, was struck in the mouth by the tiller of his boat as it swung in a gust of wind. In another case a woman felt labor pains at the time her daughter had a premature baby, although it was five weeks before the baby was expected. Psychiatrist Carl Jung tells about waking up one night with the sensation of a blow at the back of his head. The next day he heard that a patient of his had shot himself in the head that night.

Has ESP ever come as a taste sensation?

Every kind of physical sensation can be experienced through ESP. In one experiment a hypnotist placed different foods in his mouth, while his hypnotized subject in the next room correctly identified each substance.

Have there been ESP experiences involving more than one sense?

Yes. In 1913 the British ship *Volturno* caught fire in the Atlantic Ocean. During a séance in London the members of the group all "saw" the burning ship, "heard" several explosions, "smelled" the charred wood and burning flesh, and "felt" cold gusts of air sweep into the room. It was almost a total clairvoyant experience.

Are there cases of collective telepathy or clairvoyance?

Quite a few. The *Volturno* case mentioned above is one. In another, eight members of a New York family were seized with a feeling of anguish at the very moment their son and brother was dying in an automobile accident in Michigan.

Are most ESP experiences pleasurable or unpleasant?

Mostly unpleasant. Danger, accidents, mental or physical pain are more dramatic than their opposites and seem to make a greater impression on both the conscious and subliminal mind. Psychic distress signals are sent out and received most often when ordinary channels are not open.

Are there "trivial" communications?

Many, although they may be ignored or forgotten sooner than the unpleasant experiences. An example is going to the telephone to call someone who is just about to call you, or suddenly "knowing" that a certain letter is on its way. The principle of emotional association applies even to seemingly trivial matters, however, when a friend or relative is involved.

Are there ESP communications of happy thoughts and events?

Yes, and if the emotional impact is strong, it is more likely to be remembered and reported. Rosalind Heywood tells of a mother who got a psychic feeling that her son had passed a very important examination. There seems to have been a three-way involvement here, as the ESP signal came when her son was telling the news to his brother.

In laboratory tests for ESP, what is the "quantitative" approach?

The quantitative tests measure the actual amount of ESP that shows, using statistical methods. For example, when the Rhines set up the Parapsychology Laboratory at Duke University in 1930, they used a quantitative approach. In the clairvoyance experiments the subject would try to guess which of five symbols would appear when a card was drawn from a pack of twenty-five. Statistically, a correct guess of one out of five or five out of twenty-five cards over many runs through the deck would indicate that chance was operating, not ESP. A score above five out of twenty-five, maintained over hundreds of such runs, would be statistical proof of clairvoyance.

What is the "qualitative" approach?

There is more subjectivity in evaluating the results. For example, when the percipient is asked to draw an object that might be in the sender's mind, the sketch might be similar in form or details to the mental picture, but it would be difficult to evaluate statistically.

What is the "target" in an ESP test?

Whatever the subject is trying to guess—playing cards, pictures of animals, words, letters, colors, etc. In the ESP experiments at the Dream Laboratory (the Maimonides Medical Center in Brooklyn, N.Y.), the target was a print of a famous painting. The subject went to sleep in an isolated room and tried to incorporate into his dreams the details of the painting that the agent was looking at in another room. (See Chapter 7.)

What is the difference between a telepathy and a clairvoyance experiment?

In a test for telepathy, the agent or sender tries to beam his thoughts to the subject's mind. In clairvoyance tests, the agent may handle the object, but he does not know what it is. If it is a playing card or picture, it is laid face down, put in an envelope, or otherwise hidden from his view.

Who is the "experimenter" in an ESP test?

Generally a parapsychologist who has charge of the experiment. He may also have designed the test or adapted it from another laboratory procedure.

What are Zener cards?

The Zener cards, named after an associate of Dr. Rhine's, were first used in the clairvoyance tests at Duke University in the early 1930s. They are now called ESP cards. Each card face has one of five symbols—circle, star, rectangle, cross, and three wavy vertical lines. These symbols are used because they are simple and clearly understood.

Who were Rhine's subjects at Duke and what was his original goal?

Rhine tested mostly students at the university, sometimes well-known psychics such as Eileen Garrett. His first objective was merely to find out if anyone had psi ability. Some of the students scored as high as eight and nine per twenty-five cards over several hundred trial runs.

Who was Rhine's outstanding student subject?

Hubert Pearce, a divinity student, not only scored consistently higher than chance, but once made twenty-five correct guesses in a row. The odds against this are an astronomical 298,023,223,876,953,125 to 1.

What was the highest score ever made in ESP card tests?

In 1937 a female student at Hunter College in New York City had an average of more than eighteen hits per twenty-five guesses in seventy-four runs through the deck—1,349 correct responses in 1,859 tries. If ESP had not been operating, there would have been only 370 correct guesses.

Do well-known psychics get high scores in laboratory tests?

Generally they don't like a formal testing situation in which they are restricted to such prosaic targets as card symbols. When Mrs. Garrett was tested at Duke, she objected to the cards as, in Rhine's words, "an overmechanization of the extrasensory process." Although her scores were only at chance on the clairvoyance tests, she did much better in the telepathy experiments, when another mind was involved, that is, when the agent held an image of the card in his mind. The personal element seems to be just as important in laboratory tests as in spontaneous cases of ESP, particularly when mediums and other sensitives are tested.

What are the general conditions for success in an ESP experiment?

Aside from the unknown ESP ability of the subject, the experimenter must have a friendly rapport with sender and subject and must be optimistic about their success. He must try to keep the interest of the subject at a high level throughout the experiment. The subject himself must be relaxed, yet concentrating and interested in his task, not tense or nervous. He must also be confident that he will succeed and he must not think too much about what he is doing. He must, of course, have some kind of rapport with the other half of the team, the agent. It helps if there is an element of novelty introduced from time to time, if the test presents a challenge, and if the experimenter and other members of the laboratory staff keep the subject in a relaxed, good-humored mood.

What conditions interfere with the success of the experiment?

The subject must not be pressured during the test nor distracted in any way from it. He must have no physical problems, such as illness, that will hinder his concentration. Emotional upset, fatigue, nervousness, anxiety about the outcome, and intellectualizing will defeat the purpose of the test.

What is the "decline" effect?

Dr. Rhine found that generally at the beginning of a series of tests, the novelty or gamelike quality of the situation resulted in high scores, but that both the interest of the subject and his score declined somewhere in the middle of the testing. The score would generally rise again in the later stages.

Who are the "sheep" and "goats" in ESP tests?

Dr. Gertrude Schmeidler of City College of New York found that subjects who are friendly and outgoing and believe in ESP and their ability to produce it do better in tests than introverted, skeptical subjects. She called the former "sheep" and the latter "goats."

What is "psi-missing"?

Surprisingly, many "goats" prove that they have psi ability by consistently scoring below chance. This indicates to the sharp mind of the experimenter that they could as easily hit the target if they want to but choose, consciously or unconsciously, to be "psi-missers" by avoiding the target.

Are women better at ESP tests than men?

Although women seem to show more interest in psychic phenomena, laboratory tests have not conclusively demonstrated that they have more psi ability then men. However, when the agent and subject are of different sexes, it often stimulates more interest and higher scores. Although parapsychologists are not in total agreement on this point, it is thought that men are better senders and women better subjects.

Does age make a difference in ESP tests?

According to Rhine, "age is not a limiting factor." Children as a group seem to make the highest scores, possibly because they do not have the self-doubts and inhibitions of their elders. (See Chapter 12.) Gardner Murphy, past president of the American Society for Psychical Research, points out that the physical deterioration of old age has some effect on ESP capacity, but most parapsychologists, including Rhine and

Murphy, feel that one's attitude toward the tests is more significant than age.

Do intellectuals make higher scores on ESP tests than those of average intelligence?

Not necessarily. Intellect, in fact, may inhibit ESP if the subject analyzes what he is doing. Members of MENSA, an organization of individuals with genius IQs, showed strong interest in ESP tests but did not score above chance as a group.

Are blind persons good ESP subjects?

On some tests they did better than persons with normal vision. Perhaps a more acute psychic sense compensates for the loss of sight.

Does "psi" run in families?

There is good evidence that it does. Many of Rhine's best subjects said that other members of their families were psychic. Most mediums claim that the faculty is inherited. There are many cases, in both spontaneous and test situations, of psychic interaction between twins. (See Chapter 11.)

Is "psi" ability universal?

After years of testing subjects and evaluating spontaneous cases, most parapsychologists now believe that everyone has the psychic sense to some degree. Outstanding psychics, however, have certain temperamental qualities that free them from the kind of inhibitions that prevent ESP from surfacing. These qualities are discussed in later chapters.

Does ESP decline with distance?

There is no solid proof that it does. Dr. Karlis Osis, director of research for the American Society for Psychical Research, has conducted clairvoyance experiments with ESP cards as far as 10,000 miles away from the subjects. Although these tests indicate a slight decline in scores as the agents get farther away, the results are not conclusive. In the experiments at Duke, scores were just as high and sometimes higher when the distance between sender and subject was increased.

Does the target itself ever carry an "emotional charge"?

Psychologist Charles Tart, William Roll, and others believe that the target used in ESP tests may have psychical properties that affect the subject's responses. According to the theory of psychometry, all physical objects have psychic histories. (See Chapter 8.)

What is the main objection of scientists to the ESP tests?

The failure to achieve "repeatability"—doing the same experiment over and over again under identical conditions and getting identical results.

Why is "repeatability" a problem in ESP tests?

The mind cannot be captured and pigeonholed the way physical and chemical substances are isolated in a laboratory. There are many factors that seem to operate in an ESP experiment, and they may change from one experiment to the next, even though the laboratory conditions are ostensibly the same. The personality and attitude of the experimenter, the physical and emotional condition of the subject and agent, the unsettling presence of skeptical observers, even the weather may subtly alter the circumstances of the experiment. However, distinguished psychologists such as Gardner Murphy have pointed out that ESP experiments with elementary school children have been successfully repeated many times. (See Chapter 12.)

How are machines being used today in ESP testing?

The computer acts as a kind of agent when it randomly generates numbers that are guessed by subjects in tests. Another instrument is the plethysmograph, which measures the rush of blood to the fingers and toes of a subject when the agent thinks of a name that has emotional meaning for him. The EEG (electroencephalograph) records the kind of brain waves that accompany ESP experience (see Chapter 6). The polygraph records psychic responses of plants. There are many electronic devices in use, in particular those designed by physicist Helmut Schmidt for different kinds of experiments. The American Society for Psychical Research uses closed-circuit television in its ESP experiments. A device called the electrosleep machine, developed in Russia to cure insomnia, uses a mild electric current to bring on ESP through bodily relaxation.

2

YOUR QUESTIONS ANSWERED ABOUT
THE SERIOUS STUDY OF PSYCHIC PHENOMENA
FROM THE MIDDLE OF THE NINETEENTH CENTURY
TO THE PRESENT DAY; CLASSIC CASES IN
LITERATURE AND THE LABORATORY;
UNIVERSITY PROGRAMS IN PARAPSYCHOLOGY;
THE CENSUS OF HALLUCINATIONS . . .

When did the scientific study of psychic phenomena begin?

In the last half of the nineteenth century, more particuarly in the last quarter with the formation in 1882 of the British Society for Psychical Research.

How did the discovery of evolution lead to the science of parapsychology?

Darwin's discovery was a blow to religious institutions and fostered the belief that the universe is a soulless mechanism, operating blindly and without purpose. Students of psychic phenomena such as the classical scholar Frederic Myers organized the British Society for Psychical Research (SPR) to test this belief by making an exhaustive investigation and evaluation of the supernormal, particularly the after-death survival of human personality.

How did the rise of spiritualism spur the study of psychic phenomena?

The spiritualistic movement began in 1848, when strange rappings were heard in the home of the Fox family in Hydesville, New York. As in poltergeist phenomena (see Chapter 4), the noises occurred in the presence of two young girls, who later toured as professional mediums. As spiritualism spread and séances became popular in England and America, critics claimed that the girls had faked the noises and that gullible persons were being duped by fraudulent mediums.

Myers, Sidgwick, and other founders of the SPR were determined to make an impartial, scientific study of spiritualistic phenomena along with other aspects of the psychic.

What scientific paper written in 1876 was a landmark in the history of parapsychology?

Sir William Barrett, a distinguished physicist who later helped form the SPR, appeared before the British Society for the Advancement of Science and described how he had telepathically communicated sensations of pain, taste, and smell to a man in a hypnotic trance. His subject had also experienced "traveling clairvoyance," sending his mind to faraway scenes and describing what went on there. Barrett's scientific colleagues gave him a cold reception.

Who were some early members of the SPR?

In addition to scientist Barrett and poet Myers, there were physicists Oliver Lodge and William Crookes, astronomer Camille Flammarion, American psychologist William James, and many other outstanding men of their time. Still in existence today, the SPR has voluminous records on file of investigations covering the last ninety years.

What kind of psychic phenomena did the SPR investigate?

In the beginning six committees were appointed to study apparitions, ESP under hypnosis, spiritualistic phenomena, and spontaneous cases of telepathy and clairvoyance, and to evaluate and collate their findings.

Did the SPR conduct laboratory experiments?

Not at first. The nearest approach was to test persons who reported spontaneous experiences. The Society investigated hundreds of such cases, interviewed witnesses, and set criteria for accepting or rejecting the validity of these claims.

What was the first case investigated by the SPR?

The five Creery sisters, daughters of an English clergyman, demonstrated striking telepathic and clairvoyant powers with words, numbers, and objects. They were very successful in early tests by the SPR investigators but later showed the "decline" effect.

What was the Census of Hallucinations?

In 1890 the SPR distributed a questionnaire throughout England asking for psychic experiences. One of the questions read: "Have you ever, when believing yourself to be completely awake, had a vivid impression of seeing or being touched by a living or inanimate object, or of hearing a voice; which impression, so far as you can discover, was not due to any external physical cause?"

What were the results of the Census?

The SPR received 17,000 replies, of which 10 per cent answered "yes" to the above question. Of the affirmative answers, 32 per cent said they had seen apparitions of living persons, 14.3 per cent of dead persons, and 33.2 per cent of unidentified individuals.

Did William James investigate psychic phenomena?

James, along with Richard Hodgson and other SPR researchers, made a careful study of mediums. He spent a considerable time observing the famous American medium Leonora Piper and concluded that she was a genuine psychic. (See Chapter 17.)

What classic book was the first to explore psychic phenomena thoroughly?

Human Personality and Its Survival of Bodily Death, written by Frederic Myers, one of the founders of the SPR. Myers first coined the terms "telepathy" and "clairvoyance." Another landmark work was *Phantasms of the Living*, which described cases collected by the SPR.

When was the American Society for Psychical Research formed?

The ASPR, organized in 1885, later became a branch of the SPR. In 1905 it was set up once again as an independent group, with James Hyslop, Columbia University professor of logic, as its first secretary and director.

Who first discovered ESP during a hypnosis experiment?

In the eighteenth century the German physician Mesmer coined the first term for what is known today as hypnotism

—"animal magnetism." (See Chapter 6.) While one of his patients was in a trance, she "saw" the location of a dog that had been lost. The first serious experiments in ESP during the nineteenth century were done while the subject was in a hypnotic trance.

Which teacher of Sigmund Freud experimented with ESP under hypnosis?

The French psychologist Pierre Janet reported that twenty of his patients had telepathic experiences when he hypnotized them.

How did Janet conduct long-distance telepathic tests?

In 1884 he hypnotized one of his patients, Léonie, and sent mental commands to her from a great distance. Once he suggested mentally that she light a lamp, which she did. Another of Janet's hypnotized subjects "saw" a fire in his (Janet's) laboratory in Paris.

How was pain "communicated" during a hypnotic trance?

When Paul Janet, Pierre's brother, once accidentally bruised his arm, his hypnotized patient some distance away screamed and rubbed her elbow.

Who was the first experimenter to use statistical methods?

Charles Richet, an outstanding French physiologist of the late nineteenth and early twentieth centuries, put playing cards in opaque envelopes and asked his hypnotized subjects to "see" them clairvoyantly. He then scored the results mathematically.

Who was the first to do ESP experiments without hypnosis?

Charles Richet. Since the time of Mesmer, it had been assumed that telepathy and clairvoyance were natural to the hypnotic state. (See Chapter 6 on altered states of consciousness.) Richet believed that ESP could also function when the subject was in his normal state of consciousness.

What educator conducted the first long-range ESP tests with playing cards?

Dr. John E. Coover published a six-hundred-page book describing seven years of testing at Stanford University, using scientific controls and evaluating the results statistically. The tests, begun in 1912, covered 10,000 guesses with the playing cards as targets and 105 students as subjects. Coover thought his results were negative, but later analysis by parapsychologists showed otherwise.

What was the famous "checkerboard" ESP test in 1921?

The experiment by Dr. Gerardus Heymans and Dr. Henri Brugmans at the University of Groningen in the Netherlands anticipated a modern ESP test employing closed circuit TV. The subject was blindfolded and put in one room, with the agent in the room overhead. The agent looked through a glass-covered hole in the ceiling at the subject's hands and tried to influence their movements over the squares on a checkerboard. In 180 trials, the subject was correct 60 times, or 56 more than would have occurred by chance. Today, fifty years later, the American Society for Psychical Research is using a similar test, in which the agent watches the subject's hands on a television screen.

What was the "jawbone" experiment in 1925?

In René Warcollier's experiment the agent, a woman, was handed a jawbone from the crypt of a dead woman. Rather than concentrating on the object itself, she mentally "sent" her associations to it to the subject in the next room: "Horns of a little deer, or rather a roe . . . wild animal . . . stag's horn . . ." The subject drew sketches of a pitchfork, a claw, and antlers. This was obviously a case of telepathy rather than clairvoyance, reading the agent's mind rather than mentally seeing the object she was holding.

Who used a red light as sense stimulation in an ESP experiment?

This was another classic experiment in the 1920s, designed by Dr. G. H. Estabrooks, a Harvard psychologist. With playing cards as targets, the agent switched on a red light whenever he turned up a red card. Although the subject in the next room couldn't see the light, it was intended to stimulate his psi ability clairvoyantly. Estabrooks' subjects got very high scores. Today experimenters at the Maimonides Medical

Center Dream Laboratory and elsewhere are also using sensory stimulation in the form of vivid colors, paintings, music, etc., for a clairvoyant emotional impact on the subject. (See Chapter 7.)

What was the unique ESP test designed by Whately Carington?

Another classic experiment in the 1920s. Carington felt, as do many present-day parapsychologists, that cards lose their novelty quickly and can contribute to low scores. On each night of his experiment, he made a sketch of an object chosen from the dictionary and pinned it overnight on his bookcase. The subjects, in their own homes, tried to duplicate the drawings, often showing the "displacement" effect when they drew objects that had been pinned up on a previous night or one that would be used on a later night.

What famous author did ESP experiments with his wife?

Upton Sinclair, who wrote *The Jungle* and other popular books, described his experiments with Mrs. Sinclair in his book *Mental Radio*. Sinclair would make drawings, place them in opaque envelopes, then give them to Mrs. Sinclair as she sat in a dark room. Mrs. Sinclair held the envelopes, then sketched her impressions of their contents. In other experiments she would get mental impressions of drawings made 40 miles away. Of 290 drawings, she sketched 220 that in varying degrees matched the target.

What well-known literary figure could picture scenes in his daughter's mind?

Gilbert Murray would leave the room while his daughter thought of a scene, wrote it down, then called him in. In one experiment she thought of Napoleon standing on a hill and looking down at his soldiers. Murray: "This is a war scene . . . on the hill looking down on the artillery . . . I get the bursting of shells." Once she thought of Rupert Brooke, the English poet, meeting Natasha, Tolstoi's fictional heroine of *War and Peace*. Murray: "Well, I thought when I came in the room it was about Rupert. Yes, it's fantastic. He's meeting somebody out of a book. He's meeting Natasha in *War and Peace*."

Did Murray do as well with strangers?

As is generally true of telepathic communication, there had to be something of an emotional bond between Murray and the other person or persons in the room during the experiment. The presence of certain individuals "turned off" Murray's psi ability.

What do parapsychologists study today?

Almost anything connected with psychic phenomena (and some things that may not be of psychic origin): telepathy, clairvoyance, precognition, psychokinesis; ESP between mother and child, ESP under hypnosis, dream telepathy, dowsing, reincarnation, mental healing, out-of-body experiences, animal ESP, psychometry, ghosts and spirits, mediums and psychics, auras, etc. (See appropriate chapters.) Parapsychologists evaluate reports of spontaneous experiences in these areas and try to reproduce the same phenomena in the laboratory.

How do modern researchers differ in approach from the early SPR investigators?

In the 1880s and for several later decades, the object was to prove or disprove the existence of psychic phenomena. Today, many branches of psi are considered proven as a result of extensive laboratory experiments—telepathy, clairvoyance, precognition, and psychokinesis. The emphasis now is on learning the nature of psi and the psychological and physical factors that make it happen.

What contemporary organizations do psychical research?

The American Society for Psychical Research and the British SPR are still going strong. The Parapsychology Foundation in New York City gives grants for research, maintains a library for students and researchers, holds international seminars, and publishes a newsletter with information about the latest developments in parapsychology. The Psychical Research Foundation in Durham, North Carolina, is doing research into the after-death survival of human personality. The Parapsychological Association is an international organization composed of researchers in the field. The Foundation for Research into the Nature of Man (FRNM), started by Dr. Rhine in Durham, does research, gives grants, and has its own journal and newsletter. The Association for Research and Enlightenment (ARE), devoted to the study and application of the Edgar Cayce trance readings, has chapters throughout the country, sponsors seminars and lectures, and acts as a clearinghouse for literature on psychic phenomena. The Spiritual Frontiers Fellowship sponsors study groups and lecture programs. There are research organizations in Illinois, Southern California, New Jersey, other states, and many countries of the world.

How do these organizations publicize their findings?

The ASPR puts out a newsletter in addition to the *ASPR Journal*. The SPR also prints a quarterly journal. The FRNM publishes the *Journal of Parapsychology* and a news bulletin. The Parapsychology Foundation sends out the *Parapsychology Review*. The Psychical Research Foundation has a quarterly newsletter called *Theta*. The ARE and SFF print journals and newsletters. Many of the smaller organizations publish their own newsletters. In addition, there are professional journals of psychology and psychiatry that print articles on psi research, and several popular magazines on psychic phenomena.

What is the College of Psychic Studies?

Formerly known as the College of Psychic Science, it is a London organization that trains mediums, psychics, and sensitives. One of its famous graduates was the late Eileen Garrett, who developed her talents at the college in a five-year training course. The contemporary British medium Douglas Johnson is a teacher at the college. (See Chapter 11.)

What is the attitude of modern governments toward psychical research?

Although official attitudes are generally unfavorable, the climate has been changing in recent years. There are many new and exciting experiments in Russia, including the Kirlian photographic process, which has detected auras around all living matter. The Russian government, while not openly supporting the work of its scientist-parapsychologists, allows it to go on. Bulgaria has an official seer. And while the United States government won't admit it openly, there have been some inquiries and also testing by the military.

What is the position of American universities on psychical research?

It depends on the university administration and the departmental attitudes in each school. In some instances, as in the case of the Coover experiments at Stanford, sizable private endowments have enabled the work to go forward. Research has been encouraged at Harvard, Duke, and City College of New York, but relatively few courses in parapsychology have been offered. Although few universities here and abroad offer in-depth programs in parapsychology, many give single courses in their regular curricula and extension divisions. In many cases students, particularly those studying for advanced degrees, have been encouraged to write theses on parapsychology. Many instructors in other disciplines have done research on their own and in some cases have had the active cooperation of their universities. (See the next few questions.)

What was the first university research center for the study of parapsychology?

The Parapsychology Laboratory at Duke University, headed by J. B. Rhine for about thirty years. (See Chapter 1.) The laboratory was supported in part by the university but mostly by grants from private individuals and foundations.

What was the first university to establish a separate department of parapsychology?

The State University in Utrecht, Holland, with the first Chair held by Dr. W. H. C. Tenhaeff. In 1969 the first Department of Parapsychology in America was activated as part of the Department of Psychiatry, University of Virginia School of Medicine. Dr. Ian Stevenson, who has investigated precognition, reincarnation, mediumship, and other aspects of psychic phenomena, was named first incumbent of the chair.

What four American universities gave courses in parapsychology in 1882?

Harvard, Bryn Mawr, Smith, and Minnesota.

In the last hundred years, what university has been most active in psychical research?

In 1857 three Harvard professors were chosen to study the spiritualistic phenomena of the Fox sisters. Since then, many Harvard instructors have encouraged study of the psychic at the university. William James devoted much time in his courses to a discussion of psychic matters. Psychologist William McDougall, who brought the Rhines to Duke, Gardner Murphy, Estabrooks, and many others taught courses and did research at Harvard. Dr. Gertrude Schmeidler, a student of Dr. Murphy's, later went to City College, where she has been active in parapsychological research.

What was the first American university to be given a grant for psychical research?

The University of Pennsylvania, in the 1880s. The sum of $60,000 was given by Henry Seybert to found a chair of philosophy, with the stipulation that the university appoint a commission to investigate spiritualism.

Who received the first American doctorate for research in parapsychology?

In 1956 Harmon Bro received his Ph.D. from the University of Chicago for a thesis on Edgar Cayce, the sleeping prophet of Virginia Beach, Virginia. Several doctorates have since been granted at Duke University for papers on some aspect of psi. The first doctorate in the world was earned at a French university in 1893. In England, Cambridge, Oxford, and the University of London have given doctorates for work on psi projects.

What usually generates interest in psi at universities?

The enthusiasm and active interest of one or more professors. Examples are biophysicist R. A. McConnell at the University of Pittsburgh, Gertrude Schmeidler at City College of New York, Carroll B. Nash at St. Joseph's College in Philadelphia. When such instructors, who teach other courses, use their spare time to stimulate interest in the psychic, students follow suit by forming study groups and seminars, bringing in lecturers, and persuading the administration to give courses.

What is the leading Asian country in psychical research?

India, where there is an active interest in the universities. Courses in parapsychology are offered in undergraduate and graduate schools, there is much research by students and faculty, and many higher degrees have been awarded. Indian parapsychologists have studied in America and publish their own professional journals.

Is parapsychology taught in Russian universities?

Although no official pronouncements are made, in 1960 a state-supported parapsychological research laboratory was established at Leningrad State University, under the direction of L. L. Vasiliev. Since that time many Russian scientists have been actively experimenting in psi.

Which university departments favor, and which oppose the work of parapsychologists?

Strangely enough, most opposition comes from departments of psychology, which should show the greatest interest. The physical scientists, however, particularly physicists, seem to be open to the idea of psychic phenomena. Some of them, like R. A. McConnell at the University of Pittsburgh, are active in psychical research. However, most of the young and older parapsychologists now in the field are graduate psychologists.

How many full-time parapsychologists are there in the United States?

Not very many. In most universities parapsychologists teach other subjects and devote their spare time to research in psi. They are dependent on occasional grants from individuals or foundations, and these are few and far between and are quickly used up. It has been estimated that there are about fifteen full-time parapsychologists and about two hundred part-time workers in the field.

How does one become a parapsychologist?

In the Winter 1972 issue of the *ASPR Newsletter,* Dr. Gertrude Schmeidler suggests taking whatever courses are available in colleges, also enrolling in workshops and summer apprenticeships where parapsychologists train students in research methods. "Since parapsychology is not a recognized college major," says Dr. Schmeidler, "you must major in some other field. But this is good, because the skills you learn will almost surely be applicable to parapsychology. Almost everything is, from psychology and biology and physics to computer programing or anthropological field studies or mathematical theory." Dr. Schmeidler suggests writing to Mrs. Nester, Director of Education at the ASPR, for information. The ASPR's address is 5 West 73rd Street, New York, New York 10023.

3 YOUR QUESTIONS ANSWERED ABOUT PRECOGNITION AND PREMONITIONS: KNOWLEDGE OF THE FUTURE THAT COMES THROUGH PSYCHIC CHANNELS—DREAMS, VISIONS, VOICES, HUNCHES, PHYSICAL AND MENTAL DISTRESS; FAMOUS CASES—THE *Titanic* DISASTER, THE ABERFAN COAL SLIDE, THE DREAM OF A SEVERED HEAD, PREDICTIONS OF MURDER, ABRAHAM LINCOLN'S "MIRROR" PREMONITION . . .

What is precognition?

The ability to sense future events psychically. Scenes from the future may unfold in dreams or visions, a prediction may be given by a disembodied voice, or a person may have a sudden hunch that something is going to happen. Sometimes there are undefined feelings of mental or physical stress before a disaster.

What are premonitions?

The unpleasant side of precognition—forebodings of deaths, assassinations, catastrophes, etc. Two hundred people in England had premonitions, most of them coming in dreams, of the 1966 coal slide that killed 144 adults and children in Aberfan, Wales.

What brings on a premonition?

Usually there is an emotional link to those who will be affected by what happens. A person may have a premonition of his own death or of misfortune that will overtake relatives or friends. The link may be to small children, as in the Aberfan disaster, when the coal slide crushed two schools in the village. The link may be to people in the news, to those who live in the same community, or to the leader of one's country.

39

It was estimated that thousands of persons sensed that President Kennedy would be killed.

What was Abraham Lincoln's "mirror" premonition?

When Lincoln returned home after the 1860 presidential election, he saw two images of himself in a bureau mirror; in one his face was normal, in the other it had a deathlike pallor. His wife Mary's interpretation was that he would enjoy good health in his first term but die in his second.

How did an inscription in a tomb foreshadow the assassination of Julius Caesar?

The inscription, written in Greek, was found in a tomb in the Roman colony of Capua just before the assassination. It read: "When once the graves of Capua are brought to light, then a branch of the Julian House will be slain by the hand of one of his kindred." Caesar was also warned by the soothsayer Vestricius Spurrina to "beware the Ides of March [March 15]." Caesar himself dreamed on the night before his murder that he was taken up to heaven and greeted by Jupiter, while his wife Calpurnia dreamed that he had been stabbed to death and lay bleeding in her arms.

Were there any predictions of Hitler's death?

Many, but few gave the correct date. Wilhelm Wulff, the favorite psychic of Himmler, predicted that Hitler would die "under mysterious circumstances" before May 7, 1945. Hitler committed suicide a week before the predicted time—April 30, 1945.

Has anyone ever predicted the exact time of his own death?

There are innumerable cases on record. Dr. Gustave Geley, a French physician, had a patient in excellent health who announced eight days before his death that he would die on All Saints' Day precisely at midnight. At exactly twelve midnight eight days later, he turned over in bed, pointed to the clock, and died.

Who "saw" his own gravestone seventy years before he died?

The eminent French physiologist Charles Richet wrote about a schoolboy who in 1813 saw his gravestone in a dream and on it the date "Jun 9, 1883" (the "e" in the June was missing). On June 9, 1835, the dreamer's son died, and the dreamer died January 9, 1883. The dream had combined the dates of his own and his son's death.

Did Bishop Pike know he was going to die in the Israeli desert?

In an interview published in *Psychic* magazine (August 1971), Pike's widow, Diane Kennedy, stated that he had had a strange dream two days before the fatal trip to the desert. He awoke in the middle of the night after dreaming that his mother had fallen and hit her head. He thought the dream was precognitive of his mother's death, but the next morning he had a headache which felt, he said, as though it was caused by a blow. "Looking back," said Mrs. Pike in the interview, "it seems that Jim's dream was precognitive of his own death, not his mother's."

Who dreamed that he would be killed during a celebration in his honor?

Robert Morris, Sr., father of one of the framers of the United States Constitution, was an agent for a Liverpool shipping firm. When the company's ship arrived in Maryland, he dreamed that he was killed during a salvo fired in welcome. The next day he refused to board the ship, but the captain took him in a boat and started to row out of firing range before giving the signal for the salute. However, a fly lighted on the captain's nose and as he lifted his arm to brush it away, the sailors thought it was the signal and fired, killing Morris.

Who foresaw a famous volcanic eruption in 1902?

An engineer named J. W. Dunne, who later wrote about his precognitive dreams in *An Experiment with Time*, dreamed that he was on the island of Martinique in the West Indies. In the dream Mount Pelée erupted, causing thousands of deaths. The dreamer pleaded with the French authorities to send ships and woke up in a state of panic. A later newspaper article confirmed the premonition.

Do premonitions of natural disasters generally come true?

Not necessarily. Fear and hysteria can generate many false premonitions. For example, many psychics thought that California would sink into the sea in April 1969, a belief triggered by Edgar Cayce's prediction of cataclysmic disasters during the forty-year period from 1958 to 1998. A young woman had seven frightening visions of the disaster, which, of course, never occurred. Later the young woman died suddenly. Her visions were probably symbolic of her own physical condition, unknown to her at the time.

Should premonitions of natural disasters be ignored?

No, but neither should they be a cause for hysteria. Generally, the more cosmic and global the disaster predicted, the less likely it will happen. Disasters on a smaller scale, however, may sometimes be sent in dreams or visions as warnings. The Aberfan disaster, in which there was probably a close psychic link between the children and the dreamers, might have been averted if the authorities had been warned in time. The children could have been taken to a safe area, or the coal waste could have been removed before it slid down the mountain.

Were there premonitions of the Pakistani tidal wave disaster in 1970?

Not in the United States, so far as is known. Aside from a few psychics who are sensitive to events all over the world, most persons get intimations of natural disasters affecting just the geographical area in which they live. The emotional link in such cases is to the people in their community or country.

Have there been predictions of plane and train crashes that came true?

Very many. In this jet age much anxiety seems to be generated that links travelers in fast-moving vehicles to psychic dreamers. Lorna Middleton, an English psychic, has accurately forecast many plane and train accidents. In January 1970 she had a vision of "a holiday camp . . . the worst train crash I have ever known . . . hundreds of people killed . . . blood gushing into the air like fountains . . ." A week later a train in Buenos Aires, Argentina, crashed into another train return-ing from a resort area. One hundred and fifty persons were killed.

Who predicted the 1967 plane accident in Cyprus?

Alan Hencher, a British psychic, dreamed that a jet plane would crash in Nicosia and 124 persons would die. A few weeks later a plane did crash there, 124 persons dying imme-diately and another one later.

Were there predictions of trouble during the space flights?

Yes. A psychic in New York and a German actress both had premonitions of the problem that kept Gemini 6 from taking off on schedule—a plastic cap had not been removed from the fuel line. The actress dreamed that her daughter was an astronaut and a man with her was choking to death from a plastic cap in his throat. There were also many premonitions about the moon flights, several predicting danger to Apollo 13. A woman in Chicago "heard" a cry for help from outer space four months before the April 1970 flight of the space-craft. Lorna Middleton of London, England, wrote a letter five hours before the oxygen tank in the service module ex-ploded, predicting trouble. However, while the astronauts were in mortal danger 200,000 miles from home, Alan Vaughan of Brooklyn had a vision in which he saw them safely back on earth, riding in a car during a parade in a large city. His vision was matched in almost every detail by a picture that appeared in *The New York Times* of May 2, 1970.

Were there premonitions before the Titanic sank in 1912?

The *Titanic* case is one of the classics. Dr. Ian Stevenson of the University of Virginia investigated nineteen cases of psychic links to the disaster, and several books have been written about the many premonitions that the ship would sink on its maiden voyage from England to New York. One man, J. Connon Middleton, dreamed twice that, as the ship went down, he was floating a little above it. He canceled pas-sage, as did many others who had uneasy feelings about the ship. One member of the crew, convinced that the *Titanic* would sink, deserted at Queenstown before it sailed into open sea.

Who predicted the Titanic *disaster in a novel?*

Morgan Robertson wrote *The Wreck of the Titan* in 1898, fourteen years before the *Titanic* sank and before it was even built, in 1911. The voyage of the fictitious *Titan* almost exactly matched that of the later *Titanic*. Both ships sank after hitting an iceberg. Nautically, they were almost identical—in ship speed, number of lifeboats, passenger capacity, displacement tonnage, "watertight" bulkheads, etc.

What was the "emotional link" of the author to the Titanic?

Psychics tend to have premonitions connected with their business, profession, or other areas of interest. Robertson, for example, was not only a writer of novels about the sea but had been a sailor from the age of sixteen. His involvement with the sea and ships forged a strong link between him and the *Titanic.*

What is a "subliminal" premonition?

A premonition that does not arise to conscious awareness. Many persons, for example, cancel plane or train reservations without knowing why and save themselves from injury or death. There were many such cancellations before the *Titanic* sailed. W. E. Cox, a parapsychologist, compared the number of passengers on trains during ordinary runs with those on board during accidents and found that in some cases there was a drop of up to 600 per cent on the accident days.

Have psychics had dreams and visions of future wars?

This kind of premonition is quite common. Precognition of future wars, however, follows the principle that the larger in scope the event, the more unreliable the prediction. Maurice Maeterlinck, the Belgian writer who studied psychic phenomena, was struck by the scarcity of predictions preceding World War I.

When is a wartime prediction likely to come true?

When the premonition is of someone *in* the war or of a community of persons who will be affected by the war, it may be valid. Many mothers, for example, have had premonitions that their sons would be killed in battle. In one of many wartime premonitions investigated by Dr. Hans Bender of the University of Freiburg in Germany, a resident of Freiburg had a vision in 1939 that the city would be destroyed, with only the cathedral left standing. Five years later Freiburg was devastated by bombing, and only the cathedral in the main section of town escaped intact.

Can the setting of a future tragedy convey a sense of disaster?

Yes. Raynor Johnson tells in *The Imprisoned Splendour* about a young Australian woman who took a stroll through a park and was suddenly filled with a sense of terror and acute suffering. A week later a plane crashed where she had been sitting, and the pilot died in agony. A house, park, etc., may also have vibrations of tragedies that have occurred in the past, and these are felt by sensitive persons.

When does precognition or a premonition happen?

Any time of day or night but mostly in dreams or during other "altered states of consciousness"—the twilight period between sleeping and waking up, periods of relaxation or daydreaming, when one is quietly meditating, etc. (See Chapter 6.)

What is the time span between a premonition and its fulfillment?

Premonitions are generally most intense a week or two before death or disaster occurs. The Central Premonitions Registry in New York City, for example, has found that premonitions may first come as vague warnings, then grow in intensity, with the details gradually filling in, finally reaching a climax about two weeks before the disaster.

Are there any exceptions to this time factor?

The exception depends on the strength of the emotional link between the psychic and the future event. In one of Dr. Bender's most striking cases, the German mother of an infant son dreamed in 1919 that she was searching for his body in the sand. The dream kept coming back in the form of a nightmare as the boy was growing up. During World War II her son died in a French concentration camp and was buried in the dunes near the sea—just as in her dream.

Does more than one person ever have the same premonition?

This happens many times. Three psychics foresaw the blinding and death of King Henry II of France in a duel, one of them the famous Nostradamus. Three persons had premonitions of the murder of Archduke Ferdinand of Austria and his wife in 1914, one psychic correctly forecasting that both would die from the same bullet.

Is a recurrent premonition more likely to come true?

Recurring dreams give strength to a premonition. John Williams, who dreamed in 1812 that Prime Minister Spencer Perceval of England would be shot in the House of Commons lobby, had the same dream several times in one night, about a week before the shooting. Abraham Lincoln dreamed several times that he was in a boat drifting farther and farther out to sea—perhaps symbolic of his imminent death.

Is most precognition of happy or sad events?

The unpleasant premonitions seem to far outnumber the other kind. The Central Premonitions Registry receives three times as many forecasts of unhappy events as of pleasant ones. It may be that the dramatic nature of death and disaster makes a greater impact on the mind.

Don't people ever dream of good fortune coming their way?

Of course they do, although not as often as the other kind. There are many dreams of money about to materialize, and sometimes it does. Cicero, the Roman statesman, tells about a man who dreamed of an egg hanging on his bedpost. His dream interpreter told him to dig through the floor under the bed. Here he found many pieces of gold surrounded by silver, as symbolized by the yolk and white of the egg.

Do dreams of future romance ever come true?

Most young women like to think so, and popular songs have encouraged this belief. Such dreams are mostly wish-fulfilling, but occasionally a girl does get a vivid picture of her future lover. The dancer Romola dreamed many times of a lithe young man who was also a dancer, whom she finally married in her last dream. A year later she met Nijinsky, who was an exact counterpart of her dream lover, and married him.

How about sports? Has any psychic ever beaten the gambling table or a bookmaker's odds?

One Australian gentleman dreamed of the exact order in which three horses would finish in a race. On the radio the next day he heard their names in the same sequence as in the dream. Unfortunately, he was not a betting man and had no interest in racing. In another case, an Englishman who followed the horses dreamed that he was on trial for stabbing a man to death. When the judge gave him a very light sentence, the grateful dreamer leaned over and whispered to him, "Solario for the Ledger." The next day a horse named Solario won his race and the dreamer collected a large sum of money.

Has any psychic ever predicted which baseball teams would win the pennant?

In the spring of 1959 Peter Hurkos was asked by *This Week* magazine to predict the winners of the American and National League races. He visited the training camps of all sixteen clubs and predicted that the Los Angeles Dodgers, who had finished next to last the year before, would be first in the National League, and the Chicago White Sox would win in the American League. However, the brash confidence of the New York Yankees, perennial winners during the 1950s, made him change his mind and pick the Yankees. The Dodgers and White Sox won.

What is a "witchcraft" football club in Africa?

In Nairobi, Kenya, there are associations that bet on football games after consultations with witch doctors. One such club paid $3000 in consultant fees to its psychics.

What novelist wrote about the two Martian moons long before they were discovered?

In Jonathan Swift's *Gulliver's Travels,* written in 1726, astronomers in the country of Laputa said that Mars had two satellites, Phobos and Deimos. Swift's description of the moons was verified later, as recently as the Martian missile probes by NASA. Among other things, Swift said that Phobos traveled three times as fast as Mars itself, an unusual fact now known to astronomers. In 1877, 150 years later, the moons were discovered by astronomer Asaph Hall.

Do psychics ever "see" future newspaper headlines?

Not only headlines but also articles and photos. During World War I psychic Arthur Ford woke up each morning and visualized the casualty list that appeared in the afternoon papers, with the names printed in the same order. Lady Rhys-Williams, a British economist, often "saw" nonexistent items in the newspaper that were related to her work. When she asked her secretary to clip and file the article, the bewildered secretary could never find it. A day or two later the news article would be printed, with the same information Lady Rhys-Williams thought she had read.

Has anyone ever "seen" or "heard" future television or radio broadcasts?

Yes. Lady Rhys-Williams often "heard" broadcasts before they were on the air. The day before the Aberfan coal slide, a woman had a vision of a small boy in the village looking on as a worker in an unusual peaked cap dug through the rubble. Three days later the exact scene appeared on a BBC television broadcast, including the small boy with a "fringe of hair" and the worker with the peaked cap.

Does anyone ever "smell" the future?

Any or all senses may be involved in psychic contact with the future, just as in the present. In one case a woman watching a movie suddenly "smelled" an odor she remembered from her college days in a biology course. The smell lasted for fifteen minutes, until another film came on in which an actress opened a bottle containing a specimen of fish and made a wry face.

Who had a premonition about a severed head?

In 1917 Walter Franklin Prince, a parapsychologist, dreamed that a woman came to him with an order for her own beheading. He held her hand while the execution was taking place, and felt his other hand on top of her head as it was cut off from her body. The next evening a woman named Mrs. Hand, the same age and appearance as the woman in the dream, was decapitated when she placed her head on a railroad track in front of a moving train. She left a note saying that her head would continue to live after the death of her body, as it did in the dream.

Is it possible to prevent a premonition from coming true?

Many cases suggest that premonitions may serve as warnings. Louisa Rhine tells about a young mother who dreamed one night that a chandelier had fallen and crushed her baby, who was asleep in a crib in the next room. She took the baby into her own room, and a few hours later there was a loud crash—the chandelier had fallen on the crib. In other instances, however, attempts to prevent a dream premonition from coming true were not successful.

How is precognition being proved today?

Through premonitions bureaus that receive forecasts through the mail and check them with later news articles; by laboratory tests for precognition such as those at the Maimonides Medical Center (see Chapter 7); by the observations of psychiatrists who can match the precognitive dream of a patient with a later event; and by careful investigations made by parapsychologists after a disaster has occurred.

How can the validity of a premonition be established after it comes true?

Certain questions are asked to rule out coincidence or fraud: Was the event unlikely to occur—that is, it could not be inferred from facts known in the present? Do the details of the prediction and the disaster match closely? Was the prediction made within a short time of the event? Were there witnesses and written evidence such as diaries and dream journals? The time factor can be discounted if the other criteria are met.

What is the function of the Central Premonitions Registry?

The Registry has several goals: To strengthen the case for precognition by having forecasts on record that can be matched with later events; to prevent future tragedies by sounding an "early warning" alert when enough premonitions are received that point unmistakably to the same potential disaster; and to develop as many new psychics as possible. The Registry's mailing address is P.O. Box 482, Times Square Station, New York, New York 10036. Send in only premonitions about items of public interest—natural or mechanical disasters, assassinations, deaths of prominent persons, plane or train crashes, space flights, political predictions, and other newsworthy events, good or bad. If you live in Great Britain, write to the British Premonitions Bureau, T.V. Times, 247 Tottenham Court Road, London W1P 0AU, England.

What is the "chair test" for precognition?

In Holland, Dr. W. H. C. Tenhaeff conducts this test with his star psychic, Gerard Croiset. A chair in a hall is pointed out to Croiset, who then describes in accurate detail a person unknown to him who will sit in it at a later meeting. Once Croiset visualized a young man who had almost lost a finger in an electric saw and on another occasion a policeman who had a leaking fountain pen. Both sat in the designated chair and verified these and other details given by the psychic.

What is the computer test for precognition in top business executives?

Douglas Dean, a parapsychologist, asks the executives to guess in advance which numbers will be randomly generated by a computer. The tests have shown that businessmen who use intuition to make important decisions usually score well above chance and are highly successful in running their companies. Executives who use logic and go by the book when making their business decisions are less successful in guessing what the computer is going to do, and the profits of their companies are not as high.

Do psychiatrists believe in precognition?

Many of them do, having observed it in their practice. Dr. Jule Eisenbud has written about many such cases in several books and professional papers. He gives a classic example of a patient who dreamed that he was swimming in the lobby of a hotel. The next day an explosion caused flooding in the lobby of the hotel named.

What was the "emotional link" of the patient to the explosion?

Dr. Eisenbud adroitly traced the symbolic details of the dream to the patient's emotional conflicts, one of them with the doctor. The dream was a bid for the psychiatrist's attention.

Who predicts that the earth will be hit by a comet in 1984?

Psychic Jeane Dixon. She refuses, however, to reveal where the comet will strike but says there will be great devastation.

What two psychics forecast rising water level in New York City?

Alan Vaughan of New York, a regular contributor to the Central Premonitions Registry, and Malcolm Bessent, the young English psychic who was the subject of experiments in the Dream Laboratory at the Maimonides Medical Center. According to Vaughan and Bessent, this will begin in 1972 or 1973, but it will be gradual and will allow time for an orderly evacuation.

Must every prediction by a well-known psychic be taken seriously?

Generally predictions about personal fortunes are much more reliable than those of large-scale cosmic events such as wars and world-shaking cataclysms—what Dr. Bender calls "general, oracle-like" prophecies. Also, the political and religious bias of the psychic must be discounted.

4

YOUR QUESTIONS ANSWERED ABOUT
PSYCHOKINESIS—THE MENTAL POWER THAT MOVES
OBJECTS OR ALTERS MATTER WITHOUT PHYSICAL
CONTACT OR THE USE OF KNOWN PHYSICAL
ENERGIES; LEVITATION, TABLE-TURNING, APPORTS,
POLTERGEISTS, PSYCHIC PHOTOGRAPHY, ETC. . . .

What is psychokinesis?

Mind over matter. Also known as PK, it is the ability, by
purely psychic means, to change the composition of physical
objects, animate or inanimate, or move them around in space.
Two examples of PK are "willing" specific numbers to come
up when dice are thrown and impressing mental images on
unexposed film. It has also been theorized that the human
mind (and possibly the animal mind) can psychokinetically
influence future events, but there is no conclusive proof of
this power.

Could an unknown physical energy be the basis of psycho-kinetic power?

Although no such energy has been pinpointed as yet,
many parapsychologists, particularly in Russia, believe that
the human mind can send magnetic or electrical pulses into
space. Whatever it is that can move objects without contact
or perform other acts of PK may be the same force that operates in telepathy, clairvoyance, and other areas of the paranormal.

What woman can mentally move objects on a table?

The remarkable Russian Nelya Mikhailova sits at a table
and makes passes over matchboxes, saltshakers, glass tum-
blers, and other objects, which travel slowly over the table-
cloth. Sometimes when a glass containing water is moving,

the water is motionless. Before her demonstrations, Nelya warms up by practicing with a compass needle. Although she has been accused of fraud, Nelya has been observed by both Russian and American scientists, who found no evidence of chicanery.

Does Nelya have physical sensations when she is doing PK?

She says she feels a palpitation starting in her solar plexus and traveling up her spine to her head.

Who moved objects with a "psychic thread?"

A Polish psychic, Mlle. Stanislawa Tomczyk, would place her hands on either side of an object, which would then rise and float unsupported. Dr. Julien Ochorowicz, who hypnotized her, said that he could feel a psychic thread or "line of force" in the air. When Mlle. Tomczyk moved her hands farther away, the thread became thinner. Other experimenters have observed very fine threads that connect mediums to objects and people in the room. One medium said that she could feel cobwebs on her face.

Who could extinguish jets of gas by PK?

Along with his other astonishing feats, the celebrated nineteenth-century medium D. D. Home could sit in one room and put out the jets in another. Once he caused a disembodied hand to hover over a jet of gas. Immediately eight jets in other parts of the house went out.

Who played billiards without touching the table, balls, or cues?

The "game" was played in darkness in a Milwaukee pool hall. Unless spirits were present, it was the PK of two mediums, the Davenport brothers, that was operating. In other instances, invisible typists inserted paper in typewriters, addressed and sealed envelopes.

Have musical instruments played without a performer?

There have been many cases of this kind attributed to spirits, but the PK of a medium may have been responsible. Sometimes the instruments have been invisible; other times they have been seen playing by themselves. A piano once gave a recital, although it was locked.

What was the case of the moving cigar?

While the medium Eusapia Palladino was giving a séance, an observer was astonished when his cigar left his coat pocket and inserted itself between his teeth.

Whose fur coat disappeared during a séance?

Florence Marryat, a nineteenth-century writer and psychic investigator, was sitting in the circle when her fur coat suddenly left her shoulders, seemed to vanish, then came down from the ceiling and wrapped itself around her again.

Do liquids ever "travel" by psychic force?

Alcoholic beverages, probably for a good reason, are high on the list of liquids that disappear and sometimes reappear somewhere else. When D. D. Home once held a glass of brandy over his head, it became empty. A man present then put his hand over the empty glass, whereupon the brandy suddenly came down from above and spilled over him. Writer Robert Graves tells of a New Year's Eve party when either a spirit or an unidentified PK artist emptied out a glass of liquor he was about to drink.

What is levitation?

The power, through PK, to lift heavy objects such as pianos, tables, even one's own body, into the air with no apparent means of support. Among the self-levitators was Daniel Home, who was observed floating out of one window and into another by several persons, including physicist William Crookes. Crookes witnessed one demonstration in which Home willed a chair with a woman sitting in it to rise half a foot above the ground.

Which President of the United States saw two pianos levitate?

Abraham Lincoln watched the pianos lift off the ground in the presence of an eleven-year-old child. In another case, a grand piano hovered a foot and a half above the ground for three minutes before returning. Psychic investigators have also reported seeing a table rise in the air with eight men standing on it.

What is "table turning"?

During séances, the members of the group often touch the table with their fingertips, causing it to rock back and forth or even rise off the floor. Strictly speaking, PK may not be involved because of the finger contact, but the fact that no physical energy is expended would indicate the operation of a psychic force.

Do ballet dancers ever levitate?

Most of them do not, of course. Their leaps, pirouettes, and other movements are normal and well-rehearsed routines. Certain outstanding dancers, however, may have used a form of PK to keep themselves in the air. It was said of the famous Nijinsky that "in the execution of leaps he displayed . . . the ability to remain in the air at the highest point of elevation before descending."

What mental state most often accompanies self-levitation?

Religious ecstasy. There are countless cases of self-levitation at the altar of a church. St. Joseph of Copertino levitated fifteen times in front of images of the Holy Virgin.

Why do clocks often stop when someone dies?

As in poltergeist cases (see later questions), the clock-stopping force may come from an energy generated by a living person, but the timing of the phenomenon suggests that a departed spirit may be responsible. The clock often stops in the room where the person dies, but when he dies in the hospital, the clock frequently stops at home. In one case two timepieces were involved. As the man died sitting in a chair, his watch and a large clock in the next room stopped at the same time. Some of the clocks never run again. Conversely, clocks that have not been working often start running again at the time of death. Once an old clock that had not worked for many years started ticking loudly exactly twenty-four hours after the death of the man who owned it.

What other mysterious PK phenomena occur when someone dies?

Bells start ringing, lights go off and on, dishes break, and pictures fall off the wall. These objects are usually closely associated with the person who is dying or has just died. J. B. Rhine tells about a professor friend whose dying neighbor promised that she would give a PK signal if her soul survived. The night after her death, an old flashlight that had stopped working came on at 1 A.M. When the professor turned it off, he couldn't reactivate it, but the next night at 1 A.M. it flashed on again.

What are apports?

Objects that are moved great distances by PK, sometimes thousands of miles. The objects often disappear for a time, pass through physical barriers such as walls, then reappear at their destination. During a séance attended by Sherwood Eddy in 1941, a heavy wrought-iron ashtray left an apartment in Chicago and almost simultaneously appeared in the séance room in New York City. Eddy tells about the incident in *You Will Survive After Death* (Holt, Rinehart, and Winston, 1950).

What is teleportation?

If it were possible, the epitome of psychic experience would be the ability of a person to transport his body instantaneously from one location to another. There is no documented case of this kind, although the Bible tells how Elijah disappeared in a chariot of fire, leaving his garments behind. (See Chapter 18.)

Who dissolved clouds through PK?

Many persons have reported seeing this happen. In *The Search for the Girl with the Blue Eyes,* Jess Stearn describes how Rolph Alexander did a cloud-dissolving act in a Canadian park.

Are stigmata a form of PK?

Stigmata—the appearance of wounds, bleeding, and other physical marks on the body during periods of religious fervor or psychological stress—are an example of the close mind-body relationship seen in psychosomatic medicine. If physical objects can be mentally influenced at a distance, the same force may operate within one's own body.

What is "skin-writing"?

Skin-writing, or dermography, is a phenomenon in which mysterious writing appears spontaneously on the arm or another part of the body. Madame Kahl, a Frenchwoman, received drawings telepathically and reproduced them on her skin. In another case the writing appeared in raised letters that could be felt as three-dimensional.

How did Jung demonstrate PK for Freud?

During a discussion about psychic phenomena in 1910, Jung had a strange feeling of intense heat in his diaphragm. The next moment there was an explosive sound in the bookcase. Jung said he could make the sound repeat, but Freud ridiculed him. Again there was an explosion. Freud would not admit that PK was operating, but it must have made him do a bit of thinking. Jung's exploit could have been a combination of PK and precognition.

Has PK been tested in the laboratory?

Dr. Rhine at Duke University and other parapsychologists have tested subjects with dice. In the first experiments the subjects rolled the dice by hand or shook them in a dice cup and "willed" which die faces would appear when they were thrown. In later tests the dice were rotated in an electrically operated cage, rolled mechanically down a runway, or shaken in other kinds of mechanical or automated devices, so that the subject would have no physical contact with them. The overall results, evaluated by statistical methods, indicated that PK was operating.

What was the "coin" test for PK?

In an experiment by Dr. Robert Thouless, a British psychologist, coins were spun while the subject willed them to come up heads or tails. Over a two-month period the coins were spun 4000 times, with the side called on each spin coming up 42 more times than it would have appeared by chance.

Does PK get weaker with the object farther away?

In one test half of the dice throws were made with the subjects 3 feet away and half when they were 30 feet away. The results were inconclusive, which might indicate that psi ability in PK, as well as in other forms of the paranormal, does not lessen with distance.

Do men or women have more PK ability?

Since more men like to gamble, it might be assumed that they would do better in PK dice tests. In one test, however, the women had more PK than their husbands. In another test, a female psychical researcher tried to counteract the PK ability of a man by willing him to get low scores. She was successful, although the man had made high scores when he had no such opposition. In a series of tests with twenty women and twenty-five men, the women had significantly higher scores.

Do children do better than adults in PK tests?

In an experiment with children, colored discs were used to sustain their interest, but the results were not conclusive. Although children tend to do better than adults in other forms of psi, there have not been enough experiments in PK to indicate any difference.

Are gamblers better dice-throwers than preachers?

In one experiment four students who liked to gamble were matched with four divinity students in a PK dice game. The divinity students prayed each time before the dice were thrown. Both sides scored significantly higher than chance and did about equally well. It may be that the divinity students were using the religious equivalent of "Baby needs a new pair of shoes," intoned by successful crapshooters.

How does mental attitude affect PK success?

As in other forms of psi, the PK subject should be relaxed, should be motivated to succeed without being too intense and anxious about it, and should look upon it as a game, a "fun thing." In a book on how to do better at cassino, the authors suggested that a good gambler, whether at the gaming table or in a PK test, feels that luck is on his side.

Who tested cockroaches for PK ability?

Dr. Helmut Schmidt, a physicist who designs ingenious tests for psi, placed cockroaches on an electric grid attached to an RNG (Random Number Generator). The RNG was set to generate electric shocks 50 per cent of the time, and the task of the cockroaches was to psychically cause the machine to give them fewer shocks. However, there were more rather than fewer shocks generated, a fact that was extremely puzzling to the experimenter.

How were chicken embryos tested for PK?

The embryos need warmth, and the object of the test was to see if they could keep a lamp burning. The lamp was placed near them and set to light up 50 per cent of the time and be off the other 50 per cent. During the experiment the lamp was on more than 50 per cent of the time, which may or may not prove that the embryos were using PK.

What were the PK tests with one-celled animals?

In this series of experiments an attempt was made through PK to influence the movements of paramecia. An Englishman, Nigel Richmond, divided a microscope into four sections with crosshairs and "willed" the paramecia to swim into view on one of the four quadrants. After nearly 1500 tests, the results indicated that the paramecia had been influenced by the PK of the experimenter. Telepathy rather than PK may have been involved, but even this would be startling evidence that human beings can communicate with one-celled animals.

What are poltergeists?

In poltergeist ("noisy spirit") phenomena, there are mysterious disturbances in a house—objects flying around a room or shattering into many pieces. Sometimes mischievous ghosts are responsible, but when they are ruled out, it is believed that the PK force comes from a member of the household.

Who is usually responsible for the disturbances?

Parapsychologists who have studied poltergeist phenomena believe they can be traced to boys and girls in their teens, sometimes to adults.

What is the psychic force behind a poltergeist disturbance?

In general, an adolescent in the home has a repressed hostility toward other members of the family. This hostility cannot be expressed overtly, and the energy it presumably generates is powerful enough to cause objects to fly through the air and other PK phenomena.

Does the "villain" in a poltergeist drama know what he is doing?

Psychological tests given to a suspected PK agent usually show no conscious awareness of his connection with the disturbance. The subliminal mind, however, as in other kinds of paranormal situations, may possess psychic force that can explode into tremendous displays of energy.

Where is the PK agent when poltergeists are active?

Somewhere in the "haunted house." He may be sitting down, standing or walking, lying in bed, or even sleeping when the disturbances are taking place.

What is the "attenuation" effect in poltergeist cases?

After many careful investigations, psychical researcher William Roll concluded that the frequency of the disturbances was directly related to the distance between them and the PK agent. For example, when one suspected teen-ager was from 1 to 5 feet away, there were fifteen poltergeist happenings. As he moved farther away, these decreased in number. When he was 25 feet away, there were only two disturbances.

How do objects move in a poltergeist household?

Roll found that objects start to move when they are directly in front of the boy or girl who energizes them. They may move straight ahead or follow curved paths. Sometimes they turn around or rotate, or just float. In a Newark, New Jersey, case, a bottle did a jig and a lamp bulb unscrewed itself.

Do the moving objects ever hurt anyone?

There is a tendency for the objects to point toward the rooms occupied by family members who are objects of hostility, but these persons are never harmed.

What is psychic photography?

The appearance on film of objects to which the film has not been exposed. These may be pictures of living or dead persons, buildings, sometimes composites of many images.

What is spirit photography?

Spirit photographs show images of persons who have died. Sometimes this was done in a séance room, with the medium holding photographic plates or merely sitting in a chair while the photograph was taken. During the latter part of the nineteenth century there were many photographers who discovered they were also mediums when they took pictures of living persons and got "extras" on the film in the form of human or animal spirits.

When was the first psychic photograph produced on film?

In 1861 an engraver, W. H. Mumler of Boston, produced an "extra" by accident. He became a spirit photographer and, though he was tried for fraud many times, he was acquitted through the testimony of witnesses.

What is "thought-photography (thoughtography)"?

Impressing one's thoughts on film. In 1896 a Parisian, Dr. Baraduc, had his subjects put their hands on photographic plates and concentrate on mental objects. These thought-forms were partially reproduced on the plates. In 1911 a psychology professor in Japan did a successful experiment in which a psychic transferred mental images onto photographic plates that were wrapped in several layers of black paper. There have also been cases of thoughtography at a distance, a combination of telepathy and psychokinesis.

How does Ted Serios impress mental images on film?

Dr. Jule Eisenbud, a Denver psychiatrist, has done extensive experiments with Serios and wrote about him in *The World of Ted Serios*. Serios, holding what he calls a gizmo in his hand (a small object which apparently has no part in the process but helps him to concentrate) usually stares into the lens of the camera, which contains unexposed film. Sometimes the camera is turned away from him and pointed at the wall or an object. Clairvoyance has sometimes been combined with PK—Serios would try to "see" a picture hidden from him in an opaque envelope, and impress it on the film.

How successful is Serios?

It takes enormous concentration and expenditure of energy to produce a thought-form on film, and Serios has been very successful at times, partially successful at other times, and he often draws a blank. Sometimes the film has come out white, black, blotched, or blurred. Frequently there is a partial image or a composite of many images. During a television program in Toronto, he took a Polaroid camera that had just been loaded with fresh film and pointed it at his head. The picture that emerged ten seconds later was of a city scene from an aerial viewpoint. No one could identify the scene.

Are the Serios photographs genuine?

In the early days of spirit photography, there were probably many cases of fraud, since it is easy to touch up films. The phenomenon itself, however, may be genuine, and in many cases fraud could not be proved. Dr. Eisenbud, a highly respected psychiatrist and parapsychologist, has conducted his experiments with Serios in a careful, scientific manner, with many skeptical professional observers present. Although fraud has been claimed, no evidence of it has ever been uncovered, and Eisenbud has offered a monetary reward if fraud can be proven. Serios has produced pictures while blindfolded and with a lensless camera. He has been examined to see if any device that could produce photographs was secreted on his body. In the later tests the Polaroid camera and film were brought in just before the experiments began, and Serios could have had no contact with them.

5 YOUR QUESTIONS ANSWERED ABOUT
THE MYSTERIOUS POWER OF PSYCHIC HEALING THAT
ALLEVIATES AND CURES PHYSICAL AILMENTS IN
PEOPLE, ANIMALS, AND PLANTS WITHOUT MEDICINES
AND OTHER CONVENTIONAL KINDS OF THERAPY . . .

What is psychic healing?

Physicians use medicines and drugs to act directly upon an ailing organ. Chiropractors and osteopaths try to stimulate the muscles and nervous system to effect internal cures. Psychic healers, however, depend more upon the power of the mind and use a minimum of physical contact. Sometimes the healing is purely mental; other times they merely touch the affected part with their fingertips, make passes over it, or hold their hands a short distance away. Cures are also brought about psychically through individual and group meditation and prayer, with the patient present or absent. Another kind of psychic healing occurs in a religious setting through a faith healer or at a shrine when self-healing seems to take place. Psychic operations are also performed with just the hands or crude instruments, and without anesthetics.

What is "laying on of hands"?

There are many natural healers who concentrate their power in their hands. When they place their hands on the affected part of a patient's body, the pain and other symptoms often disappear. This method goes back to ancient times. The symptoms often return, but sometimes the cure is permanent. (See later questions.)

What is the stroking technique in psychic healing?

A method commonly used in earlier centuries. Instead of touching the affected part, the healer tried to brush the pain away by stroking it out toward the nearest extremity. A successful stroker was Valentine Greatrakes, who cured many Englishmen in the seventeenth century.

What does the patient feel during the healing process?

Many subjects report that when the healer's hands touch them, they feel heat in the affected part, sometimes a mild electric shock. Those who are cured in the presence of faith healer Kathryn Kuhlman speak of a "dramatic change" in their bodies, a "mysterious tingling sensation," "a great electric shock."

What does the psychic healer feel?

Those who do "laying on of hands" say they feel the same kind of heat sensation reported by their subjects. This also happens when they merely make passes over the body. Sometimes there are other physical symptoms during contact or when the healer feels his power coming on. Ambrose Worrall writes in *The Gift of Healing* that once when he was in the same room with his sister, who had a paralytic neck, he felt a "mass emerging" out of his solar plexus. He then felt a force pulling him over to his sister's chair and his hands involuntarily drawn to her neck. After he had touched her for five seconds, the paralysis was gone.

Does the healer feel the patient's pain or take on his symptoms?

Since pain can be communicated telepathically, it is natural that a highly sensitive person such as a psychic healer will sometimes "absorb" the patient's symptoms. A nineteenth-century healer named Dr. Mack would often experience all the symptoms of the person he touched, and he would make passes over his own body to get rid of them. Psychologist Lawrence LeShan believes that such symptoms are only temporary and do not stay with the healer.

What is the "human chain" method of healing?

One or more psychics assist the healer by touching him while he is in contact with the patient. Dr. Mack often called in other healers, who formed a chain while he touched or manipulated the patient's body.

Does psychic healing work at a distance?

Yes. Since a mental and possibly a psychokinetic effect may be involved, space may be a negligible factor as it is in telepathy and clairvoyance. In one case a man visited Leah Fox, one of the celebrated Fox sisters who gave impetus to the spiritualist movement in the United States, and told her his wife had a bad cough. Miss Fox went into a trance and said she would cure the woman. When the man returned home, he found that his wife's cough was gone.

What is group healing?

Religious organizations and private circles believe that prayer and meditation can bring relief and cures to persons who are ill at home or in hospitals. Sometimes the patient, when physically able, is brought into the presence of the group, and the healing process is strengthened by the participation of both group members and patient.

What are "miracle healings"?

Miracle healings are usually associated with religious shrines, demonstrations by faith healers, etc., and are so called because of the instantaneous remission of incurable diseases. This happens very often in the presence of Kathryn Kuhlman. During one of her services, a man felt an electric shock in his blind eye, and the next moment he could see again. In one case a child's club foot straightened during the service.

Do all of Kathryn Kuhlman's followers receive miracle cures?

No. On the other hand, many who come without expecting help are instantaneously cured. Others are not aware until later that a cure has taken place.

What are the miracle cures at the Catholic shrine in Lourdes, France?

The reputation for miraculous cures at Lourdes began when a peasant girl named Bernadette Soubirous allegedly received a visitation from the Virgin Mary, who asked that a shrine be set up in this area. Today thousands of persons, many with crutches or on stretchers, come to Lourdes to bathe in the springs and hope for a cure. Many have been cured of such ailments as cancer, blindness, crushed spines, and other diseases thought to be irreversible. Although the waters should be polluted by those with contagious diseases, no one has ever been infected.

When is a miracle cure announced at Lourdes?

The Catholic Church proclaims a cure when medical records show that the disease had been considered incurable and the cure was instantaneous when the patient bathed in the waters. In one case, a blind woman recovered her sight, even though later tests showed that her optic nerve had atrophied. The woman, Madame Bire, was examined a month later by doctors, who said that the nerve had been restored and the cure was complete.

What is the percentage of such cures?

There may be many cures, but only a few miracles are declared. This means, however, that such cases have received the most careful medical scrutiny and have been thoroughly investigated.

Must a patient at Lourdes have absolute faith that he will be cured?

Faith is necessary, but it is not always easy to know whether one has it. The mind is full of mysteries. Many have come to Lourdes openly expressing their faith but have gone away disappointed. Others have come scoffing and skeptical but have departed cured. Faith or lack of it may have its origin in the unconscious mind.

What miracle healings took place at the tomb of the Abbé Paris?

After the Abbé died in 1731 many miracles were reported when people crowded into the churchyard. A Mlle. Coirin, who had lost her left breast after twelve years of cancer, saw it grow back at the Abbé's tomb.

What was "The Holy Coat"?

At Treves in Germany sufferers were cured in 1891 merely by touching a sacred relic known as "The Holy Coat."

What kinds of diseases are cured by psychic healing?

Practically every kind. In laying on of hands and other healer-to-patient situations, minor illnesses and psychosomatic ailments seem to get quick relief. In the miracle cures in religious halls and at shrines and tombs, the more serious ailments have allegedly been relieved or eliminated.

How permanent are psychic cures?

Sometimes the cure is instantaneous and the patient never suffers again. Often, as in the laying on of hands and other contact situations, it takes several treatments to effect a cure. In some cases the disease returns, possibly because the patient unconsciously clings to his symptoms for neurotic reasons. Dr. LeShan believes that a spiritual involvement of the subject in the healing process is likely to bring a permanent cure.

What is psychic surgery?

In the Philippine Islands, Brazil, England, and a few other countries, there are psychic individuals without medical training who perform operations without a scalpel or other instruments. Many of them claim that they work on the "astral" or "duplicate" body of the patient, and that the physical follows the astral cure. (See Chapter 14). Some psychic surgeons say that the astral body rises just above the physical body, allowing them to make their psychic incisions. Other psychic surgeons, such as the Mexican peasant Pachita, work directly on the physical body with crude instruments or just their hands.

What kind of psychic surgery did Arigo perform?

Arigo was a Brazilian peasant without a medical or other education, who operated with a penknife on thousands of peasants who filed into his office each day. Although he had no conscious knowledge of medical terms, he prescribed medicines for some of his patients and operated on the others. He used no anesthetics, and his patients did not feel pain. Arigo wielded his knife quickly and efficiently, often while talking to someone else and not even watching his own work. Almost no blood would be shed, and the patient would walk away from the operating table feeling only slightly tired.

What psychic surgeon specializes in eye disorders?

George Chapman, an English psychic, goes into a trance and works on the astral body of the patient. Bernard Hutton, a Czech journalist who was almost blind wrote about Chapman in his book *Healing Hands*, and told how Chapman restored his sight. Among Chapman's patients were nurses and a doctor's wife.

Where do psychic surgeons get their medical knowledge?

Many claim that their bodies are used by dead doctors. George Chapman's "collaborator" is a Dr. William Lang, who was an eye specialist when alive. Several persons who had known Lang were convinced from Chapman's conversation and mannerisms that Lang was indeed occupying his body. Arigo claimed that he was assisted by several spirit doctors —one German, one French, and one Japanese.

Who are the "spirit nurses"?

Along with the spirit surgeon who occupies his body, a psychic surgeon may have spirit assistants—other doctors and nurses. An English psychic surgeon, J. D. Thomas, had an invisible nurse to whom he spoke in German, the language of his spirit doctor. The dead Dr. Lang, manifesting through psychic surgeon George Chapman, has a corps of assistant spirit doctors and nurses who help with his eye operations.

Do "spirit hands" ever heal directly?

Spirits often perform healings without taking possession of a living person's body. Stainton Moses, one of England's famous psychics, said that his bronchitis was relieved when spirit hands that he had materialized made passes over his head, throat, chest, and back.

What doctor cured patients through "spirit raps"?

J. D. Dixon, a nineteenth-century homeopathist, got his prescriptions by interpreting knocks on the wall that purportedly came from spirit doctors.

Are psychic cures mentioned in the Bible?

Christ's cures of the blind, the halt, the lame, and the sick must certainly come under the heading of psychic and miracle healings. The Bible also mentions other instances of laying on of hands.

What is medical clairvoyance?

According to the Greek physician Hippocrates, medical clairvoyance is "the affection suffered by the body the soul sees with shut eyes." It is the ability to clairvoyantly "see" the internal organs and make diagnoses. There are records of servant girls who have assisted doctors by "seeing" and diagnosing the diseases of their patients. In this century the outstanding example of a medical clairvoyant was Edgar Cayce, who could make his diagnoses while in trance with the patient often hundreds of miles away.

Is Kathryn Kuhlman a medical clairvoyant?

During her services, Miss Kuhlman often calls out the symptoms of individuals sitting in her audience, although she doesn't know them by name. Sometimes she will point to the person, describe his ailment, and say, "God is healing you right now."

What is "psychometric" medical diagnosis?

Something belonging to the patient is given to a psychic, who holds the object and makes a diagnosis. Doctors have often consulted mediums for this service. Dr. Eugene Osty, a French physician, sometimes gave a photograph of his patient or a handwriting sample to the psychic. At other times he would just think of his patient and ask the psychic, through a combination of telepathy and medical clairvoyance, to make a diagnosis.

Are men or women better psychic healers?

Some psychic investigators, such as A. Campbell Holms, put in votes for the males. There is no conclusive evidence, however, that either men or women are the better healers. There are few men who can equal Kathryn Kuhlman's remarkable healing record.

Are there child psychic healers?

Not only healers but also diagnosticians. In the nineteenth century a nine-year-old boy, Daniel Offord, wrote prescriptions in Latin, a language unfamiliar to him. He foresaw a cholera epidemic in 1853 and prescribed a daily dose of half a teaspoonful of carbon as an antidote.

Can animals be cured by psychic healing?

Many pet-owners report cases of animals responding to the healing thoughts and prayers of their masters or of psychic healers. Of especial interest are the tests by Bernard Grad, a Montreal biologist. Dr. Grad took mice with ulcers and divided them into two groups. One, the control group, received no healing. The other mice were put in boxes, which a psychic healer held in his hands each day for half an hour. The psychically treated group recovered more quickly than the control group.

Have plants responded to psychic healing?

Dr. Grad used essentially the same kind of test on plants, but three healers were involved, one the psychic healer Estebany, the other two psychiatric patients. The object was to see what effect the personalities and attitudes of the healers would have on the growth of barley beans. For half-hour periods each of the would-be healers held bottles of saline later used to water barley seeds buried in soil in peat pots. The plants that grew the fastest were watered by saline bottles held by Estebany. The least successful healer was one of the psychiatric patients, who was very depressed and saw no purpose to the experiment.

What was the psychic healing test on enzymes?

There is a theory that any disease or illness can be traced to the malfunctioning of an enzyme in the cell. Sister Justa Smith, a biochemist at Rosary Hill College in Buffalo, damaged enzymes by ultraviolet light, then placed them in a bottle that was held for one-hour periods by a psychic healer. The recovery of the damaged enzymes was comparable to the therapeutic action of a strong magnetic field.

Is a kind of physical energy at work in psychic healing?

Dr. Grad seems to think so, as do other parapsychologists. Sister Smith's experiments suggest that a healer's hands may create a magnetic force. Lawrence LeShan describes this kind of healing as a current flowing between the healer's hands. There is no conclusive proof of a physical energy, however, nor does it explain healing at a distance.

Must the healer feel love for the person, animal, or plant to be healed?

All organisms seem to thrive when they are loved, and there are many examples reported by those who take care of animals and plants. (See Chapter 13.) However, in the tests by Dr. Grad, although the negative attitude of the depressed psychiatric patient seemed to inhibit healing, psychic healer Estebany felt no particular emotion when he held the bottle. In the tests by Sister Smith, psychic Malcolm Bessent spent the first five minutes concentrating his healing energy in his hands, then turned his attention to other things while he continued to hold the container. It may be that love as a conscious emotion is not necessary but that the healers, even those with a sense of detachment, are dedicated to the healing principle and this is reflected in their success.

How does the mystic sense aid healing?

Lawrence LeShan, who is training psychic healers, believes that the most effective kind of healing takes place when the healer feels "at one" with the patient. He tries to "merge" with the patient, and at the moment this happens there is biological improvement. LeShan calls this Type I healing, which does not require use of the hands. He believes that healing with the hands (Type II) is a physical method involving a "flow of current" from the hands of the healer to the body of the patient. LeShan thinks that Type I healing is far more effective than Type II and that results in Type I healing tend to be permanent.

What is the "aura"?

This is a halo of different colors that surrounds living objects. Many psychics claim that they can see the aura around human beings, animals, and plants and that its color is a key to the health of the organism. Some doctors have made diagnoses based on the change of color of an aura. The Russians claim that they have developed a process called Kirlian photography that can not only photograph the aura but also determine by its appearance when disease is about to strike.

What is the Russian theory of psychic healing?

The Russians, who insist on finding a physical basis for all phenomena, believe that a kind of energy they call bioplasma circulates through the body and may be seen as the aura through the Kirlian process. When the body is diseased, this energy shows a different pattern from when it is healthy, and it leaves the body completely at time of death. The bioplasma responds to the energy coming from the hands of psychic healers. One of them, a retired military man named Krivorotov, uses noncontact treatment by passing his hands a few inches behind the sick person's back. Both healer and patient feel intense heat radiating from each other, and the healer can pinpoint the location of the diseased organ. High-frequency photographs of the healer's hands show changes of energy patterns during the healing process.

Is the technique of psychic healing being studied in America?

Yes. Lawrence LeShan is training healers through meditation and other techniques. He claims that they have had a 40 to 50 per cent success with his cases, either individually or as a group, with the patients present or at a distance. The Southern California Society for Psychical Research has received a grant from the Parapsychology Foundation to study what happens physically during the psychic healing process. In England many physicians are making a serious study of psychic healing.

Is psychic healing merely self-suggestion?

In the final analysis, a person who is ill cures himself, either consciously or through very deep levels of the mind. This is demonstrable in hypnosis, also in the remarks of doctors who speak of the "will" of their patients to recover. Laying on of hands, passes over the body, and other kinds of unorthodox healing may actually plant the suggestion in the patient's mind, and he then consciously or unconsciously uses his mind-over-matter power to help himself. However, some cases of healing at a distance (group praying, meditation, etc.) are effective even when the patient doesn't know about them, unless PK or unconscious telepathy is at work. Psychic healing of plants and animals also rules out the self-suggestion theory. Psychic action at an unconscious, perhaps suprapersonal level may be the true explanation. At Lourdes a six-year-old child born an idiot and certainly without conscious awareness of what was happening was bathed in the waters and instantaneously cured of his brain deficiency. It would appear that the child and those who assisted him, along with the spiritual atmosphere of Lourdes, were all part of a psychic energy field in which the healing took place.

6

YOUR QUESTIONS ANSWERED ABOUT
"ALTERED STATES OF CONSCIOUSNESS"—MENTAL
STATES FAVORABLE TO PSYCHIC EXPERIENCES;
HOW THEY COME NATURALLY OR ARE INDUCED BY
ARTIFICIAL MEANS SUCH AS HYPNOSIS, DRUGS, AND
SENSORY DEPRIVATION . . .

What is an "altered state of consciousness"?

A state of mind that differs from everyday, conscious awareness, when one's attention is partially or completely withdrawn from the immediate environment. This can happen during periods of relaxation, daydreaming, drowsiness, sleep, exalted moods, trance states, drug-induced states, bursts of creativity, etc.

Do psychic phenomena tend to occur during altered states?

Yes, unless such states are brought on by psychosis or severe neurosis, which tend to inhibit the psychic sense.

Is psychic experience common during states of conscious awareness?

No. When the rational mind is functioning, spontaneous ESP or other psychic phenomena are not likely to occur. The subliminal mind, which is in the ascendant during altered states, is blocked off at this time.

At what point in the mental process is psychic experience most likely to break through?

At the point of transition from one state of mind to another. In sleep, for example, this may be when the sleeper is just beginning to fall asleep, moving from deep sleep to a lighter, dreaming sleep, or waking up. It often comes when a person concentrating on a task allows his mind to wander, that is, when his everyday, rational state of mind momentarily shifts to a fantasy or daydreaming state.

74

Why are spontaneous cases of ESP so difficult to duplicate in the laboratory?

Actually, many parapsychology laboratories today are using such altered states as dreams and the hypnotic trance in ESP experiments. In the Rhine type of testing, however, when a conscious effort is made to guess card symbols, numbers, etc., the effort itself may act as a block. Yet there is impressive evidence of success even under such controlled conditions. Rhine noticed that some of his subjects went into a slightly altered state during the tests—a state of "relaxed alertness."

What is characteristic of the "relaxed mind"?

Absence of bodily tension and a minimum of physical activity. During convalescence and similar conditions, such as recovery from childbirth, there is a state of passivity in which ESP often occurs. This state is accompanied by the brain-wave alpha pattern which can be traced on the electro-cephalograph.

What happens during the "fantasy-mind" altered state?

This is the daydreaming, reverie state, with rapidly occurring thoughts unrelated to the external environment. The fantasy-mind states occur frequently in children, who usually accept their psychic experiences without question. (See Chapter 12.) This state is sometimes artificially induced by sensory deprivation, when the subject stays for long periods in a completely darkened, soundproof room.

Does fasting bring on a fantasy-mind state?

Yes. Primitive tribes have often fasted for long periods to induce colorful visions and psychic experiences.

Are creative people psychic?

Creativity and psychic experience seem to be related. Artists, writers, and composers encourage their unconscious minds to surface and bring up much extrasensory material. In one experiment professional musicians were tested before and after ensemble performances, and it was found that a good performance stimulated their ESP ability.

Did Rhine find any connection between creativity and psychic ability?

He found many such examples among his student subjects. Two girls who had outstanding artistic talent and were unusually intuitive about other people did extremely well on the ESP card tests.

How does the "creative-mind" state differ from the "fantasy-mind" state?

The basic difference is that creativity is experienced in some kind of artistic framework and is given shape and meaning by the conscious mind. Psychic experiences, however, are common to both.

Do creative artists ever communicate mentally with each other while they work?

Yes. It is said that ideas are "in the air" and the unconscious creative minds of two or more artists will often reach out and grab them at the same time. This has been the basis of many lawsuits charging plagiarism. Writers who collaborate often communicate with each other telepathically.

How does music bring on psychic experiences?

The emotions of the listener are often stimulated and a train of associations is produced that may take him out of his immediate environment and stir up his psychic sense. The Dutch psychic Tholen once had a premonition of a plane crash when he was merely looking at notes in a music book. He "saw" the face of Queen Juliana superimposed over the notes and "heard" the music of "Ave Maria." Then a vision came to him of an airplane with forty-one funeral cars and one person walking away. A week later an airplane named the *Queen Juliana* crashed, killing forty-one passengers. The stewardess walked away from the wreckage.

Is music used as stimulation in ESP tests?

Music is often used as part of a "sensory bombardment" experiment (see Chapter 7), also in clairvoyance and precognition experiments at the Maimonides Medical Center Dream Laboratory. In one of Thelma Moss's experiments at the University of California at Los Angeles, the agent would look at pictures and listen to music that could stir him emotionally and convey his feelings telepathically to the subject in another room.

Can a physical setting or atmosphere heighten the psychic sense?

Very often. One can be lulled into something of a trance state by country scenes. A woman in Castleblaney, Ireland, was once looking dreamily at the quiet ripples in a small lake. Suddenly she "saw" a tall man in a tweed suit rising in a black cloud above the water. The man in her vision then leaped into the water and was drowned. A week later a man she did not know, identical in appearance, committed suicide where she had been watching the water.

What altered state is best for psychic experiences?

Probably dreams, along with the transition period when one is falling asleep (hypnagogic) or just waking up (hypnopompic). At this time the mental censor, or whatever keeps psychic impressions from crossing the barrier into consciousness, is almost completely off guard. When parapsychologist Louisa Rhine analyzed more than seven hundred spontaneous cases of psychic phenomena, she found that 65 per cent came in dreams.

What happens during the "twilight state" between sleep and waking?

In the hypnagogic and hypnopompic states there is a minimum of rational thinking but many dreamlike images and sounds. Alpha brain waves appear on the electroencephalograph. Many premonitions occur at this time, also many creative experiences. Much of the poem "Kubla Khan" came to Samuel Coleridge during this twilight state. In an experiment at the Maimonides Dream Laboratory, a subject in the hypnagogic state tried to clairvoyantly visualize a picture that was hanging in another room. He saw a "hunk of glass that had crossbars on it" and "a round stool." The picture of a communications satellite mounted on a round platform closely resembled the clairvoyant image.

Do psychic experiences ever come in deep sleep, that is, non-dreaming sleep?

It was thought at one time that the mind was completely nonfunctioning during deep sleep, but experiments in recent years indicate that there is probably some kind of mental activity all night long, and that psychic impressions may come in both the dreaming and nondreaming state. In another experiment at the Maimonides Dream Laboratory, a subject awakened during deep sleep accurately described a painting in another room, the "Dark Figure" by Castellon, depicting a somber figure in front of a red brick wall. The subject mentioned "a big red building . . . darkish reddish brown brick color . . . gloomy . . ."

What is the hypnotic or trance state?

A person who has been hypnotized or who puts himself into a trance has narrowed his field of consciousness until it is partially or completely withdrawn from his immediate surroundings. He is hypersuggestible but not passive.

Do ESP and other psychic phenomena happen during hypnotic trances?

Yes. For three thousand years or more, since the Egyptian priests began to heal through hypnosis, the hypnotic trance has given rise to psychic powers. After Mesmer's experiments in the eighteenth century, there was an increasing interest in ESP during the hypnotic trance, and the first controlled experiments in ESP were done with hypnosis. (See Chapter 2.) Today many parapsychologists, among them Stanley Krippner (United States), John Beloff (Great Britain), and Milan Ryzl (Czechoslovakia), frequently use hypnosis in their ESP experiments. Edgar Cayce, the sleeping prophet of Virginia Beach, put himself into trance for many years and visualized the anatomy of sick persons sometimes hundreds of miles away. (See Chapter 5.) Some Hindu yogis practise self-hypnosis to bring on extrasensory powers.

In psychiatric practice, is hypnosis ever used to induce ESP?

It has been done experimentally but generally not as part of the analytic hour. (See Chapter 2.) Dr. Jule Eisenbud of

Denver, Colorado, once made a mental suggestion to a hypnotized patient to call him long distance. A few moments
later the telephone rang.

**Who uses hypnosis as a training device to develop ESP pow-
ers?**

Several parapsychologists use hypnosis as a training tool,
but Dr. Milan Ryzl has probably made the most extensive use
of it. He has trained five hundred subjects in this technique
and says that at least fifty of them developed into good ESP
subjects. In one of his tests, his subjects were able to clairvoyantly see objects in opaque boxes.

**What four altered states were brought on during an ESP ex-
periment at the Maimonides Dream Laboratory?**

Dreaming, relaxation, fantasy, and hypnotic trance. Subjects in the Dream Laboratory were hypnotized in the
afternoon, then told to take a nap and describe what images
came to mind when they woke up. During this time an agent
sat in another room and concentrated on a famous painting.
Then the subjects went home and kept records of their
dreams for the following week. (See Chapter 7.)

What were the results of this "multiple mind state" test?

The fantasy images following the hypnotic induction and
daytime naps showed more ESP than later nighttime dreams.
Dr. Krippner, director of the Dream Laboratory, theorized
that hypnosis may have speeded up the telepathic process.

**If the agent in an ESP test is hypnotized, will the subject's
scores be higher?**

Such tests have indicated how close the rapport can be
between agent and subject. Dr. Morris Paulson, working with
parapsychologist Thelma Moss at the University of California
at Los Angeles, found that if either agent or subject was hypnotized, the results exceeded chance by 1000 to 1. When only
the agent was hypnotized, the subject reported that the ESP
messages were in sharper focus.

Do the Russians use hypnosis in their ESP experiments?

It is one of their primary tools and is frequently used in

long-distance telepathy. Subjects in Moscow may be put to sleep telepathically by hypnotists in Leningrad.

How does hypnotic age regression improve ESP ability?

Parapsychologist J. G. van Busschbach of the Netherlands believes that when an adult is regressed to his earlier child-mind state, psi ability is released. This would tie in with the general belief that children are more in tune with their psychic sense.

Is there a "séance-mind" state of consciousness?

Evidently there is, since all kinds of psychic experiences may occur during a séance. One example is the woman who saw the boy with the "fringe of hair" before the Aberfan coal slide. (See Chapter 3.) Another is the collective experience of the group that witnessed the sinking of the *Volturno* as they sat in an apartment (See Chapter 1.) Materializations, disembodied voices, telepathy, and clairvoyance may all occur because of the altered mind states of the medium and the members of the circle.

What is the "floodlight" state of consciousness?

If deep sleep represents the most unaware state of consciousness, at the other end of the spectrum is the "floodlight" or "superconscious" state, one of hyperawareness. It has been experienced by mystics and others who practice religious disciplines. Sometimes it comes without preparation to both psychics and ordinary persons. In its purest form it is called "cosmic consciousness." The floodlight state may be induced through hypnosis, hallucinogenic drugs, meditation, and the exercise of creativity.

What happens when the floodlight mind is turned on?

The experient feels a lessening of his own ego, a sense of unity with others, sometimes "oceanic feelings" that extend to everything in the universe. In his mind there is no division between subject and object—they are one. Logic and thinking are abandoned, time and space are blurred. This experience is called by different names in different religions: "transcendence" (Christian); "satori" (Zen); "samadhi" (Hindu), etc.

Does psychic experience come easily during the floodlight state?

Yes. Poets George Russell (Æ) and William Yeats had many floodlight experiences accompanied by ESP. Many dreamers who have out-of-body adventures report feelings of ecstasy and expanded awareness during this time. (See Chapter 14.)

What remarkable PK feat often occurs during a state of religious ecstasy?

Levitation. Many saints levitated, including St. Francis of Assisi, St. Teresa of Avila, and St. Joseph of Copertino. (See Chapter 4.)

Does the practice of meditation develop psi?

Yes. This is a technique used by nearly every psychic and those interested in sharpening their psychic sense. Groups that meet for ESP testing at the American Society for Psychical Research hold periods of silent meditation before the tests begin.

What is the procedure in meditation?

The meditator sits in one of several positions, generally cross-legged on the floor or in a chair. He relaxes both mind and body and watches the inflow and outflow of his breath. He may make his mind a blank, try to solve a seemingly paradoxical problem (called a koan in Zen meditation), or merely observe his thoughts as they pass through his mind until he feels detached from them. Meditation may be silent or may be accompanied by chanting. It leads to gradual withdrawal from the outer environment and into the inner self. The ultimate goal is to become egoless and to experience a sense of oneness with others.

Does caffein help or hinder psi performance?

Coffee seems to improve ESP, as reported by Rhine and other researchers.

How does alcohol affect ESP powers?

A small quantity gets rid of inhibitions that block ESP, but more than that may befog the mind and defeat the purpose of the experiment. During the checkerboard ESP test described in Chapter 2, the subject went from 21 per cent to 75 per cent success after taking a small drink of liquor.

Do drugs heighten ESP powers?

Sometimes but not invariably. It depends on the drug and the amount that is used, on the state of mind of the subject, and emotional and other factors. Dr. Rhine found that such drugs as sodium amobarbital inhibited ESP during laboratory tests.

What is the effect of psychedelic drugs on psychic powers?

The overall results of testing with psychedelic drugs are inconclusive, but some striking experiences have been reported after the subject took LSD, mescaline, or psilocybin.

Who heard music out of listening range after taking mescaline?

The Spanish pharmacologist Bascompto Lakanal reported that subjects in an experiment reproduced not only music sung in a different room but also drawings and spoken words. The Russian parapsychologist Vasiliev also found that mescaline facilitated ESP.

What was the strange case of the "psychedelic mushroom"?

Dr. Margaret Paul was a psychiatrist who experimented with the *Amanita pantherina* mushroom, which has a psychedelic effect. While she was enjoying a three-hour fantasy, one of her patients went into an irrational state, while another "lost" three hours during which he couldn't think straight and had the impulse to eat mushrooms for the first time in his life. Neither patient was aware of what was happening to Dr. Paul.

Do primitive tribes use drugs to stimulate their psychic powers?

Many tribes have taken drugs for this purpose. Natives in Latin America took ololiuqui, a morning-glory seed, before the arrival of the Spanish missionaries. The Spanish conquistadors told of American Indians who used peyote so that they could predict when enemies would attack or to find the hiding place of stolen goods.

How does yage, an Indian drink, bring on clairvoyance?

When South American Indians drink yage, they go into a deep trance and become both telepathic and clairvoyant. During this time they know what is happening in a village hundreds of miles away.

What did the Incas chew to enhance their ESP powers?

When Spanish missionaries arrived in Mexico, they found the Incan soothsayers chewing coca leaves.

What is the consensus among researchers about psi ability in drug-induced states?

The late Dr. Walter N. Pahnke, Director of Clinical Sciences at the Maryland Psychiatric Research Center in Baltimore, Maryland, said this in an article in the *Parapsychology Review* (July–August 1971): "Up to the present, no clear-cut or substantial effect of any drug has been demonstrated, perhaps with the exception of the depressing effects of a barbiturate like sodium amobarbital on ESP scoring as reported by Rhine." However, the experience of primitive tribes plus the reports that come from individual and laboratory experiments, indicates that certain drugs, in the right circumstances, particularly when there is rapport with the experimenter and others involved, will bring on an altered state in which psychic experiences do occur.

How does an ESP subject change consciousness through the "feedback" technique?

According to dream researcher Joseph Kamiya, anyone can learn how to control his brain activity. Machines are now being used to signal when a subject is in the alpha brainwave state that is favorable to ESP, a state of relaxed alertness in which mind and body are quiet and free of tension. In the Kamiya experiment a bell would ring when the subject was in the alpha state, as recorded on the electroencephalograph, thus confirming the kind of mood he should maintain. Experiments at the American Society for Psychical

Research are also improving the ESP of subjects through feedback. The dynograph sounds a tone when the subject is in alpha. Another machine in use at the ASPR is the ESPa-teacher, which has five colored lights that flash on and off. When the subject in the next room guesses which light is flashing, he punches a button. If his guess is right, a chime will sound, thus indicating that he is in the right altered state and reinforcing his ESP powers.

What did William James say about the importance of altered states of consciousness?

"Our normal waking consciousness . . . is but one special type of consciousness, whilst all about it, parted from it by the flimsiest of screens, there lie potential forms of consciousness entirely different. We may go through life without suspecting their existence; but apply the requisite stimulus, and at a touch they are there in all their completeness. . . . No account of the universe in its totality can be final which leaves these other forms of consciousness quite disregarded."

7

What kinds of psychic experience happen in dreams?

Many kinds: clairvoyance—seeing distant objects and events taking place at the time of the dream; telepathy—making contact with another mind while dreaming; out-of-body experiences (see Chapter 14); precognition—knowing through the dream what is going to happen in the future; and possibly contact with spirits. Dreams are the most active channel for psychic experience.

Are most ESP dreams pleasant or unpleasant?

Although Freud believed that wish-fulfillment is the underlying motive of all dreams, most dreams are unpleasant, and this includes the extrasensory kind. The emotional tone of an unpleasant dream probably makes a stronger impact on the dreamer than pleasant or neutral dreams do. Death is common in dreams, coming to the dreamer, his relatives, or friends.

What was Mark Twain's death dream?

Twain dreamed that he saw the body of his brother Henry lying in a metal coffin, supported by two chairs. On Henry's breast was a bouquet of white flowers, a single red flower in the middle. Two days after the dream Henry was killed in a steamboat explosion. When Mark Twain entered the room, he saw the same details as in the dream, except for the flowers. A moment later a woman came in carrying a large white bouquet with a single red rose in the middle.

What was the dream of the "blue coffin"?

This dream is on record with the Society for Psychical Research. A young mother dreamed that a cart drove up to her house bearing three coffins, two white and one blue, the blue coffin the largest. The driver left the larger white coffin and drove off with the others. A few days later the woman's little boy died at the same time that the infant son of her neighbor also died. There were three coffins at the funeral, two white and one blue. The infant was put in the smaller white coffin, the dreamer's son in the larger white coffin, while a third child who had died, older than the other two, was laid in the blue one.

Who "witnessed" the murder of her brother in a dream?

A Chicago girl of nineteen "saw" her brother, a farmer living fifty miles away, being killed by a neighbor. The next day she went with another brother to the neighbor's house and found blood in the kitchen. She sensed that her brother was buried in the henhouse, where they found his body five feet underground.

Did Abraham Lincoln "see" his assassination in a dream?

He didn't dream of the actual assassination but saw in astonishing detail what followed. About six weeks before his death, Lincoln dreamed that he woke up in the White House to the sound of sobbing and was told by a guard that the President had been killed and was lying in the East Room. Lincoln also had a recurring dream in which he was drifting away in a boat to an unknown shore. (See Chapter 3.) He described this dream to the members of his cabinet several hours before he was shot.

What famous "dream letter" predicted the killing of a royal couple?

The murder of Austrian Archduke Franz Ferdinand in June 1914 triggered World War I. Twelve hours before the Archduke and his wife were killed by the same bullet, Bishop Joseph de Lanyi of Grosswarden, who had been his teacher, dreamed that he received a letter from the Archduke bordered in black and reading: "Your Eminence, dear Dr. de

Lanyi, my wife and I have been victims of a political crime at Sarajevo." Superimposed on the letter was the scene that took place the next day when the assassin fired into a car in which the Archduke and his wife were sitting.

What dream foreshadowed the death of three astronauts?

In her dream a German actress, Mrs. M., witnessed a countdown and felt "tragedy in the dream because of stupidity and carelessness." That same night in January 1967, Apollo 6 went up in flames with three astronauts.

How many dreams were there of the 1966 tragedy in Aberfan, Wales?

Of the two hundred reported premonitions of the disaster that killed 144 adults and children, the vast majority came in dreams, starting about four weeks earlier and hitting a peak about two weeks before the coal slide. Of sixty premonitions investigated by Dr. J. C. Barker, thirty-six came in dreams.

Were the Aberfan dreams exactly like the later disaster?

Some of the dreams reproduced the exact details, while others were in symbols. One woman dreamed of "children standing by a building [the school] below a black mountain. Hundreds of black horses then thunder down the hillside dragging hearses." Another woman had a nightmare of a child enshrouded in black steam.

In what dream was a woman commanded to choose death for either her husband or her daughter?

This dream was reported by the French astronomer Camille Flammarion. A ghost appeared to the woman in the dream and said that the agonizing choice of death for either one was up to her. She tried to put the dream out of mind but finally decided that, if she had to make a choice, she would spare her daughter. A few days later her husband, who had been in perfect health, died suddenly.

What was the warning dream of the "triangular dagger"?

This dream saved the life of a young man, who told the story to writer Arthur Conan Doyle. While on vacation in

Switzerland, he dreamed one night that a big man menaced him with a triangular dagger. The next day he was exploring an abandoned tunnel when he paused beneath a massive triangular icicle hanging from the roof and coming to a sharp point. Remembering his dream, he stepped back quickly and the next moment the icicle, which weighed about two hundred pounds, crashed on the spot where he had been standing.

Who put his nephew in jail because of a warning dream?

Nicholas Wotton, Dean of Canterbury, dreamed in 1553 that his nephew Thomas Wotton was involved in a plot to prevent the marriage of Queen Mary of England to King Philip of Spain. He then arranged with the Queen to have the young man incarcerated on a trumped-up charge. This ruse saved his nephew's life because, while he was in jail, the other conspirators were rounded up and executed.

Are lost objects ever located in dreams?

Many times. In the fifth century B.C., a valuable golden vessel was stolen from the temple of Herakles in Greece. The playwright Sophocles, who wrote *Oedipus Rex*, dreamed three times that the god Herakles visited him and gave the name of the thief. The accused man confessed and returned the vessel.

What was the famous "scarab" dream reported by psychiatrist Carl Jung?

Jung's patient, a young lady who had resisted all attempts to get well, told him about a dream in which someone had handed her a golden scarab. While she was describing the dream, an insect tapped on the window. Jung opened the window and took it in. It was a scarabaeoid bettle, very close in appearance to the golden scarab. Just as in the dream, Jung handed the insect to the girl, saying, "Here is your scarab." The dream and its aftermath, in Jung's words, "punctured the desired hole in her rationalism and broke the ice of her intellectual resistance."

Who dreamed in 1886 of a new comet in the sky?

This was either a clairvoyant or precognitive dream covering one of the greatest distances on record. Charles L. Tweedale, an amateur astronomer, had his dream at four A.M., then ran to his telescope and peered at the eastern sky, where the comet came into view. The dream may also have been telepathic, because at the same time two astronomers, Barnard and Hartwig, were announcing their discovery of the comet.

Who perfected the sewing machine in a dream?

The inventor Elias Howe dreamed that he had been captured by a savage tribe, whose king warned him that he would die if he did not find a solution to his problem within twenty-four hours. At the end of that period in his dream, the savages menaced him with their spears, and he saw the points coming at him, each spear with an eye-shaped hole. He woke up with the realization that, for his sewing machine, the eye should be near the point, not at the top or in the middle. There have been many other scientists and inventors who used dreams in this way to solve problems, among them James Watt, Louis Agassiz, and Niels Bohr, the physicist.

What famous author watched his characters perform in dreams?

Robert Louis Stevenson said that his dreams were filled with "little people" who provided him with "truncheons of tales upon their lighted theatre." The idea for *Dr. Jekyll and Mr. Hyde* was first dramatized in a dream.

What well-known composition was written by the Devil in a dream?

The composer Giuseppe Tartini dreamed that he handed a violin to Satan, who then played a piece "so singularly beautiful, and executed with such taste and precision, that it surpassed all that he had ever heard or conceived in his life." Later Tartini used the dream musical theme in his best work, "The Devil's Trill."

Why is dream telepathy difficult to prove?

Generally the dream is not reported or recalled until the dreamer learns from other sources that it may have been psychic. Writing down the details upon awakening and telling others help to verify it later. Experiments in dream laboratories (see later questions) are also making it easier to prove dream telepathy and clairvoyance.

What Swedish psychic gives proof for her extrasensory dreams?

Eva Hellstrom of Stockholm is not only a psychic but also the founder of the Swedish Society for Psychical Research. By writing her dreams in a diary each morning and having them witnessed by members of her family, she documents those that prove to be psychic. In addition, she has trained herself to analyze the qualities of a psychic dream.

What is the strongest motivation for psychic dreams?

The dreamer's emotional link to persons, events, and settings—just as in other psychic states. Mrs. Hellstrom often has extrasensory dreams of illness and death involving relatives. In her dreams of accidents friends have often played a role, sometimes because they lived in the vicinity of the accident. As for settings, once when Mrs. Hellstrom was visiting in Egypt, she had a dream of the forthcoming war between England and Egypt.

What is the significance of symbols in psychic dreams?

Symbols are important in any kind of dream, of course, in representing people, attitudes of mind, etc. In Mrs. Hellstrom's dream of the English-Egyptian war, she saw a "Scotsman in a kilt" and this symbolized for her the presence of the British.

What is the dreamer's role in a psychic dream?

Mrs. Hellstrom and other psychics have discovered that their dreams are more likely to be extrasensory when they are observers of the dream action rather than participants in it.

Are most extrasensory dreams in color?

Psychics, and creative persons in general, report that they have more dreams in color than in black and white. Color seems to be an attribute of extrasensory dreams.

What else is characteristic of an extrasensory dream?

The dream is very vivid, much more realistic than an ordinary dream. The dreamer usually has a strong conviction that his dream is extrasensory.

Have two or more persons ever had the same dream on the same night?

There are many such cases on record. Once, back in the middle of the nineteenth century, a young law student dreamed that he was being choked to death by a ruffian who finally hit him with an ax and killed him. In the dream he saw his friends rushing to his rescue and heard their anguished cries when they were unable to help. The next day a fellow student described the same dream, which he had had at the same time, in which he was rushing to help the dreamer. A week later the dreamer talked to another friend in another city who had had the same dream on the same night and was also hurrying to rescue him. Fortunately, only telepathy was involved, for the dreaded murder never occurred, as it would have if the dream had been precognitive.

What are the dream telepathy laboratory experiments?

In the last ten or fifteen years there have been several experiments of this kind by parapsychologists and dream researchers, but the best-known and most impressive are those at the Dream Laboratory of the Maimonides Medical Center in Brooklyn, New York. The dreamer sleeps in a soundproof room while he is hooked up to an electroencephalograph (EEG) in another room, the control room, where the experimenter watches his brain-wave patterns traced on graph paper. The agent sits in a third room and tries to beam the details of an art print to the dreamer's mind. The dreamer, of course, does not know what the painting is, as it is chosen through a random procedure after he has retired for the night. When the EEG shows that the sleeper is dreaming, the experimenter wakes him up over the intercom and asks him to describe his dreams, and his words are tape-recorded. Later the dreams are compared with the target painting for evidence of ESP.

What have been the results of these experiments?

Both the dreamer and three professional judges not connected with the Dream Laboratory compare the dreams with the paintings used on different nights, and their evaluations are given a statistical rating. The results have often been "statistically significant." Some of the experiments described below give an idea of how closely many of the dreams matched the paintings.

When one target painting was of the Dempsey-Firpo prize fight in 1923, what did the sleeper dream about?

He dreamed of Madison Square Garden in New York City, the scene of the fight, and of a boxing match. This was a direct "hit."

How did one series of dreams match the painting of a "nude, dark-skinned girl by a stream of water"?

The painting was "The Moon and the Earth" by Gauguin. The sleeper, a female secretary, dreamed she was in a bathing suit getting out of a tub of water. She also dreamed of another girl with a "dark tan skin."

How close did one dream come to Chagall's "The Yellow Rabbi"?

The painting shows an elderly rabbi sitting at a table, reading a book. The dreamer, a male psychologist, dreamed of "a man in his sixties . . . a minister or priest . . . sitting and reading from a book."

How did one set of dreams match Dali's "Sacrament of the Last Supper"?

Dali's painting depicts Christ at a table surrounded by his twelve disciples. A glass of wine and a loaf of bread are on the table, while a body of water and a fishing boat can be seen in the background. The sleeper dreamed of "Christmas," "the Mediterranean Ocean," "Biblical times," "twelve men pulling a fishing boat," a "fish," and "a loaf."

When did "meat" and "a black rock" appear in both the target painting and the dreams?

The painting was Tamoyo's "Animals": two dogs eating pieces of meat, a huge black rock in the background. The sleeper, a female teacher, dreamed about a banquet where people were eating meat, and of a "mermaid from Black Rock."

When did the dreamer catch the "Hollywood" mood of a target painting?

The painting for the night was Orozco's "Zapatistas," which could have depicted a Hollywood extravaganza with its group of Mexican revolutionaries on the move, clouds and mountains in the background. The sleeper dreamed of a "De-Mille super-type colossal production" set in New Mexico, with travelers and Indians, pueblos, mountains, and cloudy weather.

How did the dream word "poisse" match a target painting?

The painting was de Chirico's "The Sacred Fish," showing two dead fish on a wooden slab which had been placed in front of a candle. The sleeper, a female artist, dreamed of the word "poisse," which in French is short for "poisson," or fish. She also dreamed of "lighting a candle" and of "death."

How did one dreamer clairvoyantly see the "whirling football" in a painting?

The painting was called "Football Players" and it showed the moving football and some men dressed in turn-of-the-century clothes. The sleeper dreamed of "a revolving something . . . spinning like a top," also of "sports events," and of a "design that was considered very artistic around 1903 or 1904."

Were these dreams examples of telepathy or clairvoyance?

Probably both. Since the agent looked at the picture, telepathy could have been involved. However, the sleeper may have "seen" the picture clairvoyantly without the mind of the agent taking part in the transmission.

Were men or women the better ESP dreamers in the experiments?

An analysis was made of 74 sessions involving 14 male agents, 41 male subjects or sleepers, 9 female agents, and 33 female subjects. The pairing of female subject and female agent produced inconclusive results, as did the pairing of male agent and female subject. There were more impressive results from female agent–male subject and male agent–male subject pairings. In general, however, ESP comes more easily when there is an emotional affinity between the persons involved, with the females usually better receivers, the males better senders. (See Chapter 1.)

How did emotional stimulation sharpen the dreamer's telepathic images?

Art paintings with vivid colors, archetypal themes, and emotional associations were chosen for their subliminal effect on the dreamer. Psychics in other kinds of ESP situations are also stimulated by music and paintings out of sensory range.

How was music used as an emotional stimulus in a long-distance dream-telepathy experiment?

While the subjects were dreaming, the agents were in a "sensory bombardment chamber" fourteen miles from the Dream Laboratory. Here they tried to transmit mentally images from forty different slide sequences of art paintings, while listening to music with a strong emotional content. The results were spectacular. For example, when the theme of one set of slides was "Far Eastern Religions," one of the sleepers dreamed of paintings, sculptures, and statues of the Buddha. The dreamer said: "I saw a rather beautiful face, squarish, with slanty eyes. Eastern, I would think . . ."

How did precognition happen accidentally in the Dream Laboratory experiments?

Dr. Krippner, director of the Dream Laboratory, noticed that often the sleeper would dream about a painting that would not be shown until several weeks later, a clear example of precognition. One subject dreamed of "a Negro man on a boat being tossed by waves." The target picture some weeks later was Homer's "The Gulf Stream," depicting a black man on a raft with a hurricane approaching.

What were the experiments in dream precognition at Maimonides?

In two series of experiments, one in 1969 and the other in 1970, the young English psychic Malcolm Bessent slept in the laboratory and tried to dream about paintings that would not be chosen until the next day. There were no agents as in the telepathy/clairvoyance experiments, and no one knew at the time which pictures would be selected.

How was sensory stimulation brought into the precognition tests?

This was similar to the "sensory bombardment" effect except that the emotional and sensory stimuli were created *after* the night of dreams on the theory that cause and effect could be reversed in time. For example, after the first night of dreams, when the painting chosen was Van Gogh's "Corridor of the Saint Paul Hospital," Krippner created a kind of psychodrama for Bessent, using the senses of movement, touch, taste, hearing, and smell. These were based on the theme of the picture, which showed a mental hospital.

How did Bessent's dreams match the Van Gogh painting?

He dreamed about a mental hospital, people drinking water, doctors and psychiatrists, a female patient running down the corridor and escaping, a feeling of hostility. The next morning, after choosing the Van Gogh painting in a randomized procedure, Dr. Krippner played the part of a mad psychiatrist, while he showed Bessent weird pictures presumably drawn by mental patients and ordered him to swallow a pill with a glass of water. The correspondence between the Van Gogh painting and the dreams was so striking that when Bessent walked into Krippner's office and saw the painting on the wall, he exclaimed, "My God, that's my dream!"

How did a picture of Alaska affect Bessent's dreams the previous night?

The target painting chosen after the night of dreams was Akpaliapik's "Walrus Hunter." In the morning Bessent was shown white northern lights from a color organ and sheets draped over furniture to resemble ice and snow. Ice was applied to his face and back while several fans blew air on him. In one of his dreams he was "standing in a room, surrounded by white. Every imaginable thing in the room was white . . . the light was very bright . . . predominant colors were pale and ice blues and whites . . ."

What was the design of the second series of dream-precognition tests in 1970?

Bessent was asked to dream about the content of a slide sequence that he would not see until the following evening. No one in the laboratory knew what the slides would be until they were chosen at random many hours after the dreams were over.

When the slides showed Christ on the Cross, what did Bessent dream about the night before?

"Religious overtones and symbology . . . three men on camels . . . The main theme was religious, philosophical, mystical. . . ."

How did Bessent's precognitive dreams match a slide sequence on Egyptian art?

He dreamed of "a boy and girl on some Mediterranean island . . . someone being transported to the Middle East." When the theme of one sequence was of birds, he dreamed the night before of the sky, the color blue, and different kinds of doves. In the morning he said, "I just have the feeling that the next target material will be about birds."

How was hypnosis used at the Dream Laboratory to induce ESP dreams?

This experiment, mentioned in Chapter 6, began during the day with two groups, one hypnotized and the other acting as a "control" group. As in the other telepathy experiments, the agent sat in another room and "sent out" his impressions of the paintings. The subjects in both groups then took a nap and told what images came to mind when they woke up. Then they went home and kept records of their night dreams for the following week.

What were the results of this experiment?

For the hypnotized group, the daytime images showed striking similarities to the paintings, but the later nighttime dreams were less impressive. For the control group, however, the results were just the opposite. When the target picture was Robinson's "Windmill," with the setting in Virginia, one of the hypnotized subjects had images of "down South" and visualized grass, a pasture, and a country road, all of which were in the picture.

What happened unexpectedly when Chagall's "Rabbi With a Lemon" was the target painting?

A friend of one of the hypnotized subjects was sitting in another room when he had the urge to sketch a bearded man in a derby. This was a likeness of the rabbi in the painting.

8

YOUR QUESTIONS ANSWERED ABOUT OBJECTS USED AS "PROPS" TO BRING ON PSYCHIC EXPERIENCES: TEA LEAVES, STROBE LIGHTS, MAGIC MIRRORS, EGGSHELLS, PLAYING CARDS, TAROT CARDS, ETC.; SEEING VISIONS IN CRYSTAL BALLS, HEARING VOICES IN A SEASHELL, HOLDING OBJECTS THAT CONTAIN A PSYCHIC RECORD OF THE PAST; THE THEORY AND PRACTICE OF PSYCHOMETRY; HOW TO BECOME A CRYSTAL-GAZER . . .

What is "scrying"?

Scrying is a method of getting psychic information of the past, present, and future through images in a reflecting surface—crystal balls, mirrors, water, etc.

How widespread is the practice of scrying?

Scryers—crystal-gazers and others—were prominent in ancient Assyria, Persia, Egypt, and China. The practice spread all over the world to practically all countries and continents.

What is "crystal vision"?

A form of scrying in which the psychic gazes into a crystal ball until images appear. In ancient times this practice was called crystallomancy.

What does a crystal ball look like?

Generally it is a small sphere, although sometimes it is six-sided, from three to five inches in diameter, made of quartz and colored white, blue, yellow, or green. It may be translucent or transparent. Some crystals were shaped like pyramids or cylinders, and often small pieces of crystal were embedded in rings or other objects. An ancient practice was to lower the crystal into water before staring at it.

Do primitive tribes practice crystal vision?

Yes. Among them are the Zulus, Australian aborigines, and other tribes. Andrew Lang writes of a Malagasy woman who saw two French vessels in her crystal ball and predicted the day of their arrival.

Are crystal balls in active use today?

Yes. They are still used as psychic props. Jeane Dixon has a ball that was given to her by a gypsy. Mrs. Dixon looked into it and saw where the gypsy was born. Another psychic who uses a crystal ball is Ann Jensen of Dallas, Texas.

How can the average person become a crystal-gazer?

Lewis Spence in his *Encyclopedia of Occultism* suggests getting a crystal ball that is "a perfect sphere, free from speck or flaw, highly polished and contained in a stand of polished ebony, ivory, or boxwood." Other scryers recommend that the ball be kept clean at all times and that no one else hold it except the person for whom the scryer does a reading.

How well should the room be lighted?

The crystal ball should be placed against a dark background, with no distracting reflections from other objects. The ball can be held in one's lap or in the hand, or placed on a dark cloth. The light should be at the scryer's rear, but total darkness in a room is not advisable. Many psychics believe that a dim light is best.

How far away should the scryer be from the ball?

About the distance one would hold a book when reading.

What should be the scryer's state of mind?

He should be relaxed but with his attention concentrated on the ball, and should gaze into it for as long as necessary before a vision appears and before his eyes tire.

What happens when visions come into the ball?

First the ball clouds over; then the images appear. They may be very tiny in size or fill the surface of the ball. The scenes may be colored or in black and white. Sometimes the crystal itself disappears from view and life-size pictures fill the room.

What is the explanation for crystal vision?

The "rational" explanation is that the images are projections from the unconscious mind of the psychic, symbolic representations of personal problems or fragments of forgotten memories. Frederic Myers, one of the founders of the British Society for Psychical Research, believed it was a means for the subliminal mind to send messages to the conscious self. This theory foreshadowed the views of Freud and later psychiatrists.

How does the subliminal-mind theory explain unfamiliar scenes that appear in the ball?

We may keep a mental store of objects and events that were never registered by the conscious mind. Miss Goodrich Freer, a writer and psychical researcher, once saw in her crystal ball a newspaper announcing the death of an acquaintance. At first she thought this was a clairvoyant experience, then discovered that, although she had not read the previous day's newspaper, she had used the page on which the announcement appeared as a screen to shield her face from the light. In this way the news item may have been implanted in her mind without conscious awareness.

Are some crystal visions extrasensory?

Yes. The subliminal-mind theory does not hold in every case. Ann Jensen, the Dallas psychic, once looked in her crystal ball and witnessed a bank holdup. This was verified later in the day by a television broadcast giving the same details as in the vision. On another occasion Mrs. Jensen saw a scene with a brown bear reclining in a basket chair. When her newspaper was delivered later, the identical picture was on the front page. These are definite instances of clairvoyance.

What was the crystal-ball experiment with lighted candles?

This was an unusual ESP experiment conducted by Miss Goodrich Freer, whose studies of the crystal ball have given us much information on how it works. First she sent her friend into the dining room, where there were unlighted candles on the table. Then she mentally projected the scene into her crystal ball and "lighted" the candles in her vision. Her friend immediately called out, "But why have they lighted the candles in broad daylight?"

Does the crystal ball ever reveal the future?

Psychics report many cases of predicting the future for their clients, using the ball as a prop or center of focus for visions which probably originate in their minds. Physicist W. F. Barrett, a member of the Society for Psychical Research, tells of a lady seer who was reading for a friend. First she handed the ball to her friend to hold. When it was handed back to her, she saw a tall, rather bald man take a gun and shoot himself. Three days later the woman's husband, the man in the vision, shot himself.

Do the images ever have a physical reality?

Some of the pictures have appeared larger when seen through a magnifying glass. The images have also been photographed. A child's head in a crystal was photographed and reproduced in a magazine in 1920.

Have there been cases of collective scrying?

Yes. One was reported during a session with the nineteenth-century medium D. D. Home. With the crystal ball on his head, those present saw an image of the ocean as though they were on top of a cliff. Sir Arthur Conan Doyle, creator of Sherlock Holmes, reports that both he and a medium saw the same message written in a crystal ball. Ann Jensen's friends often witness the same scenes she sees in her crystal.

Do spirits ever communicate through the crystal ball?

If spirits do exist, the crystal ball is as good as any other "prop" through which to send their messages. Nandor Fodor, the parapsychologist who became a psychiatrist, believed that in some cases spirits might communicate just as they may do through the ouija board and automatic writing (see Chapter 9). Sometimes these messages have been written backwards, which could be evidence of spirit communication.

How many persons in the general population have crystal vision?

Charles Richet, the physiologist who investigated every phase of the paranormal, believed that one in twenty may have this ability. Others can develop it, however, through meditation and other techniques, along with actual practice.

Was a book or play ever "written" in a crystal ball?

We go back again to Miss Goodrich Freer, who was a novelist. She often projected her characters into her crystal and, by observing what they did, got her ideas for the next scenes and chapters in her book. The part that fictitious characters have played in the dreams of authors and playwrights such as Robert Louis Stevenson suggests that they may have a kind of reality of their own.

How are other reflecting surfaces used in scrying?

Any such surface will do for either spontaneous experiences or experimental purposes—a mirror, a river, a spring, polished glass, the blade of a sword, etc. A young lady once saw in a doorknob a death scene that came true nine months later.

How does the "magic mirror" work?

The mirror has been a source of psychic information for thousands of years. The queen in "Snow White and the Seven Dwarfs" was practicing catoptromancy when she asked the mirror on the wall who was the fairest lady of all. The mirror, as we know, gave her an answer she didn't want to hear. A true case of "magic mirrors" occurred during the French Revolution when a young lady saw the killing of Robespierre in her door mirror, although the scene took place many miles away.

How were mirrors used to diagnose disease?

The Greeks used a form of catoptromancy and hydromancy (seeing visions in water) at the Temple of Cerae at Patrae. Here a sick person would lower a mirror suspended from a thread until it touched the surface of the water. Then his image in the mirror would presage death or recovery. Among some American Indian tribes, those who were ill gazed into the water until they saw images of foods and medicines that would cure them.

How does the "magic mirror" bring love and romance?

In certain parts of the United States, a young girl often walks backwards down the cellar stairs on Halloween, looking intently into her mirror. If she doesn't trip and break her neck first, the image of her future husband may appear. In Greece and elsewhere, maidens hold mirrors over a well and watch for the image of their dream man to appear.

How did "magic mirrors" trap unfaithful wives?

In many cultures, including the Berbers, cuckolded husbands had a sure way to get the evidence: they looked into their mirrors and saw the faces of Don Juans who were wooing their wives.

How have thieves been caught through scrying?

In Scotland a bucket would be filled with water, which would then reveal the face of the thief. In Polynesia a robber is caught in the following way: the priest prays, then a hole is dug in the floor and filled with water. As he looks intently into the water, the face of the thief appears.

Can lost objects be found through scrying?

Yes. The concentration on the crystal ball and other scrying devices may stir up memories in the unconscious mind, or clairvoyance may even operate. Apache medicine men were probably using clairvoyance when they located lost ponies by gazing into crystals.

Is scrying mentioned in the Bible?

According to the Old Testament, Joseph and his brothers scried into a cup. The Hebrew Talmud tells of brass objects used for scrying, along with mirrors, crystals, and water poured into the palm of the hand.

What is "fingernail" scrying?

This was called onychomancy: a young boy's fingernails were covered with oil and turned to the sun to reveal mystic messages. Other offbeat scrying devices are gems, eggshells, and ivory handles. The Seeress of Prevorst, a psychic of the early nineteenth century, saw visions in soapbubbles. Anne Harmon, a New York actress, once saw a man's occupation reflected in his eyeball.

Why have children often been used as scryers?

Probably because of their ostensible innocence and purity, qualities associated with mysticism. The celebrated eighteenth-century occultist Count Alessandro Cagliostro gave the following requisites for a young lady assistant: "She must be of a purity unexcelled, except by the angels; she was to be born under a given constellation, have delicate nerves, great susceptibility, and blue eyes."

Has scrying ever been a salaried occupation?

John Dee, a notorious occultist of the sixteenth century, had a number of scryers on his payroll, the best-known being Edward Kelly, whom he paid fifty pounds a year. Astrologer William Lilly also writes of a "speculatrix, Sarah Skehorn, who did crystal ball readings for a doctor," but no salary is mentioned.

How do psychic messages come from a seashell?

A clairaudient psychic can put the seashell to his ear and hear voices that may be coming from a distant source or from the past, or even may be saying words that will be spoken in the future. Sometimes the words cannot be traced to any living person but may be a spirit communication or a psychic message of unknown origin.

What is psychometry?

In psychometry the psychic holds an object and gets impressions of the person to whom it belongs or who may have had contact with it. The psychometric object, like the crystal ball and other scrying devices, thus becomes a "prop" that stimulates the psychic powers.

Does a psychometric object have emotional associations?

As stated earlier, every object has a psychic history and may give off emotional vibrations absorbed from persons who have handled it. Charles Richet mentions a psychic who held an object concealed in several folds of paper. She said it was either a rope or a necktie and that it had killed a man. It was a necktie with which a condemned man had hanged himself.

Who held a piece of string and "saw" a firebomb explode?

Gustav Pagenstecher was a German doctor practicing in Mexico who discovered a "natural" psychometrist, a Mrs. Zierold. He conducted forty experiments with her during an eight-month period, with spectacular results. One of the thirty-seven objects he used was a string that had been attached to an identification plate belonging to a German soldier in World War I. Mrs. Zierold got the impression of a firebomb exploding in a group of soldiers. The owner of the string said that this event had made the greatest impact on him during the war.

Has psychometry ever been used to solve crimes?

Many times. The psychic is handed an object belonging to a missing person or found at the scene of the crime, and this often leads him to a solution. Peter Hurkos and Gerard Croiset have been called in many times by European police departments to use psychometry as a detection aid.

Who was the famous "vanished man" located through psychometry?

In February 1966, a physician disappeared from a hotel in a Midwestern city. The late Eileen Garrett was called into the case and handed a two-inch square of cloth that had been cut from one of his shirts. Mrs. Garrett said the doctor had traveled toward California and was now in La Jolla, a suburb of San Diego. On the same day the doctor's wife received a letter from him, saying that he was ill in La Jolla. Mrs. Garrett gave the doctor's correct age and other facts about him and his family that she could not have known.

Can a psychometric object "carry" a disease?

Yes, although fortunately this is not common. (See Chapter 5.) In one case a psychic developed a liver ailment after holding an object belonging to the man with the disease. The unconscious mind of the psychic was probably more to blame than the object.

Do psychometric objects reflect past events as well as personalities?

Yes. Gerard Croiset, in one series of experiments, was handed fossil fragments that he was able to place in the correct period and culture. Objects are strongly impregnated with the vibrations of disasters. One psychic who held a piece of lava from a volcano trembled with a feeling of terror she could not shake off for an hour.

Does psychometry work when the object is concealed?

Yes. Many psychics hold objects that are hidden in opaque envelopes, and they correctly describe the object and the persons and events associated with it. In one of Croiset's tests, he was given a sealed envelope containing a medieval manuscript. He got an image of a pope, a knight, and a monk.

Is a fragment of the object enough for psychometry to work?

In this case the part is as good as the whole. The journalist and psychic investigator William T. Stead handed psychometrists blank squares of paper that had been cut from letters written by famous persons, and they were able to identify the writers.

Does the psychometric power of an object depend on what it is made of?

William Roll of the Psychical Research Foundation in Durham, North Carolina, believes that objects derived from animal or vegetable sources have much stronger psychic properties than inorganic matter such as metal. In one test, psychics responded more to cardboard than to aluminum objects.

How does the theory of "memory traces" explain psychometry?

According to this theory, each object acts like the human unconscious in storing impressions of people, events, and surroundings that have been associated with it. This would also explain some kinds of ghosts, which may merely be thought-forms released into a house during a traumatic event in the past. The house has "memories" of everything that has happened in it, especially scenes of emotional content.

What is the "psi field" theory of psychometry?

William Roll believes that every object is surrounded by an energy field and that events leave traces in this field. Psi fields are also created when people interact with each other or with objects and events.

Are tea leaves psychic "props"?

Yes. According to the late Eileen Garrett, "Tea leaves, crystal balls, cards, and the like . . . probably serve as a form of concentration which allows the unconscious to reveal inner aspects of the mind."

What is an "aurameter"?

Another prop, a rodlike device invented by Verne Cameron of California for psychically diagnosing disease. (See Chapter 10.) The psychic passes the aurameter over the patient's body, and when it reaches a trouble spot it begins to turn.

How do psychedelic strobe lights activate the psychic sense?

In many experiments today an attempt is made to stimulate the agent or sender of the telepathic message through both the emotions and the senses. (See Chapter 7.) In a Russian experiment, with the subject a mile away, the agent watches a series of numbers flashed by strobe lights, and he keeps repeating the numbers out loud. In one test the subject, psychically stimulated at his end, got 100 numbers correct out of 134, a phenomenal result.

9 YOUR QUESTIONS ANSWERED ABOUT
MYSTERIOUS MESSAGES RECEIVED WHEN THE HAND
AND ARM MOVE INVOLUNTARILY IN AUTOMATIC
WRITING AND OUIJA BOARD PHENOMENA; THE
STRANGE CASE OF PATIENCE WORTH, THE
SEVENTEENTH-CENTURY WOMAN WHO "WROTE" NOVELS
AND POEMS IN THE TWENTIETH CENTURY . . .

What is automatic writing?

The psychic holds a pen or pencil over a sheet of paper, and the hand writes without any conscious effort or thought by the writer.

Does the psychic know what he is writing?

Not always. He can watch what is being written or he can ignore it. While his hand and arm write, he can be thinking of something else, talking with someone on another subject, or even consciously writing different words with his other hand. He may be blindfolded when he writes or in a state of trance.

Where are the messages coming from?

The message may come from a discarnate entity, from the unconscious mind of the writer, from another living mind, or from a source that cannot be identified.

What kind of messages come through automatic writing?

Sometimes the psychic acts as a medium and writes the same kind of messages that are received at a séance. The "writing spirit" may identify himself as a deceased friend or relative or may be just a casual spirit using the hand and arm of the psychic. The message may be personal, trivial, or even philosophical, as in the case of the Imperator Group that came through medium Stainton Moses. (See Chapter 16.) If the writing comes from the unconscious mind of the psychic, it may mirror some deep-seated conflict or other psychological problem, or it may give advice.

Who received telepathic messages through his hand from a living person?

On rare occasions a message may come from a friend some distance away, be registered in the unconscious mind and then written down automatically. W. T. Stead, a journalist and psychic investigator, received such messages from friends over a period of fifteen years, many of whom were astonished to hear that they had been sending telepathic messages.

Can automatic messages from the living be totally unconscious?

If the automatic writer is busy with other tasks while his hand and arm write, and if the sender is unaware that he is communicating, the whole process becomes unconscious. It is possible that many spirits are not aware they are sending messages during séances. Telepathy, clairvoyance, psychokinesis—all forms of psychic phenomena may take place on an unconscious level.

Is the automatic script in the psychic's own handwriting?

Not always. Sometimes the handwriting can be identified as that of someone who has died. Mediums who write automatically often have two or more spirit guides, each with a characteristic script.

What are automatic "doodles"?

The script frequently begins with little circles and curlicues as if the communicator is collecting his thoughts and trying out the hand before sending his message. These gradually form into words and sentences.

How fast does the arm move during automatic writing?

The writing may go slowly and haltingly, it may move at normal speeds, or it may fly over the paper. Some messages received by medium Geraldine Cummins were written at the rate of two thousand words a minute.

What is "mirror writing"?

The automatic script is written backwards and makes sense only when seen through a mirror.

What are other peculiarities of automatic writing?

It often appears that the communicator is playing a game. Sometimes every other word is written backwards. Sometimes the writing is so small it can be seen only through a microscope. Occasionally the message will start at the bottom right-hand corner of the page and be written completely backwards up to the top left-hand corner. And sometimes the script is upside down.

What happens to the psychic mentally before automatic writing takes place?

Some writers, such as the famous Mrs. Piper, first go into a trance. Others remain conscious but are in a relaxed state, with tension absent, as in other kinds of psychic experiences. It is best to be occupied with another task and let the writing take care of itself.

What happens to the psychic physically?

Stainton Moses, the nineteenth-century medium, had his first experience in 1878, when his "right arm was seized about the middle of the forearm, and dashed violently up and down . . ." Another psychic, William Howitt, felt an electric shock in his arm while he was holding a pencil, which began to whirl around in a rotary motion. Other psychics feel a tingling sensation in the arm that announces the presence of a communicator. Many psychics have no physical symptoms but just feel an urge to get pencil and paper and begin writing.

Who began to write automatically at the age of five months?

The infant son of Kate Fox (one of the Hydesville Fox sisters) held a pencil in his hand and wrote messages purportedly from deceased friends of the family.

Who received two messages simultaneously, one through automatic writing, the other through her voice?

Mrs. Piper. While in trance one of her spirit guides, Phinuit, spoke through her vocal cords, while the other, George Pelham, wrote with her hand.

How can two psychics "collaborate" on an automatic script, although only one does the writing?

The second psychic touches the wrist of the writer, and this may increase the clarity and strength of the communication. In one case the attempts of a married couple to write separate scripts ended in failure, but the wrist-touching method worked.

Has illness ever been cured through automatic writing?

Yes. A spirit guide called "Humnur Stafford," who wrote through the hand of medium Mme. D'Espérance, not only told the medium's friends what was wrong with them but prescribed treatment, just as Edgar Cayce did later in trance.

Who gave answers in automatic writing to scientific and philosophical questions?

"Humnur" was one. This versatile spirit guide wrote discourses of a depth and complexity far beyond the knowledge of Mme. D'Espérance and others present.

Are automatic scripts ever written in a foreign language?

Yes, often one unfamiliar to the writer. Dr. Charles Richet, the eminent French physiologist, tells about a psychic with no knowledge of Greek who wrote several pages in perfect Greek. In another case an eleven-year-old girl wrote in Chinese and Kaffir, two languages completely unfamiliar to her.

Have books been written through automatic writing?

Many of them. An uneducated accountant, Charles Linton, "received" a manuscript of a hundred thousand words, The Healing of the Nation, through his hand. A fourteen-year-old French girl automatically wrote The Life of Jeanne d'Arc and Confessions of Louis XI.

Who completed a book by Dickens after his death?

It may have been the spirit of Dickens himself. The last chapters of The Mystery of Edwin Drood came through the hand of an American mechanic.

What "dead" nineteenth-century playwright wrote character sketches through a medium's hand?

British psychic Hester Travers Smith allegedly received messages from Oscar Wilde analyzing other writers of his time, among them George Bernard Shaw. The style, handwriting, and signature matched those of Wilde when alive.

Who received a message in automatic writing from the Lusitania as it sank?

The ship was torpedoed by the Germans in 1915. The message came the same night through the hand of Mrs. Travers Smith, from the spirit of Sir Hugh Lane, a passenger, who described what had happened.

Who solved the mystery of Glastonbury Abbey in England through automatic writing?

Starting in 1907, two Englishmen, Frederick Bligh Bond and Captain John Allen Bartlett, spent many years deciphering messages about the abbey received from medieval monks. The monks gave the history of the abbey and instructions on how to find two lost chapels. The chapels were located in the ruins.

What was the language of the Glastonbury scripts?

Sometimes they were written in modern English, sometimes in medieval English, and often in Latin, which was the official Church tongue of the time. The messages came from several different personalities associated with the abbey.

What strange predictions of war were received with the Glastonbury scripts?

Over a period of about ten years, Bartlett's hand recorded the sequence of events in World War I and some puzzling predictions that foreshadowed World War II twenty years later. For example: "When the West falls, Britain shall endure. . . . In May the advance carries the foe down the fair lands that lie to the west of him . . . slower, slower grows the advance. . . . The pact is near its end in Europe. . . ." These passages could refer to the Nazi advance in May 1940, Britain's stubborn resistance after the fall of France, and the end of the pact between Germany and Russia when the Nazis invaded the Ukraine in the summer of 1941.

How did Captain Bartlett make an automatic sketch of Glastonbury Abbey?

He started at the left-hand top corner and sketched toward the bottom. His completed drawing was as detailed and accurate as those done by cartographers.

What is automatic drawing?

The same as automatic writing except that the psychic finds himself sketching and painting rather than writing words. Captain Bartlett's automatic line drawing of Glastonbury Abbey is an example. Sometimes the drawings are in oils or watercolors. In one case colored chalk was used.

Who did an "upside-down" automatic drawing while blindfolded?

Psychic Susannah Harris did an oil painting in two hours while in this condition. Dr. John Ballou Newbrough painted in total darkness, using both hands simultaneously.

Who did automatic portraits of spirits?

Mme. D'Espérance could see the spirits in the dark and automatically sketched their portraits, which were recognized by friends of the deceased. She drew very quickly, sometimes in half a minute, and it appeared that her hand was controlled by another force.

Who automatically sketched geometric designs?

An early nineteenth-century psychic, the Seeress of Prevorst, drew flawless intricate diagrams and perfect circles, without using a compass or ruler. She worked without conscious effort and at great speed.

What is the ouija board and how does it work?

This is another form of automatic writing, using, instead of pencil and paper, a polished rectangular board and a triangular piece of wood called a planchette. The board is imprinted with the letters of the alphabet, ten numerals, and the words "yes" and "no." One or two persons place their fingers lightly and with no conscious pressure upon the planchette, which may begin to move over the board, spelling out words and answering questions. As with automatic writing, the motive force may come from the unconscious mind of one or both persons or from an invisible entity or unknown agency.

Must the psychic look at the planchette as it moves?

No. Some psychics have worked the ouija board while blindfolded. A third person would record the message.

When was the ouija board invented?

No one knows for certain, but a form of it was popular in ancient Greece as far back as the sixth century B.C. Pythagoras and his followers held séances with signs inscribed on a stone slab and a table on wheels that moved over the slab toward the signs.

In what famous experiments was the ouija board turned upside down?

Sir William Barrett, a physicist and member of the British Society for Psychical Research, did several unorthodox tests with the board. In one series, although the board was turned around, the messages came at incredible speeds.

Have ouija board messages ever come in a foreign tongue?

Ambrose and Olga Worrall, in *The Gift of Healing*, tell about a ouija board message spelled out in Welsh, although no one present knew the language. The message purportedly came from the Welsh grandmother of one of the spectators.

What else may be used in place of the planchette?

A coin, an inverted tumbler, even a pendulum moved slowly over the letters of the board.

What seventeenth-century personality "dictated" novels and poems through the ouija board in the twentieth century?

In 1913 a St. Louis housewife, Mrs. Pearl Curran, and a friend were experimenting with the board when a message came through: "Many moons ago I lived. Again I come— Patience Worth my name." The association between Mrs. Curran and Patience Worth lasted twenty-four years and resulted in several published novels, stories, and poems.

Could Patience Worth have been created in Mrs. Curran's unconscious mind?

If so, Patience would be what is called a "secondary personality" of Mrs. Curran. However, the differences between Mrs. Curran and Patience were so striking that this theory is not convincing. Mrs. Curran, who had gone only as far as the eighth grade in school, was a pleasant and plain-spoken housewife with no knowledge of poetry or history, while Patience Worth was extremely witty, revealed an outstanding intellect, and composed novels, stories, and poems that were praised by professors and literary critics as works of genius.

What was unusual about Patience's writing style?

She wrote her books in several styles or mixtures of styles covering the period from the time of Christ to the twentieth century. *Hope Trueblood* was written in modern English and described an English village (Mrs. Curran had never been to England). Another novel, *Telka*, was almost completely in Anglo-Saxon, with archaic forms of words in use today— "athin" for "within," etc.

Did Patience's books describe her native seventeenth-century England?

Telka may have been close to the period in which Patience lived. *The Sorry Tale*, however, was laid in the period of Christ and was declared by literary critics to be as realistic as if Patience had lived there during the Christian era. She seemed to have the remarkable faculty of reaching back into the history of all times and places and identifying with the characters, speech, and customs of the period she was describing. Mrs. Curran, on the other hand, was completely unfamiliar with any of the periods or locales of the novels.

How long did it take Patience to write her stories and poems?

The writing appeared to be spontaneous, although some of it may have been worked out before the ouija board sessions. *Telka* was written in thirty-five hours, with no editing. Sometimes a visitor would request a poem or story and it would be spelled out immediately on the ouija board.

Why did Patience manifest through Mrs. Curran?

Even though Mrs. Curran had limited ability and education, Patience explained that she was a perfect instrument for her literary output. "We throb," said Patience, meaning they were on the same wavelength.

Was Patience anxious to identify herself?

No. She felt that the facts about herself and her life on earth were not important, but that her literary, spiritual, and philosophical ideas were.

What was an example of Patience's quaint way of speaking?

In describing the value of a literary man, she said: "He who buildeth with peg and cudgel but buildeth a toy for an age who will but cast aside the bauble as naught; but he who buildeth with word, a quill and a fluid, buildeth well."

What did Patience's speech reveal about life in the seventeenth century?

Casper Yost, in his 1916 book about Patience, speaks of her as being "essentially feminine . . . profoundly versed in the method of housekeeping of two centuries or more ago . . . familiar with all the domestic machinery and utensils of that olden time—the operation of the loom and spinning wheel, the art of cooking at an open hearth, the sanding of floors." Patience complained that "in thy day housewifery is a sorry trade. . . ."

What were some obsolete words used by Patience?

Patience particularly mentioned articles of dress completely unfamiliar to Mrs. Curran and her guests: "wimple," "kirtle," "pettieskirt," "points." In one story she spoke of "fingering the regal," referring to a small medieval pipe organ.

Did Mrs. Curran receive Patience's messages in trance?

No. As in automatic writing and other mediumistic experiences, the psychic may be conscious or in various stages of trance. Mrs. Curran was always aware of what was going on.

Did all of Patience's speech and writing come through the ouija board?

After a few years Mrs. Curran discarded the board and received mental impressions, first in the form of letters and later words, which she dictated to a stenographer. She also received mental pictures from Patience. On occasion Mrs. Curran wrote Patience's poems "automatically" on the typewriter.

Is it safe to use the ouija board for "kicks"?

Louisa Rhine, writer and parapsychologist, cautions against excessive use of the board if one is inclined to be unstable or to become too seriously involved (which is true of any involvement in psychic experiments): "The general verdict is that these automatic responses may be intriguing to the uninformed, but may possibly have unhealthy effects on naïve, suggestible persons." There is always the danger of being overwhelmed by problems buried in the unconscious mind.

10

YOUR QUESTIONS ANSWERED ABOUT
THE USE OF THE DIVINING ROD TO FIND
UNDERGROUND STREAMS OF WATER, VEINS OF ORE,
LOST OBJECTS, AND MISSING PEOPLE; HOW THE
DIVINING ROD SOLVES CRIMES, DIAGNOSES
ILLNESSES, LOCATES ENEMY MINES IN WARTIME,
FINDS BREAKS IN PIPES, ETC. . . .

What is dowsing?

Dowsing, or water-witching, is basically the practice of using a Y-shaped twig cut from a tree to locate underground sources of water on farmland and other sites.

How does the dowser work?

He walks over the property, holding the twig, or divining rod, with both hands until it begins to revolve or dip toward the ground. This movement usually indicates that he is near or directly over a hidden vein of water.

How does the dowser hold the rod?

Generally he holds the forks close to his chest, the rod pointing directly ahead, elevated, or dipping toward the ground. Although this is the popular method, there are variations, depending on the dowser and the kind of rod he uses.

What makes the rod turn?

No one knows for certain. One theory is that unconscious or involuntary muscular movements act upon the rod, and when the dowser grasps it more tightly to prevent it from turning, conflicting sets of muscles create the strong movement. Another theory is that an electromagnetic field acts upon the rod in the presence of earth and water.

How fast and how often does the rod turn?

There seems to be no limit. Some rods have made as many as eighty revolutions a minute.

Is there a chemical attraction between the rod and the water?

Hardly likely. No chemical action has been discovered that would operate from the water to the rod.

What kind of wood works best in the rod?

Almost any kind, with maple or hazelwood highly recommended by dowsers. Verne Cameron, a leading American dowser, suggests cutting a slender green branch up to three feet long from a live tree. More important than the kind of wood is the weight, symmetry, and balance of the rod.

Does the rod have to be Y-shaped?

No, although that is the popular shape of the wood. Sometimes a straight stick is merely laid across the fingers of both hands, and it revolves without resistance in the presence of water. Another rod used in the past was a straight stick cut in two, one extremity hollowed out, the other half sharpened at one end and inserted in the hollow. When over water, the pointed stick would rotate in the cavity.

Does the rod have to be made of wood?

No. There are many kinds of rods in use, made of all kinds of materials. It depends on the dowser and what material suits him best. There have been rods made of wire, whalebone, and nylon. One woman dowser held a hairpin. Dowsers have used pliers, crowbars, horseshoes, even a rubber ball suspended from a string. Pendulums are used in map-dowsing. (See later questions.)

Who used a cone-shaped cork to find water?

In 1930 the Abbé Gabriel Lambert, a French dowser, looked for water with a bobbin made of cork and suspended from a thread. When he walked over hidden springs, the bobbin would spin wildly in widening circles.

Will the rod move over stagnant water?

No. For some reason, the water must be in motion for the rod to work.

How does the dowser estimate the depth of the water?

There are different methods of finding out. Sometimes the rod starts to dip and rise several times before it is directly over the water, then points straight down. The dowser calculates the depth in feet by the number of dips. Other dowsers note where they first feel the tug of the rod, then count their steps until they are directly over the water.

How does the "dialogue" between dowser and rod determine the rate of flow?

The late John Shelley, president of the American Society of Dowsers, asked his rod such questions as "How much water will I find at this point? Is it more than four gallons per minute?" If the rod swung to the right, it meant yes. The next question was "More than five gallons?" Shelley kept up this kind of questioning until he got a swing to the left, thus narrowing down the actual rate of flow of gallons per day. He used the same question-and-answer method to find the depth of the water. Other dowsers use variations of this dialogue technique.

What does the dowser "feel" when he is over water?

The famous British dowser John Mullins said he felt an electric shock and his arms ached all night after he found the water. Other dowsers become excited, feel a tingling sensation, are chilled or nauseated, and sometimes faint. Some dowsers spit blood, and one begins to wheeze when he is near water.

What is the "contact" effect in dowsing?

Sometimes the dowser can transfer his ability to another person merely by touching him or holding his wrists. It may work in reverse: in a Russian experiment it was also found that when a skeptic touched a dowser, the rod refused to turn.

Can the divining rod dowse metals as well as water?

Yes. This seems to have been its purpose in Germany during the Middle Ages, when dowsing first became widely known. A manuscript of 1430 indicated how the rod was used to find ore. In 1530 an essay by Agricola recommended the rod as a practical help in mining. The mining technique was brought over to England in the seventeenth century, where it is still practiced in Cornwall. Today some miners bend metal clothes-hangers into L shapes and hold one in each hand pointing forward as they dowse. The hangers swing wide when they are over metals in the ground.

Has the divining rod ever been used to find oil?

Yes. One of the best-known dowsers, Evelyn Penrose of England, was once employed by the government of British Columbia to locate oil through dowsing. She found twelve wells this way.

What is the "witness"?

The "witness" is a sample of whatever the dowser is trying to locate. The dowser carries it while at work, presumably to attract its like or to stimulate his powers. A small portion of water will be attracted to a hidden stream, metal will find metal, a thimbleful of oil will lead to oil, or a personal object belonging to a missing person will help to locate him. In the last instance the witness acts as a psychometric device.

What kind of materials can interfere with dowsing?

In many cases it has been stopped by a silken or woolen glove, rubber-soled shoes, or a tight bandage on the arm or leg of the dowser. The Russians claim that lightning storms inhibit dowsing.

Can dowsers work without a rod?

Yes. Some claim that they can see water or metals through the ground. The Abbé Bouly, in a lecture in 1928, said: "I no longer require a rod. I can see the stream with my eyes; I attune my mind; I am looking for lead, I fix my eyes; I feel a wavy sensation like hot air over a radiator; I see it."

What woman dowser could find water without a rod?

Many of them, but one of the best-known was Clarissa Miles, who told how she was physically drawn to water: "I get violently attracted to certain spots. . . . The rest of the ground seems to disappear and I see only the spots where the water is. In an open field, one glance is enough to show me the exact spot. . . ."

What is a hydroscope?

A name given to those who react strongly in the presence of water, with or without the divining rod. Bleton, a famous seventeenth-century hydroscope, had convulsions whenever he walked over running water. A Marseilles hydroscope, Jean-Jacques Parangue, was filled with horror whenever he approached unseen water. One man reacted strongly to the presence of water, coal, or salt. Many contemporary dowsers are unable to sleep if a water pipe is located under the bedroom.

Can dowsing be explained by extrasensory perception?

Yes. The experience of actually seeing water through the ground is a form of clairvoyance. When the rod is used, the dowser probably located the water or metal clairvoyantly but not consciously, and the subliminal information is communicated to the hands holding the rod, causing it to turn as a signal to his conscious mind. Thus the rod acts as a "prop" to stimulate his clairvoyant powers.

What is map-dowsing?

If anything could prove that dowsing is extrasensory, it is dowsing for water or metals over a map of the property. The map must be fairly large and detailed, and the rod smaller than one used over the actual property. John Shelley used a small V-shaped nylon rod. Others, including woman dowser Evelyn Penrose, use a pendulum over the map.

How close must the map be to the property dowsed?

It can be hundreds, even thousands of miles away. If the dowsing faculty is extrasensory, it will work at great distances, just as ESP does in other situations. In one instance reported by writer Beverley Nichols, Evelyn Penrose dowsed a map of a South African mining area while she was in a living room in England. Henry Gross, the New England dowser who was the subject of books by Kenneth Roberts, dowsed a well site in Bermuda while he was looking at a map in Maine.

Ray Willey, of the American Society of Dowsers, dowses with a road map. Once he found water in Point Roberts, Washington, while he was in Schenectady, New York, three thousand miles away.

Who located a school of lobsters in the Atlantic while map-dowsing?

There is no limit to the kinds of objects that can be found with the divining rod. John Shelley was once asked by a fisherman to pinpoint a good source for lobsters because the offshore Maine waters where he plied his trade were becoming lobster-poor. Shelley, using a large map of the Maine coast, found a better area farther south. The fisherman went there and immediately pulled in a very large specimen.

Can dowsing be used to find lost objects?

Lost or misplaced coins, jewelry, and other valuables have all been found through dowsing. In India a dowser finds lost or stolen objects by holding two bamboo rods. When the object is near, they cross horizontally, then alternately rise and descend. Henry Gross reports that a friend once lost her bracelet in the ocean at the shoreline. His divining rod pointed to the exact spot where it was buried in the wet sand.

Can dead bodies be located through dowsing?

Any person, dead or alive, is fair game for the divining rod. John Shelley, while in Maine, was once asked to trace the movements of a college student in California who had left his dormitory and had not returned. Sitting with his rod over a map on the table, Shelley traced the boy's movements to the Pacific Ocean and there "saw" his dead body.

Has the divining rod tracked down criminals?

Yes. The most famous case is that of Jacques Aymar, a French peasant with the dowsing talent who lived in the seventeenth century. Aymar once located the murderers of a wine merchant and his wife by following the path of the killers over land and sea, his divining rod pointing in front of him.

Have dowsers worked for the police?

Although it is not advertised, the police of some European countries have called upon the rod when other methods failed to find criminals. The French police in the seventeenth century frequently employed Aymar and his rod. In recent times a dowser helped the Belgian police locate the missing body of a murdered policeman through map-dowsing.

What was the historical attitude of the Church toward the divining rod?

Officially, dowsers were frowned upon, but through the centuries some of the best ones have been priests and ministers. In 1518 Martin Luther issued a proclamation against using the rod. The movements of the rod were often ascribed to the Devil, and there were elaborate rituals to keep from being contaminated by it. In 1701 the Church decreed that the rod could not be used in criminal prosecution.

What is the official attitude of governments toward dowsing and the divining rod?

Skeptical, for the most part. Yet there have been many instances of armies using the rod, and until the early part of this century dowsing was recognized by the United States government as a legitimate activity, probably because homesteaders in drought areas had a desperate need for water. Experiments in dowsing are going on today in Russia. Some governments have hired dowsers to find oil or water. In addition to Evelyn Penrose, who worked for the British Columbia government, Major Pogson was official water diviner in India during the 1920s.

Has the divining rod ever been used on the battlefield?

Marine engineers in Vietnam used coat-hangers as rods to locate enemy tunnels, mines, and buried rifles. The rods, bent into L shapes, were held in each hand pointing forward as the dowser walked. When over a mine or tunnel, they swung apart to form a straight line. In another case a British expeditionary force suffering from the intense heat of the tropics and a lack of water was saved when one of the soldiers used a bent copper band to find water.

Who made biological predictions with his divining rod?

A French dowser named Bossuet could predict the sex of eggs.

What historical discovery was made by a young girl and her rod?

Maria Mattaloni, an Italian peasant, led the authorities to several Etruscan tombs near Rome.

Is the divining rod used for medical diagnosis?

In many ways. Reference has been made to Verne Cameron's aurameter (see Chapter 8), an instrument which is passed near a human body and reacts when a weak area is located. A French veterinarian uses a pendulum to diagnose an animal's illness.

How ancient is the use of the divining rod?

Historically, the rod was mentioned as early as 3000 years ago, but paintings in North African caves dating back 30,000 years show prehistoric man with a rod in his hand.

Did Julius Caesar dowse?

Yes. He took dowsers into the deserts of Africa to find water for his troops. Cleopatra had five dowsers on her barges, who used silken cords with a gold-nugget pendulum.

Who was Great Britain's outstanding dowser?

John Mullins, who lived about seventy-five years ago, was said to locate water in 99 out of every 100 attempts. He was subjected to many tests and even dowsed successfully when blindfolded.

Who were some outstanding French dowsers?

Many of them were Jesuit priests: the Abbé Gabriel Lambert; the Abbé Paramelle, who found 10,275 sources of water in twenty-five years, most of them at depths of more than fifty feet; the Abbé Bouly; and many more. Jacques Aymar must be mentioned, along with Bleton, the hydroscope.

How many dowsers are there in the United States?

No count has been taken, but one estimate places the number of dowsers at fifty thousand.

Do women dowse?

Several outstanding examples have been given—Evelyn Penrose and Clarissa Miles among them. An early woman dowser was the Baroness of Beau-Soleil, the first person to dowse for water in France. Lady Milbanke, the mother-in-law of Lord Byron, was a dowser.

Do animals dowse?

They are natural dowsers and do not need divining rods. Dogs have been used to dowse mines in Vietnam. Among the best animal dowsers are donkeys, horses, and armadillos. In Mexico people living in deserts depend upon their burros to find water. The animals dig down until their bodies and faces are almost completely covered, and they never stop until the water appears.

Do plants dowse?

They are the most natural dowsers of all life forms. A plant depends upon water for its life. There is an oak tree with a 140-foot-long root that wandered horizontally underground to find a water supply.

Who dowsed on a television program?

In a televised experiment in England, six drums were filled with water, and salt was added to five of them. They were then buried in a gravel bed along with three cardboard boxes, two filled with stones, one containing a kitchen knife. The dowser's job was to locate the objects buried and to differentiate between the salt and other ingredients. He was almost 100 per cent successful. In another television broadcast, five cans of water and a carton containing a knife were buried at wide intervals. The dowser found three of the five cans of water.

Are dowsers better at finding water than geologists?

The geologist relies on his knowledge of the terrain and surface features that may indicate the presence of underground water. In many tests dowsers have succeeded in finding water after the geologists failed. In some experiments the geologists found the general location of the water site, but the dowsers went to the exact spot. Many geologists, engineers, and other trained scientists are now enthusiastic dowsers in their own right. They regard the rod as another detection tool along with their Geiger counters and magnetometers.

Have dowsers been employed by commercial firms?

Yes. Mining companies often use dowsers to locate bodies of ore. Power companies and water-supply firms call in dowsers to locate breaks in pipes. Railroad companies and breweries have had dowsers on the payroll. In a case reported by *Scientific American* magazine (November 1933), a geologist-dowser, Dr. Kurt Oswald, went over the proposed site for a canal with his dowsing rod and found that the force of the flowing water would cause pressure breaks during the building of the canal.

What are the "physical" theories that explain dowsing?

Most of these theories are based on possible interaction of magnetic fields involving the earth and water with dowser and rod. Another theory is that dowsers respond to radio waves, a third that they are affected by radiations from the earth. Some or all of these theories may be partially true, but they do not explain dowsing at a distance. Whatever physical elements are involved, clairvoyance seems to play a large part in the dowser's success.

What is "food dowsing"?

Unless Verne Cameron is pulling our leg, he suggests that it is possible to dowse the dinner table to determine the quality of the food. If so, we may soon have housewives waving their rods in supermarkets and diners in restaurants taking out their pocket rods before beginning a meal.

11
YOUR QUESTIONS ANSWERED ABOUT
WELL-KNOWN PSYCHICS—EILEEN GARRETT,
ARTHUR FORD, EDGAR CAYCE, JEANE DIXON,
DANIEL LOGAN, DOUGLAS JOHNSON, AND MANY
OTHERS; WHAT KIND OF PEOPLE THEY ARE, HOW
PSYCHIC IMPRESSIONS COME TO THEM, MANY OF
THEIR UNUSUAL EXPERIENCES; WHERE PSYCHICS ARE
TRAINED AND HOW THEY KEEP IN PRACTICE;
PSYCHIC FAMILIES . . .

What is a psychic?

A psychic is a person who constantly receives extrasensory impressions. He may pick up thoughts in someone else's mind, mentally see events that are happening elsewhere, or get glimpses of what is going to happen in the future. He is sensitive to any or all supernormal phenomena.

What is the difference between a psychic and a medium?

A medium allegedly communicates with spirits or can cause objects to materialize or move in his presence, particularly in the séance room. Although many psychics do not claim spiritualistic powers, there are some who are also mediums—the late Eileen Garrett, for example. (See Chapter 16.) Both psychics and mediums are also known as sensitives.

Was Arthur Ford a psychic or a medium?

Although he was known primarily as a trance medium (among his famous cases are the breaking of the Houdini survival code and the alleged communication with Bishop Pike's son), Ford also had many spontaneous telepathic and clairvoyant impressions while in his conscious state.

Was Edgar Cayce primarily a psychic?

Yes. His diagnoses of illnesses while in trance were based on clairvoyance plus a subliminal knowledge of medical terms and cures. Cayce also gave "life readings" and told people about their former incarnations, a purely psychic process if it was not a fantasy of his unconscious mind. Cayce was also somewhat of a medium and had occasional contact with spirits. (See Chapter 17.)

Could Cayce read the human aura?

Yes. This is another psychic gift. His son writes that Cayce once was concerned about a neighbor who had no aura, and he feared for her life. Two days later she died. On another occasion he had a premonition when he saw a strange woman on the steps of the post office. He touched her elbow and said, "Please don't go on an auto ride today." The woman was puzzled, but she begged off a ride with a friend, who went alone and had a bad accident.

How do psychics get their "impressions"?

Each psychic has his or her individual style. Some emphasize clairvoyance ("seeing" objects and events); others read minds; many are primarily seers who can divine the future. In many cases one sense is predominant; Arthur Ford, for example, spoke of himself as "clairaudient." Some psychics work on hunches, others have external or mental visions, the clairaudient "hear" voices, many have physical symptoms that signal a psychic experience. Some psychics get extrasensory information in dreams, others in their waking state. Some have purely mental impressions, while others use "props"— tea leaves, psychometric objects, cards, crystal balls, etc. Psychics function on every level of consciousness. (See Chapter 6.)

What kind of psychic "sees" pictures in other minds?

The visual-minded do, and they are very successful in telepathic experiments of this kind. One example was Mrs. Upton Sinclair, who would sketch animals, trees, and other objects in the mind of a sender in another room.

In what form do mental pictures come?

Each visual-minded psychic "sees" the pictures in a different way. Douglas Johnson, the English medium-psychic, gets scenes in the center of his forehead that are small but sharply etched, either in color or black and white.

Who saw the past and future unfolding like a movie film?

Vincent Turvey, a psychic who predicted the sinking of the *Titanic* in 1912, could see an actual film moving in his visions and could distinguish each frame of the film. If the pictures appeared to be engraved on the frames, he knew he was viewing past events. Those that looked like pale blue photographs stuck on the film were scenes from the future.

Who saw the future on "tiny screens" in her mind?

In her book *Adventures in the Supernormal*, Eileen Garrett wrote that she "began to see events occurring in the lives of many of my friends before they actually happened. A tiny screen, containing images, places, and events of which I knew nothing, would sometimes interrupt my normal vision. A few days later, or perhaps months later, I would meet and recognize someone who had played a part in these episodes."

Whose psychic impressions come as television pictures?

Peter Hurkos is a psychometrist; that is, he can take an object in his hand and describe the person to whom it belongs. He has located lost persons and solved many crimes through this method. He says that when he holds the psychometric object he must "blank everything out and make mental pictures, like a TV picture." In one case he visualized a murderer who owned a trailer and a motorbike. The killer was later picked up in his trailer.

What modern Joan of Arc hears a voice that gives her psychic information?

Jeanne Gardner, a housewife in Elkins, Virginia, is one of our leading clairaudients. She gets her knowledge of future events from a voice that accompanies her everywhere. The voice told her three days in advance that Senator Kennedy would be killed and said it would happen in a "galley" (kitchen).

What writer-psychic gets mental "orders" when she is needed?
Rosalind Heywood tells of an incident in a hospital when she was wondering how to help a delirious postoperative patient. Suddenly a voice in her mind said, "Think him quiet." She did so, and at once the man fell into a calm sleep. She calls this kind of experience a psychic "order."

What other sensory impressions do psychics get?
Sometimes they "taste" or "smell" faraway objects. Psychics frequently feel pain or other physical symptoms of persons who are ill or have accidents. (See the blow-in-the-mouth case in Chapter 1.) Some psychics "know" the future through bodily distress.

Who gets headaches when he thinks a plane will crash?
Alan Hencher of England. He is not the only one, however. Lorna Middleton, also English, frequently has headaches before plane or train crashes or when she senses a forthcoming natural disaster such as an earthquake.

Is the solar plexus a psychic center?
It is one of several areas in the body that may be psychic channels. Many sensitives feel a disturbance in the solar plexus (diaphragm area) when a valid psychic experience is coming on. The solar plexus is also involved in out-of-body experiences. (See Chapter 14.)

What is a "human seismograph"?
The term was coined by the late Dr. J. C. Barker, who founded the British Premonitions Bureau. Dr. Barker discovered that there are many persons in the general population, psychics and non-psychics, who have feelings of nausea, choking sensations, and other kinds of physical distress a short time before a natural disaster, an assassination, or similar traumatic events.

Who became a psychic after he fell on his head?
Peter Hurkos was a house painter, with thoughts of ESP furthest from his mind. During World War II he fell off a ladder and landed on his head. While in the hospital he

began to tell other patients about themselves and make predictions.

Which psychics use props?

John Shelley, Henry Gross, and other dowsers are in this category. Many psychics are psychometrists. Jeane Dixon, Paul Neary, and Ann Jensen often turn to their crystal balls for psychic information. Mrs. Jensen once saw an explosion in her crystal ball while a niece and nephew from Arizona were visiting her in Texas. The next day they received a long-distance call that there had been an explosion on their property at the time Mrs. Jensen had her crystal-ball vision.

What psychic "sees" the future in a deck of cards?

Many do, but Mrs. Katharine Sabin of San Diego has probably the most unique system. Mrs. Sabin, who is a regular contributor to the Central Premonitions Registry, assigns her own symbols to each card, then shuffles the deck and lays the cards out in a certain order that reveals the future for her. Once she predicted that there would be an attack by a foreign power in the San Diego area. A few months later a Mexican vessel fired at an American tuna boat. Fortunately war did not break out over the incident, but the prediction was accurate.

What psychic once stayed in a closed coffin for three days?

Wolf Messing, who escaped from Poland to Russia during World War II, was an amazing, somewhat unorthodox psychic. He was able to put himself into a cataleptic trance and remain in that condition while "buried" in the coffin. Very few psychics, especially in the Western world, could emulate this feat of Indian fakirs and of Harry Houdini, the magician who tried to debunk mediums and psychics but probably had psychic ability himself.

Whose psychic impressions come first as "ripples of thought"?

In an interview with *Psychic* magazine (August 1970), the English psychic Douglas Johnson said that he "believes in a period of quietness first and a sort of tuning in. You have to dissociate your mind from your surroundings so that your mind is like a pond. And then you get ripples of thought in it, just as when a pebble is thrown into this pond. . . ."

What is a "cool" psychic?

A new kind of psychic has been emerging in recent years, one who takes a thoughtful, somewhat detached attitude toward his psychic gift and tries to separate true paranormal experiences from mere fancies. He is somewhat analytical and philosophical, also spiritual, though not attached to any religious institution. The general impression he gives is one of "coolness."

What young Englishman is an example of a "cool" psychic?

Malcolm Bessent, who has been the subject of many tests at American parapsychology laboratories in the last few years, started as a psychometrist, but he has discarded props for the most part and now gets many of his psychic impressions in the form of mental statements. As a "cool" psychic, he can often stand apart from his own mental impressions.

What psychic combines logic with intuition?

Alan Vaughan of Brooklyn, New York, also takes a "cool" approach to his psychic experiences. As a former science editor and now a writer and editor in the psychic field, he tends to be analytical about all psychic experiences, including his own. He believes that logic and analysis should play a part in predicting the future.

How does Daniel Logan get his psychic impressions?

Logan, a radio and television performer, is also somewhat on the psychic "cool" side. He gets his impressions as thoughts and says he must first "clear his mind and tune in."

Are there still psychics with a religious orientation?

Very many. Arthur Ford was an ordained minister, as is the Reverend Adrienne Coulter Meakin of Las Vegas, Nevada. Many psychics are associated with churches and precede their readings with prayers and meditation. The predictions of Jeane Dixon and Jeanne Gardner are strongly colored by their religious affiliations.

Are good psychics also creative?

Some of them are. Parapsychologists such as Karlis Osis, director of research for the American Society for Psychical Research, seem to think there is a strong link between creativity and the psychic sense. Lorna Middleton, one of Great Britain's outstanding psychics, is a dance and piano teacher in London.

Are actors and actresses psychic?

Many of them are, possibly because they need to be unusually sensitive to the nuances of characters they are impersonating. Psychic Daniel Logan is a former actor. Peter Hurkos has spoken highly of Mary Pickford as a psychic. Arlene Dahl has been referred to as "the champion tea-leaf reader of Hollywood." Actress Monica Peterson sensed twenty-four hours in advance that Robert Kennedy would be killed. Peggy Lee, Sally Ann Howes, and Nanette Fabray have all had psychic experiences.

What psychic has unusual empathy with lost children?

Gerard Croiset, the Dutch protégé of Dr. W. H. C. Tenhaeff, has a strong emotional link to children and often locates them psychically when they are lost. Croiset's unhappy childhood has strengthened his link to children and sharpened his psychic sense in such cases. Psychics often have an extra motivation in situations similar to those in their own lives.

Is will power necessary for psychic experience?

No, just the opposite. A French psychic, Mme. Bouissou, states that she must completely exclude will power and reach a state of passivity before her powers can function.

What is the mind-calming discipline practiced by most psychics?

Many psychics meditate and often lead meditation groups. (See Chapter 6.) The late Arthur Ford recommended setting aside twenty minutes a day in a quiet place for relaxation and meditation.

Where did Eileen Garrett get formal training as a psychic?

She was a student for five years at the College of Psychic

Studies in London under Hewat McKenzie, its founder in 1920. Douglas Johnson teaches at the college, and Malcolm Bessent received his training there.

How many ways are there to teach psychic development?
According to parapsychologist Lawrence LeShan, there are about a hundred and fifty techniques, including yoga and Zen disciplines.

What two well-known seventeenth-century astronomers were psychic?
Tycho Brahe and his famous pupil, Johannes Kepler. In 1619 Kepler predicted that the emperor Mathias would die in March. Mathias died on March 20.

What Chicago psychic predicted a train crash two hours before it happened?
Joseph DeLouise walked into a Chicago bar at 11 P.M. on January 16, 1969, and announced that two trains would crash head on south of Chicago and that it would be the worst train accident in the Chicago area in twenty-five years. Two hours later, at 1 A.M., two Illinois Central trains met head on just south of Chicago. Three persons were killed and forty-seven injured.

Why do psychics often put an emotional wall between themselves and other people?
Rosalind Heywood, a perceptive psychic, points out that the person with an "ESP-prone" temperament knows that too much exposure to the emotional conflicts of others could drain the psychic of physical and emotional energy.

What kind of people become psychics?
Tenhaeff in Holland, Bender in Germany, and other parapsychologists believe that psychics are more extroverted than other persons, more imaginative and sensitive to external stimuli, but less well adjusted to reality. Dr. Gertrude Schmeidler of City College of New York points out, however, that a distinguished psychic, Mrs. Willett, was a magistrate in England and that Eileen Garrett was a successful executive as head of the Parapsychology Foundation. There is no general

rule. Among those with the psychic sense are engineers, corporation lawyers, businessmen, artists, and housewives.

Is psychic power a lifetime gift?

Generally, once the power is recognized, it stays for life, but there are cases when it suddenly disappears. Children, who are more in tune with their psychic sense than adults, often lose it as they mature or as they are discouraged by the attitude of their elders. Even among established psychics, the power cannot always be turned on at will. It comes and goes, a fact that tempts many mediums and psychics to practice fraud and not disappoint their followers. (See Chapter 16.)

Do psychics ever get collective impressions?

There are many groups interested in the paranormal who have regular meetings for this purpose, preceded by periods of meditation. New York psychic Paul Neary has often joined other psychics in receiving impressions from a crystal ball.

Are there psychic families?

Yes. Jeanne Gardner's "voice" was heard by her mother and grandmother, and today she carries on a three-way psychic communication with two relatives who also hear the voice. There have been many brother-and-sister teams among the mediums—Willi and Rudi Schneider, the Davenport brothers, the Fox sisters. Shirley Harrison, a psychic of West Buxton, Maine, has six children, three of them psychic. Her son Mark once woke up from a deep sleep, walked into another bedroom, put out his arms, and caught his baby brother as he fell out of a bunk.

Which country produces the most psychics?

No country has a monopoly. From ancient China and Persia to modern India and the rest of the world, psychics have emerged in every culture. In some countries the population is more openly sympathetic to this gift and its possessor than in others, but it will surface no matter what the cultural climate.

12

Are children better psychics than adults?

They appear to be. Children are less inhibited than adults and seem to accept extrasensory experiences as natural. Many children have mediumistic powers up to and including their teen-age years.

Why do many children lose their psychic ability as they grow older?

In the United States and other Western countries adults tend to belittle the psychic experiences of children. The children are shamed into denying their psychic sense and turning their attention to practical matters. However, this attitude may be breaking down, as more and more young children are showing phenomenal extrasensory powers.

Who was the most famous child psychic in history?

Jeanne d'Arc should get the nomination. Jeanne was both clairvoyant and clairaudient. She had visions and heard voices that told her what to do and spelled out the future for her. The voices said that she would lead the French armies in battle against the English and that she had only "a year and a little more" to accomplish her mission of saving France. It all happened just as the voices had predicted.

What child psychic later became a leading figure in ESP research?

There have been many child mediums, but the late Eileen Garrett more than fulfilled her promise by becoming the "dean" of American psychics in her adult years and by heading the Parapsychology Foundation, one of the leading organizations in the field of psychical research. As a small child in England, she saw the spirits of people who had just died and played with spirit-children who were invisible to others.

Are many young children mediums?

Yes. The Schneider brothers, Rudi and Willi, are examples. (See Chapter 16.) One of the best cases is described in Westwood's *There Is a Psychic World*. Westwood, a Unitarian minister who had previously refused to believe in a spirit world, wrote that his eleven-year-old daughter received messages from the spirits of men, women, and children. Once her body was taken over by a man of outstanding intellect and philosophical bent who spoke in a deep man's voice. His mentality was far beyond that of an eleven-year-old girl.

How did a four-year-old boy receive a spirit message in shorthand?

Two weeks after the child's father died, the boy began to scribble strange symbols on paper, which were deciphered as an old style of shorthand no longer in use. The note began with an expression the boy's mother recognized as an habitual greeting from her husband: "Dearest Beloved." The message directed her to a safe-deposit box with an important letter in it. The dead man had used the old-style shorthand when he was a young telegrapher.

Who or what was the "Watseka Wonder"?

This was a classic case of "possession" (a spirit taking over the body of a living person). In 1865 a girl named Mary Roff living in the town of Watseka, Illinois, died at the age of nineteen. Thirteen years later Lurancy Vennum, a young girl who had been an infant at the time of Mary's death, contracted a similar illness and woke up one morning as Mary Roff. She insisted that she was the dead girl, and for three months her actions and personality were those of Mary. During this time she lived with the Roffs, who she claimed were her parents. On May 21, 1878, she said good-by to the Roffs, went into a trance, and woke up again as Lurancy Vennum, in good health and cured of her illness.

Do children see apparitions?

Although parapsychologists use the cautious label "apparitions," children and more venturesome adults prefer to think of such manifestations as ghosts or spirits. Children probably see more "apparitions" than adults do and accept them with less fear and trembling. Many famous men tell about seeing, hearing, even feeling ghosts or apparitions when they were children. (See Chapter 15.) Alexandre Dumas wrote that the night his father died, when Alexandre was only four, he heard a knock on the bedroom door and felt "a strong masculine breath passing over his face."

Do children ever have premonitions of their own deaths?

Yes. Aniela Jaffe tells about a schoolboy who looked down into a well and said, "How can I be lying down there when I am standing here?" Later he was drowned in the well. Charles Richet has written of many children who not only foresaw their own deaths in the near or far future but also knew when other members of the family would die.

Do children ever travel in their astral bodies?

Yes. (See Chapter 14.) Both Sylvan Muldoon and Oliver Fox have written about their astral travels in childhood. Writer Susy Smith tells of elementary-school children who were asked to draw pictures illustrating unusual events in their lives. One child drew a picture of herself in a Sunday-school class, where she had suddenly felt herself floating up to the ceiling, her body surrounded by brilliant yellow light. Another child reported leaving her sleeping physical body and going to visit friends.

What does psychiatrist Jan Ehrenwald call "the cradle of ESP"?

Literally the cradle itself. Dr. Ehrenwald believes that what is known as the maternal instinct may be a case of telepathy between mother and infant. The ESP link is a substitute for the baby's inability to express his needs in words, and therefore has a "survival value." As the child grows older and is more able to care for himself, the ESP link is not as strong.

At what age is a child's psychic sense most acute?

Louisa Rhine, who has analyzed thousands of cases of spontaneous ESP in children, believes that the psychic sense is most active at three and four years of age. In his book *Parent-Child Telepathy* Berthold Schwarz, a New Jersey psychiatrist, reports many examples of telepathy in his children at that age.

When is a mother most sensitive to her child's ESP?

Generally when the child needs help or is in danger. In one case described by Ian Stevenson, a six-year-old boy several miles from home was adrift in a small boat and in danger of drowning. His mother "heard" him call "Mommy!" and immediately knew he was in the boat. She sent a mental message that he should not stand up but should keep sitting. The boy was rescued later by persons who said that he had remained seated in the boat all the time.

Are there ever such emergency messages from mother to child?

Yes. Very often when the mother is ill or in trouble, somehow the child picks up the telepathic impression. The case of the girl who clairvoyantly "saw" her mother lying on the floor with a heart attack is described in Chapter 1.

Is there a psychic link between father and child?

Such links are very strong between all members of a family. During World War I a three-year-old child stopped playing one day and cried out, "My daddy is choking. He's down a hole and he can't see." When his father returned from France after the war, he said that at the very hour of the child's vision, he was gassed while in a cellar and was blind for three weeks.

What small child "saw" his father at the South Pole?

In *The Eye of the Wind* Peter Scott writes about his father, Robert Scott, who in 1912 arrived at the South Pole just after Roald Amundsen. Peter was three years old at the time, and it was not known if either of the two men had reached the Pole or who got there first. Peter said suddenly, "Amundsen and Daddy both got to the Pole, Mummy, but Daddy has stopped work now." Scott had just begun the dangerous trip back. He died a few weeks later.

How does an adult's state of mind bring on a child's ESP?

In cases of psychic links between parent and child that do not involve danger to either, there still may be an emotional component—that is, the child may catch a strong feeling behind the adult's thought. Dr. Ehrenwald, who calls this an "emotional charge," tells of one occasion when his wife was thinking about a photograph of a cousin that had just arrived in the mail. At this moment her four-year-old daughter said, "Matilda," the cousin's name. Ehrenwald points out that the response was not accidental: his wife was thinking of Matilda's new baby and regretting that they (the Ehrenwalds) could not afford another child at that time.

Are there "trivial" communications between parents and children?

Apparently, although the emotional component may be well hidden, as it often is in relationships between adults. Dr. Schwarz had many such experiences with his two-year-old daughter Lisa. Once he came into the kitchen and had an impulse to do a "Nijinsky-like kick." With this thought the child did a kick herself and broke into a dance.

What was the "book of gold" case?

A mother showed a photograph of her four-year-old daughter to a friend, who remarked, "That child should have a musical education. It would be to her a book of gold with notes of silver for her in it." The child's mother was not home at the time and when she returned, the girl was asleep. The next morning the child woke up, peered under her pillows, and searched among the bedcovers. Then she opened the dresser drawer and looked inside. When her mother asked her what she was looking for, she replied, "I want a book of gold with something in it for me."

Do retarded children have ESP ability?

Psychic powers are not necessarily related to intelligence. When a child is handicapped, a "survival value" may be operating in an ESP link with the mother. One mother of a retarded six-year-old sends him mental messages when he is outside and she wants him to come home. In a few moments he appears in the doorway. Professor Marcel de Thy of France writes about his fifty-six-year-old brother Robert, who has the mental age of an eighteen-month-old baby. Robert, who never learned to speak correctly, could always speak perfectly when he was reading his brother's mind.

What was the case of the retarded child Ilga?

Ilga was a nine-year-old Lithuanian girl with an IQ of only 42—50 points below normal. Although she had a reading disability, she could read normally when her doctor was standing by, thinking about the text. She could also do complicated mathematical problems beyond her usual capacity if her teacher was mentally doing the calculations at the same time. When her mother was reading, she could recite what was in the book, even if it was written in a foreign language.

Can the psychic link between mother and child overcome physical handicaps?

Yes. Dr. Ehrenwald tells of a small boy with cataracts who normally could not see letters and figures on an eye chart, but could read them perfectly when his mother was in the room. Was his mother "reading" the chart for him telepathically or did a temporary healing process take place?

How does the "survival value" principle operate in cases of handicapped children?

The ESP link with parents may be more active when there is physical or mental abnormality than when the child is healthy. Both mother (or father) and child may not only compensate but in some way overcompensate for the handicap with an unusually strong psychic link.

Are there psychic links between children?

Yes, just as between adults. In *Hidden Channels of the Mind* Louisa Rhine tells about a three-and-a-half-year-old boy whose infant brother was staying at his grandmother's house, a block away. Suddenly the older boy ran to the window and called frantically to his mother that the other child wanted her. She found later that at the very moment of the boy's outburst, the baby had awakened, crying for his mother.

Do small children know that they have ESP?

It is evidently a subconscious process that the child responds to without thinking. He does what comes naturally. This is generally true of ESP at all ages, but older children and adults are often aware of the strangeness of their mental impressions.

Do young children have an active interest in psychic phenomena today?

Yes. With a growing adult interest in the paranormal and more ESP testing in elementary and high schools, both young and older children are eager to learn about all things psychic. Although teen-age boys and girls take a serious interest in witchcraft and other occult phenomena, the younger children seem to look upon the occult with some amusement and find ghosts especially entertaining. Both groups are cooperative subjects in ESP experiments.

How much testing is there in elementary and secondary schools today?

There is more and more of it. Parapsychologists such as J. B. Rhine, Margaret Anderson, Rhea White, and J. G. van Busschbach are designing many kinds of tests, some similar to those in the Duke University experiments, others with a highly imaginative content for young children.

Which age groups are the most successful in the tests?

Gardner Murphy has written that, taking the population as a whole, the two most successful groups are (1) elementary and junior-high students, and (2) young adults. Unfortunately, as children get older, they often lose interest in the school ESP testing, with some dropping off of scores. Parapsychologist J. G. van Busschbach of the Netherlands reported that fifth- and sixth-grade children in Holland were full of enthusiasm but when they reached the seventh and eighth grades they thought that such testing was "silly." This was some years ago, however, and ESP is taken more seriously everywhere today.

Do children make higher scores in ESP tests when they are given rewards?

Yes. In one of Louisa Rhine's examples, a young girl named Lillian was offered fifty cents to make a good score in an ESP card test. She closed her eyes and went through twenty-five cards perfectly.

How else can a child be motivated to make a high score?

A young psychologist had an eleven-year-old nephew to whom she was strongly attached. After he had made mediocre scores in a series of tests, she took him to his room one day and gave him a "pep talk," telling him how important it was for him to make a high score. She convinced him that he could "see" the cards if he really tried. On his first run with the ESP cards following this session, he got eleven right out of twenty-five, six more than if only chance had been operating. Then he got seventeen right, a phenomenal score. Finally, she offered him a prize if he could make twenty correct guesses out of twenty-five. On his next two tries he got nineteen, then twenty-two.

How does the teacher-pupil relationship affect ESP test results?

In general, children who say they like their teacher do better than those who don't like him or her. If the teacher likes them too, the scores will be even higher. When the student doesn't like the teacher, he makes a lower score and, when the dislike is mutual, still lower. Scores are highest in cases of mutual admiration.

How can a teacher help students make high scores?

Van Busschbach found that in elementary school, when the teacher looked at the cards or other targets during the tests, the children made high scores. This was not true in high school, and van Busschbach concluded that the greater "emotional closeness" between teacher and pupil in the lower grades might be responsible.

What is the "fantasy" element in ESP tests for children?

Because children respond to the imaginative and play elements in all situations, it is believed that the use of fantasy in an ESP test will result in higher scores. Dr. Margaret Anderson, a parapsychologist, did three series of tests with elementary-school children in which they worked out codes for "hearing" music in outer space and "launching" rockets into space. She chose teachers who had unusual rapport with their students.

What were the "music from outer space" ESP tests?

This was a two-year program testing clairvoyance and precognition in thirty-two fifth-grade children. Instead of the ESP card symbols (circle, star, wavy lines, etc.), seven variations were used as targets, including stars and musical notes. The students in a music-appreciation class pretended that they were the "Orchestra of Tomorrow" and were "tuning in" to outer space music. Results of the tests showed evidence of ESP in the children.

What were the "vastronaut" tests for ESP in children?

In the second of the Anderson series, a fourth-grade teacher told her students that they would mentally launch a rocket by picking the correct symbols corresponding to "computer codes." The printed tests were in the form of "rocket tubes" divided into blank spaces instead of columns as in conventional ESP card tests, and each student would fill in the spaces with numbers or colors rather than ESP card symbols. Each correct choice of number or color would "launch" the missile and "send" it into space. To stimulate the children's imagination, the teacher brought a model rocket with flashing lights and bleeps into the classroom.

In what ESP tests did an entire elementary school participate?

Dr. Anderson also planned this experiment. The testing involved 590 students in grades one through six, 22 teachers, and the principal of the school. The objective was to mentally launch a rocket, put it into orbit, and bring it back to earth. Aids to the imagination were a six-foot colored rocket and a large panel of an imaginary computer with lights that flashed on and off. Each student made a choice of colored circles, letters, or numbers for "tracking the orbital flight path." Dr. Anderson directed the tests by loudspeaker from the "control center."

How well did creative children do in this test?

Before the series began, the teachers were asked to give each of their pupils a "creativity" rating. Those thought to be the highest in creative imagination made the highest ESP scores.

What is Dr. Anderson's theory about ESP in the learning process?

In the *Journal of the American Society for Psychical Research* (April 1966), Dr. Anderson writes: "From observation over several years in classroom situations, it appeared to me that, particularly with a 'good' class, which I define as one in which the feeling of rapport is strong, something is 'caught,' so to speak, beyond the subject matter being taught. I came to the tentative conclusion then, and I hold it even more strongly today, that the learning process is an emergent characteristic of the total elements constituting any given classroom at any given time and that ESP probably plays an important part in that process."

What was the most far-reaching ESP project ever attempted in the high schools?

In the late 1960s, the Foundation for Research into the Nature of Man (FRNM) in Durham, North Carolina, directed by Dr. Rhine, did a test for precognition in junior and senior high schools in the United States and several foreign countries. Seventy-five thousand students participated, making over a million and a half guesses of the order in which ESP card symbols and words would be chosen the following day. The results showed significant evidence of precognition.

13 YOUR QUESTIONS ANSWERED ABOUT
STRANGE POWERS IN ANIMALS AND PLANTS:
"PSI-TRAILING" DOGS, CATS, AND PIGEONS WHO
TRACK DOWN THEIR MASTERS OVER THOUSANDS OF
MILES OF UNFAMILIAR TERRITORY; THE DOG
WHO PREDICTED HIS OWN DEATH; PSYCHIC HORSES;
TELEPATHY BETWEEN ANIMALS AND MAN; ANIMALS
THAT "THINK" AND "TALK"; PLANTS THAT "LISTEN" TO
MUSIC; PSYCHIC EXPERIENCES SHARED BY MASTERS
AND THEIR PETS . . .

What is "psi-trailing"?

There are many strange cases of dogs, cats, and other pets who, left behind when their owners move to another city and state, show up at the new home weeks or months later. The pet often travels hundreds or thousands of miles over unfamiliar territory. The homing and migratory direction-finding sense in birds and other animals may be related to the "psi-trailing" faculty.

How are psi-trailing animals usually identified?

Their personalities are often dead giveaways, but even better identification is a special tag or an unusual physical characteristic—color or length of hair, eye color, spots, the marks of a veterinary operation, obvious deformity, etc. A small black dog, Tony, was identified by a white line under his chin and a right-angled hole in his collar that had been made with a pocket knife.

Who was the psi-trailing cat that played the piano?

Smoky, a three-year-old Persian cat, disappeared in Oklahoma while his owners were on their way to a new home in Memphis, Tennessee. A year later the cat trotted up to the porch of the Memphis home and jumped into the lap of the

fourteen-year-old daughter of the house. The girl recognized
a tuft of red hair under Smoky's chin, but for further proof
she went to the piano and began to play. Smoky jumped on
the seat beside her and placed his front paws on the keys, as
he had done in the past.

Who was the psi-trailing cat with seven toes on two paws?

A black cat called Clementine was left with neighbors
when her owners moved from Dunkirk, New York, to Denver,
Colorado, 1600 miles away. After she had a litter, Clementine deserted her own family and her new owners and appeared four months later on the doorstep of the Denver
home. It was easy to identify her. She had seven toes on each
front paw, two white spots on her stomach, and a scar on her
left shoulder.

Who was the psi-trailing dog that "shook hands"?

A mixed-breed Belgian Shepherd named King was stolen
before his owners moved from Idaho to California. One morning three months later the dog was found lying in front of
their apartment door. King identified himself by shaking
hands with his left paw and by sitting in the back seat of the
family car and placing his paws on the shoulders of a front-
seat occupant.

What was remarkable about Pigeon 167?

Another psi-trailer. When Pigeon 167's owner, a twelve-
year-old boy, was taken to a hospital 100 miles from home for
an operation, the pigeon, his identification number attached
to his leg, flew through the snow and appeared at the window of the boy's room.

Do animals find one another through psi-trailing?

Yes, and usually affection plays a large part in their ability to do so. Just as human beings in love may follow each
other around the world, animals have been known to do like-
wise. While a California family was driving from Los Angeles
to San Francisco, one of their two pet pigeons, a male, flew
out of the car and headed back to Los Angeles. When the
family arrived in San Francisco, they hung the cage in the

window with the female pigeon in it. The male must have changed his mind about going back to Los Angeles, because the next morning he was sitting outside the window. It was the first time the two pigeons had been away from home.

Are moths psi-trailers?

In an experiment in the 1940s the female of a rare moth species was kept in a room four miles from the male. The male was released and in a few hours was beating its wings against the window screen of the room. Was a psychic sense operating?

Have psi-trailing animals been studied during their trips?

Many studies have been made of the homing sense in dogs, cats, pigeons, even mice. Although it is not psi-trailing in the sense of psychically tracking down another individual or a family, ESP seems to be working in the animal's ability to find its way home through unfamiliar territory. In one kind of experiment dogs and cats have been crated so they could not see their surroundings, then taken by rail or in a closed truck long distances from home. In a German experiment, a sheep dog was let out of a closed van 7 miles from home and carefully watched. With woods barring his way, the dog seemed puzzled at first, but he slowly gained confidence, circled the woods, and finally reached the main road. Here his tail went up and he galloped home, traveling 7 miles in 1 hour and 8 minutes. At no point was he seen sniffing the air for sensory cues.

Do birds have the psi-trailing faculty?

Migratory direction-finding in birds is closely related to the psi-trailing sense. Although their ability to fly south each year to the same location has been explained by thermal radiation, the earth's magnetic field, the position of sun and stars, etc., there are certain cases that defy analysis. In some species the young go south for the first time before their elders, taking the identical routes followed by the adults in previous years, and winding up in the same place. Another example of psi among birds is the way a flock rises and descends in unison. Two books with detailed studies of bird flight are *Bird Migration* by Donald R. Griffen and *Thought Transference (or What?) in Birds* by Edmund Selous.

Has the psi faculty in birds been studied during their long-distance flights?

Yes. Birds who fly south to almost the same spot each winter have been identified by numbered bands attached to their feathers. One white-throated sparrow was banded in Georgia. He went to Canada to breed, then returned home three years in a row to the same thicket in Georgia. Homing pigeons, trained to fly home in one direction, still found their way back when released for the first time in another direction.

What was the direction-finding test with a deer mouse?

The mouse, with a radio transmitter implanted beneath his skin to trace his route, was released 200 miles from his nest. He returned home the next night. Later he was taken in a closed container in a different direction and let out 300 miles away. Again he found his way back home.

Are green turtles psi-trailers?

Whatever it is that green turtles do, a psi faculty seems to be operating. When baby green turtles are hatched on Ascension Island in the middle of the South Atlantic, they head for the ocean 7 miles away and swim 1400 miles to their adult habitat off the coast of Brazil. A similar case is that of the European eel, which is spawned in the Atlantic east of Bermuda, then travels to the rivers of western Europe and North Africa, returning several years later as an adult to the breeding area where it was born.

Can animals sense forthcoming disasters?

Yes. In 1902, for example, just before the eruption of the Mount Pelée volcano that killed 40,000 people (see Chapter 3), the cattle became upset, snakes left the area of the volcano, dogs howled continuously, and birds flew away from their nests. In another case cows and horses refused to go down into a ravine before an avalanche. Rats have been known to leave a ship that was destined to sink.

Has an animal's ESP ever warned human beings of an approaching disaster?

There are innumerable cases on record. In one instance, a canary belonging to an Italian family fluttered wildly in its cage and tried to get out. The family, sensing that something was wrong, ran up a road that led to the top of the village just before an avalanche devastated the town, killing everyone in it.

Do animals know when a human being is going to die?

There is evidence that they do. Sometimes a dog behaves strangely before the death of its master, although the latter may be in good health at the time. Many dogs give the familiar "death howl" when their masters die in hospitals some distance away. Throughout the world the behavior of many animal species—birds, owls, gophers, etc.—is considered a harbinger of death.

Do psychic cries for help ever come from animals?

In *Animal Affinities with Man* Thurlow Craig tells about waking up in the middle of the night with the feeling that his horse Patience needed him. He went out to his fifteen-acre field and found Patience limping badly, a coil of rusty wire wrapped tightly around her leg and cutting off her blood supply. Craig had been sleeping soundly, his window closed, and could not have heard the horse.

Do animals in trouble ever communicate through dreams?

A man on a visit to London dreamed one night that his dog Mitzi came into his room, her ear almost torn off, crying with pain. He woke up at 4 A.M. in a cold sweat, and at breakfast described his dream to his hostess. At that moment the telephone rang. It was his housekeeper, who told him that Mitzi had come through his bedroom window at 4 A.M., screaming with pain. Her ear was nearly torn off.

How do animals "anticipate" the return home of their masters?

They often know the exact time their masters will appear on the doorstep and seem to clairvoyantly follow each step of the return trip. In *The Good Beasts* John T. Rowland tells of the dog Elko, who always knew which of three possible trains his master was on. When he heard each train whistle, he would run out joyfully, pause as if in thought, then walk back slowly if it wasn't the right train. If his master was actually on the train, he would run up the road to meet him, although the train might be just pulling into the station. The writer Maurice Maeterlinck also observed "anticipatory" behavior in his dog.

What dog gave the signal to start cooking dinner?

This was another example of "anticipatory" behavior. In the 1930s a dachshund called Charlotte would trot out to the front gate and sit there exactly four hours before her master would return from a trip. At this point the cook knew he should start preparing the meal.

Can dogs read a human being's mind?

They often appear to. In many cases, of course, what appears to be telepathy is merely a response to certain physical movements and other sensory cues. In other cases, ESP is strongly indicated. As with human beings, the emotional closeness between a dog and his master seems to stir up psychic communication.

What dog predicted his own death?

In *Many Lives, Many Loves,* writer Gina Cerminara tells of a remarkable man named Fred Kimball, who could carry on a "conversation" with dogs. In the presence of its owner, Kimball would orally ask the dog a question, then look into the dog's eyes and receive the answer psychically. One dog "complained" to Kimball that there was too much fat in his diet, another that he needed more exercise. A husky named Jack, who conveyed the thought that he would live only six months more, died at the end of that time.

Do dogs ever obey telepathic commands?

The owner of a dog named Dodgerfield would close his eyes and mentally command the dog to bring a card from the table, then say out loud, "Attention, Dodgerfield, bring it." The dog then trotted over and got the card. Another dog,

Roger, would spell out on lettered blocks with his paw a word that his owner was thinking of, although no word was spoken and no signal given.

How did a Russian circus trainer give telepathic commands to his dog Pikki?

The trainer, Durov, would hold the dog's head in his hands, stare into his eyes, and give him mental suggestions. Once he silently told Pikki to charge at a small stuffed wolf on the table. Pikki looked sharply at the wolf, then rushed at it, barking angrily. To rule out sensory cues from the trainer, an observer, Bechterev, also gave a silent command to pull a handkerchief from the pocket of a doctor present. Pikki jumped on the table and fetched the handkerchief.

What dog could "say" the word his master was thinking?

Happy was a five-year-old cocker spaniel owned by Mr. and Mrs. Chet Petersen of Kenosha, Wisconsin. When Mrs. Petersen thought of a word, Happy would respond with guttural sounds accompanied by movements of his body. Although the word was not distinct, Happy grunted the same number of syllables as those in the word.

How did a dog named Dozie "read" the numbers in her master's mind?

If her master was thinking of "four," Dozie would bark four times, eight times for the number eight, etc.

What canine baseball fan knew what the score was?

Probably the most famous of all "telepathic" dogs was Chris, a nine-year-old male mongrel belonging to George H. Wood. Chris, who often demonstrated his talent on television programs, was the subject of many experiments in his own home. Once he was asked the result of a baseball game that had just ended. No one present knew the score, but Chris pawed his master's arm to indicate the runs scored by each team. Chris also gave the answers to mathematical problems by the pawing method. After he was trained to understand the letters of the alphabet through a number code, he gave the answers in words.

What dog "tutored" children in arithmetic?

Rolf of Mannheim, an Airedale terrier, gave answers to complicated math problems by barking or tapping his left paw on his master's arm. He sometimes worked so fast that he had the answers before his questioners could figure them out. When the children of his owners had trouble with their homework, Rolf was called in to help them.

Who was the blind dog with ESP?

Darkey answered questions by barking and stamping and, like Rolf of Mannheim, worked so fast that he often gave the answers before they were completely asked. Since there could be no visual cues, he may have been getting the answers telepathically from someone present.

What dog predicted how many puppies she would have in a litter?

Lola was the name of this remarkable dog seer. Lola could forecast the weather, tell what time it was, and, when asked how large her new family would be, tapped out with her paw that she would have nine pups. The nine were born several days later. It appears that psychic abilities may run in dog as well as human families, for Lola was the daughter of Rolf of Mannheim.

Who were the "talking dogs" of Weimar?

Kurwenal, a dachshund, and Asra, a Great Dane, learned the alphabet through a code and barked out letters and words in answer to questions. Asra also tapped answers with her left and right front paws. The dogs were investigated by Nandor Fodor, the psychiatrist.

What dog was hired to find lost objects?

This was another Rolf, a German Shepherd who lived on the Danish island of Funen. As his owner drove with Rolf in a panel truck, he would keep telling the dog the name of the object to be found or would concentrate on it silently. Rolf dug up articles buried in ice, in swamps, even in manure piles. In seven years he located objects worth a total of $400,000.

Who was the dog "typist"?

The four-legged secretary was an Italian dog named Arli. His owner taught him the letters of the alphabet, then showed him how to manipulate a fourteen-key machine with his paws. He learned to type short words to dictation.

Have dogs been tested for ESP under laboratory conditions?

Researchers from the Parapsychology Laboratory at Duke University tested several dogs, including some mentioned above, who were apparently psychic. The dogs were taught a code in which letters and ESP symbols (cross, circle, square, etc.) were equivalent to barks and taps, then tested in their own homes just as human beings are tested in the ESP laboratory. One of the canine subjects was the remarkable Chris (the baseball fan), who pawed his responses on his master's arm. In one series with Chris, he was separated from the agent by several miles, and the tests were conducted by telephone.

How did the dog subjects compare in scoring with human psychics?

Although it was difficult to impose the same tight controls, the dogs as a group did much better than their human rivals, averaging 80 per cent correct answers. Chance level was 10 per cent.

Did the dog subjects show the "decline" effect?

The element of novelty is important in any ESP testing situation, whether human beings or animals are involved. The dogs, like human subjects, became tired and less attentive after many tests, and their scores dropped off.

How were sensory cues from the dogs' owners eliminated in the ESP tests?

One dog, Heidi, scored well above chance even when her master, acting as agent, was separated from her by a stairway. Cookie, an eleven-year-old cocker spaniel, made high scores even in a dark room. Happy, the dog who barked out answers in syllables, was separated from her master by a door and was also tested in darkness, but she still made high scores. Loud radios were sometimes played to screen out possible auditory cues.

How did the attitude of the dog's owner influence the scores?

As with human beings, any change of mood on the part of the agent, usually the owner, affected the dog's responses. In one case the dog's interest fell off when her master was tired or not feeling well.

What theory other than ESP can explain the high scores?

A dog is, of course, extremely sensitive to bodily movements, voice inflections, and other cues his master might give him consciously or unconsciously. The precautions taken during the tests, however, ruled out to a great extent the theory of sensory cues. Another theory is that the human beings present who kept score were actually ESP receivers and were reacting not to the dog's responses but to their own unconscious knowledge. However, no theory except ESP takes into account the fact that the dog's barking or tapping out answers in most cases originally came to the master's attention by accident.

Who were the "thinking horses" of Elberfeld?

These were eleven German horses trained to spell out sentences and solve complicated mathematical problems such as giving the square or even fourth power of numbers. The horses answered questions by stamping their hooves to indicate numbers or letters of the alphabet. Mohammed, one of the horses, could do mathematical problems in a few seconds that took schoolteachers, working on paper, ten times as long. A visitor once asked Mohammed what she could do for him. The horse stamped out this reply: "Please wag your tail and then go home."

Who was the famous psychic horse Lady?

Lady was a three-year-old filly of Richmond, Virginia, who was trained to work with letters and numbers. Lady would respond to both spoken and silent commands to spell words or make computations by touching her nose to the appropriate symbols printed on blocks.

How did parapsychologist J. B. Rhine test Lady?

Rhine made a series of exhaustive tests over a six-day period. At first oral commands were given by the horse's owner, Mrs. Fonda; then Rhine would write on a piece of paper a question that could be answered by a number or a word. He would show the question to Mrs. Fonda, who would ask the horse to tap the number or spell out the word she was thinking of.

What words did Lady spell out when given silent commands?

In one test Rhine wrote the words "Hindustani, Carolina, Mesopotamia" on a piece of paper and showed it to Mrs. Fonda, who said to Lady, "Spell the word." Lady touched her nose to the letter blocks and spelled each word perfectly.

What did Lady answer when Rhine asked her where he could borrow money?

Rhine showed the question to Mrs. Fonda, who "beamed" it mentally to the horse. Lady spelled out B-A-N-K.

How did Lady "find the dog"?

Among Lady's props were twenty picture blocks with figures of animals and other objects. If Mrs. Fonda said, "Find the dog," Lady would trot over to the blocks and touch the picture of a dog.

How were voice and visual cues eliminated during Lady's testing?

Mrs. Fonda was gradually separated from the horse. First she had her back to Lady. Then a screen was placed between them. Finally Rhine and others acted as agents, but Lady continued to make high scores.

How did Lady show the "decline" effect?

When Rhine tested Lady for the second time a year later, she showed almost no ESP and did not seem interested in the tests. Rhine points out that Lady's fluctuations in scoring are more indicative of ESP than if she had made perfect scores, which would be likely if she were responding to sensory cues.

Was Lady in an "altered state of consciousness" during the first series of tests?

She appeared to be. She was passive, slow-moving, dreamy, a state favorable to ESP experience. (See Chapter 6.) During the second series of tests a year later she was alert and active, more alive to her surroundings than to the testing.

What is the evolutionary theory of ESP that would explain an animal's psychic ability?

Biologist Alister Hardy, psychiatrist Sigmund Freud, and others speculated that the psychic sense may have been dominant in early forms of animal life before the senses were well developed. Tests with cockroaches, chicken embryos, paramecia, and woodlice (see Chapter 4) point to the possible truth of this theory.

What animal was born with its birth date on its body?

Rene Sudré in his book *Parapsychology* writes that a cat in Nice, France, gave birth in 1921 to a kitten bearing the date of the year on its front, formed by groups of black hairs on a white background. Investigators found that during gestation the cat had spent long periods watching for rats hidden behind a sack bearing this date. Three stars above the date on the sack appeared as spots on the kitten's fur.

Do plants have emotions?

There seems to be more and more evidence of this. Cleve Backster, a New York polygraph expert, found that when he attached the electrodes from the machine to the leaves of a plant, it responded to his thoughts and intentions. Once he thought idly about burning the plant, and the needle on the graph paper fluctuated wildly. Backster also found that chicken eggs showed an emotional response on the polygraph.

Does prayer help plants to grow?

Many plant owners swear this is true. In *The Power of Prayer over Plants*, the Reverend Franklin Loehr describes a series of 700 experiments by 150 persons with 27,000 seeds. The seeds that got the prayer treatment grew more rapidly than the "control" group of seeds that were ignored. (See experiments of Bernard Grad in Chapter 5.)

Do plants have auras?

Some psychics can see such auras. Mrs. Ethel DeLoach of Morristown, New Jersey, has spent hours watching the aura of a leaf as it dies. When the leaf is cut in half, the auras of the two halves reach out to each other. When the leaf is dead, the aura is gone. The Kirlian process developed in Russia has photographed auras of many living organisms, including plants. (See Chapter 5.)

Do plants prefer classical to rock music?

Rock fans would dispute this, but a Denver woman claims she has evidence. She says that her squash, bean, and other plants "cringe and die" when they are forced to listen to acid rock on her record-player, but turn their petals toward the music and seem to flourish when Bach or East Indian music is played. The plants also seem to like jazz and country and Western music.

14

What is the "astral" body?

According to a widely held theory among those who study psychic phenomena, every person has a duplicate body within his physical organism, exactly like the physical body in every way but made of finer, less dense material. Also called the "etheric" or "second" body or "the double," the astral body has much greater freedom of movement than the parent body.

What is an OOBE or "out-of-body" experience?

Many persons have claimed that their astral bodies have left their physical bodies during sleep and at other times, sometimes remaining in the same room, often traveling out of doors and to other cities and countries.

Where is the physical body while the astral body is traveling?

It remains in bed or in a chair, wherever it was when the astral body left, usually unconscious.

Is the traveling astral body connected to the physical body?

Yes, by what is called the silver cord. The cord has been variously described by astral travelers and witnesses as a ribbon-like strand, a silky thread, a cord, a chain, or an elastic cable, surrounded by light and connected to the head or solar plexus of the physical body. It has been compared to the umbilical cord.

How thick or strong is the silver cord?

The cord is about two or three inches thick when the two bodies are close together, but it becomes thinner and more tenuous as the astral body moves farther away.

How fast and how far can the astral body travel?

According to Oliver Fox, an astral traveler of the early twentieth century, the astral body can "move with the freedom of thought." It can walk, float, or glide, move slowly or at lightning speed, and go as far as thought will take it.

What happens if the silver cord breaks?

Ordinarily the cord is indestructible and will stretch out interminably. At death, however, the cord is severed from the physical body. There appears to be no danger that this will happen accidentally during an OOB experience.

What do psychics feel when the astral body is leaving the physical body?

Most of them report a momentary blackout or a feeling of going through a tunnel. There is usually a sensation of rising, more rarely a temporary descent before the rise. Many persons feel as though they were slipping out of a "tight glove" and one described it as a "skinning process." Others experience numbness and rigidity before their astral bodies are free. Robert Monroe, in his book *Journeys out of the Body,* tells of first feeling vibrations, followed by "turning in the air," then "diving into a tunnel" as he left his body.

Are there any physical changes in the parent body?

When the separation occurs, there may be a change in temperature, a drop in blood pressure, and an alteration of brain-wave patterns. Such changes have been observed on the electroencephalograph and other machines that record physiological changes. When the astral body is out, the physical body usually stays passive until it returns.

What is the astral body made of?

No one really knows, but it may be electrical in nature. Many OOB travelers first feel an electrical charge when their bodies separate. On one occasion Monroe believed that his astral body had traveled via telephone power lines.

What do astral travelers see or hear when they are leaving the body?

Many see a very bright light without shadows. In the first stages of some experiences, there is a kind of fog with strange entities moving about, followed by a beautiful bright light. The cord itself seems to give off light. Some travelers hear a sound like that of silk tearing.

Through what part of the physical body does the astral body leave?

Mostly through the head, sometimes by way of the solar plexus. Sylvan Muldoon, who probably had more OOB experiences than anyone else, felt a "tremendous pressure being exerted in the back of my head." Diane Kennedy, the widow of Bishop Pike, described a vision in which she saw Pike's spirit come out of his body at the back of the neck. With death the silver cord would have been severed.

Where does the astral body go when it first slips out?

Generally, it rises to a horizontal position about three feet above the physical body, then moves to a vertical position before beginning its journey. Some OOB travelers first feel themselves sinking before they rise. One astral projector slid to the floor at an angle, then shot back up at the same angle before starting his journey.

What happens when the astral body returns?

It reverses its departure sequence, assuming a horizontal position above the physical body and slipping back in with a "click." Monroe says he "rotated" back into his body and felt the same vibrations as when he left. Others report "spinning" back in.

What can cause the astral body to make an abrupt return?

Noise or an emotional disturbance such as a sudden fright. The effect of the abrupt re-entry of the astral body has been compared to a shock or concussion.

Do the ordinary senses function during astral travel?

Probably better than they do in the physical body. Astral projectors have said that thought, feeling, and awareness are much more intense in the out-of-body state. Here is what Eileen Garrett said about her OOB experiences: "The double is apparently able to use the normal activity of all five senses which work in my physical body. For example, I may be sitting in a drawing-room on a snowy day and yet be able in projection to reach a place where summer is at that moment full-blown. In that instant I can register with all my five physical senses the sight of the flowers and the sea, I can smell the scent of the blossoms and the tang of the ocean spray, and I can hear the birds sing and the waves beat against the shore. . . ."

Can the astral traveler see his own physical body?

This is how most of them realize they are having an OOB experience. Caroline Larsen, who in 1910 walked around her house in her astral body, writes that she first found herself standing beside her bed looking at her physical counterpart: "I recognized every line in that familiar face, pale and still as in death, the features drawn, the eyes tightly closed and the mouth partly open."

Can the astral body be seen by others?

Sometimes. It depends on the psychic sensitivity of the observer and perhaps, as in other paranormal experiences, the rapport between the traveler and the person he is visiting. Monroe writes that he was recognized on many of his "trips." In a case reported by psychic researcher Robert Crookall, a woman who had warned her daughter not to leave a hot iron within reach of her grandson "traveled" five miles one night to visit her sleeping daughter. The daughter said later that she saw her mother standing at the bedside with an iron in her hand.

Does the astral body appear as solid as the physical body?

At times it does. Some astral travelers, among them novelist William Gerhardi, have seen themselves reflected in a mirror.

Can the astral body be felt?

Only on rare occasions. Robert Monroe was able to put his astral hands together and feel the sensation. He could also reach and touch his physical body. Evidently the astral body, which Monroe claims has weight and is subject to gravity, has some physical characteristics. In one case a college student dreamed that he visited his fiancée's home one evening at 10 P.M., saw the young lady on the stairs, and put his astral arm around her waist. The next day a note came from the girl telling him that at 10 P.M. she had been on the stairs on her way to bed when she heard his footsteps and felt his arm around her.

Who pinched a lady friend while he was in his astral body?

Robert Monroe made this confession in his book. When he pinched the woman, she said, "Ow," and when he saw her later in his normal body, she showed him black-and-blue marks.

If an astral traveler talks, can he be heard?

Probably not, but Monroe says he once carried on a conversation with a little girl. She said, "I know who you are." "Who am I?" "You're an astral projection!"

Can an astral projector handle objects or make them move?

This is rare, but there have been such cases reported. Oliver Fox wrote that he could "mold matter into new forms." Muldoon claimed that through a process he called "externalized energy" he could move objects by will power. Once he activated a metronome.

How elastic is the astral body?

Monroe writes that his "second body" could be extended many feet, his arm to three times its length. Standing in the middle of a room, he could "stretch out" and touch a wall eight feet away.

Is the astral body ever stopped by physical objects?

Sometimes it is. Robert Crookall, who has investigated thousands of OOB cases, believes that the astral body is actually a composite of two bodies—a semi-physical substance he calls "the vehicle of vitality," and a superpsychical essence or soul body. When the composite astral body is released, physical conditions prevail to some extent, but when the vehicle of vitality is dropped off, the soul body may pass through all substances. Eileen Garrett referred to the vehicle of vitality as "the surround."

What does the astral traveler think and feel during his journeys?

He has a great sense of freedom and is often reluctant to return to his physical body, which he regards with a sense of detachment and indifference. Most astral travelers tell of a heightened consciousness. One woman said she felt "strangely linked to all the people in the world—as if their thought consciousness belonged to me also."

Are joy and bliss universally felt by the astral traveler?

That depends on which realm he is visiting. According to Crookall, if too much "vehicle of vitality" is released, the traveler may stay for a while in a murky atmosphere with "Hades-like" conditions, inhabited by unpleasant entities. Monroe reports passing through a "gray-black hungry ocean" to a world "peopled with insane or near-insane, emotionally driven beings." Once the traveler breaks through this earthbound state, he may find himself in what Crookall calls "Paradise," a realm of brilliant light and angelic creatures. One woman said, after such an experience, "Have you ever been to Paradise? If so, the memory will remain with you until you die."

Must the astral projector first go through the "Hades" realm before he reaches "Paradise"?

Crookall believes that most projectors release only their soul bodies and avoid the temporary Hades conditions. The Hades realm may be a reflection of the mental stresses of those still alive as well as of the dead.

Who are the "deliverers"?

This is a term Crookall and others give to spirits who help astral travelers out of their physical bodies and sometimes accompany them on their etheric journeys. They are benevolent souls, some known to the travelers, others not identified.

Who are the "hinderers"?

These are unpleasant entities, mostly encountered in the earthbound realm, who try to prevent the traveler from going farther.

Who are the "cooperators"?

Many astral projectors feel compelled to leave their physical bodies because someone needs their help. Crookall reports the case of a man who visited a woman astrally and in some way prevented her from performing a rash act. Although they had never met before, she saw him later in his physical body and cried out, "It is my mentor!"

Do astral projectors meet the spirits of dead persons?

Many report that they see and converse with long-dead relatives and friends. Monroe saw his father, a friend, and a recently deceased young doctor. During one projection William Gerhardi met a friend thought to be still alive who was also projecting, and the two made an astral visit to the friend's house. Here they saw that the physical body of the friend was no longer breathing and the silver cord had been broken, a fact very upsetting to the "dead" man.

When and why does astral projection occur?

OOBEs happen mostly in sleep but may also occur when a person is sitting or lying in a relaxed state. Sleepers are often not aware that they have been astral travelers. Most projectors are in good health, but projections may happen during an emotional disturbance, severe illness, shock, or an accident. In such cases, said Eileen Garrett, "the physical hold upon ourselves is less tenacious."

Can a person consciously project his astral body?

Most cases occur without volition during an altered state of consciousness, but several astral travelers—Oliver Fox, Eileen Garrett, Robert Monroe, and a few others—have trained themselves to leave their bodies almost at will. In a case reported by the Society for Psychical Research, a man projected his astral body to the home of a friend by visualizing his usual procedure of going to her house and ringing the bell. The maid heard the bell and answered the door. The man's astral body was seen in a cloud by his friend, and her daughter heard his "footsteps."

Has astral projection been tested in the laboratory?

Dr. Charles Tart, a psychologist at the University of California, Davis campus, tested two persons, one of them Monroe, the other a young woman. The woman slept in one room, while in another Tart watched her brain waves traced on the electroencephalograph. In the woman's room a five-digit number was concealed from her view on a wooden projection near the ceiling. In the morning the woman gave the numbers correctly, saying she had floated up to the ceiling during the night and read them. The electroencephalograph showed unusual brain patterns as she slept. The American Society for Psychical Research is also testing out-of-body travelers by placing objects of different design on a shelf near the ceiling. The psychic is then asked to sketch the objects he sees astrally. These experiments have been very successful.

Do patients project during hospital operations?

This is a common phenomenon. The anesthetized patients find themselves near the ceiling looking down at their bodies on the operating table and hearing conversations between the doctors and nurses which they report verbatim later, to the astonishment of the medical personnel. They often see their own silver cords connecting their astral and physical bodies.

What is the astral state of mind of these hospital cases?

A feeling of peace and pleasure and a decided reluctance to go back to their physical bodies. In one case reported by *Light* magazine, a man's heart stopped beating during an operation. For a period of "death" lasting about five minutes, he saw his deceased wife and said after he was revived that he would never again be afraid to die. There are also many cases of astral projection under anesthesia in dentists' offices.

Have there ever been astral projections during an accident?

Yes, and in some cases the person remains conscious as he

leaves his body. What probably happens is that a concussion or some other physical trauma induces an altered state of consciousness favorable to OOB experience. In *Man Is a Spirit*, J. Arthur Hill reports a fascinating OOB case during the Civil War. A soldier was thrown into the air when his gun exploded. His physical body fell unconscious to the ground while his "double" stayed in the air. He watched two medical soldiers examine the body on the ground and heard them say that he was dead. They turned his body on its side and left, and at this point he re-entered the body. Although his right arm had been torn from his shoulder and there were forty-eight scars on his face and chest, he lived to tell about his astral projection.

Has fear ever caused a person to go out of his body?

Crookall describes a very unusual case during World War II. During a bombing raid in England a woman lay on her bed, petrified with fear, then suddenly found herself out of her body and floating above the bed. Her fear immediately left her, and she was able to endure future bombings stoically and without dread of death.

What was the famous Wilmot case of astral projection?

One night in 1863, a woman whose husband was on a ship in the Atlantic dreamed that she went to visit him in his stateroom. She kissed him as he slept, then left, noticing another passenger in the berth above his, who was watching. When her husband came home from his trip, he told her he had dreamed that night of the same sequence of events. Most astonishing was that his cabinmate, who was wide awake, saw what happened and chided the man about it. Mrs. Wilmot also correctly described the upper berth as being very unusual—not directly over the lower berth but set back a distance from it.

How did Eileen Garrett travel astrally from New York to Iceland?

This was a controlled experiment, with Mrs. Garrett's objective the office of a doctor in Reykjavik, Iceland. At the prearranged time she "left" New York and found herself passing through walls and into the doctor's room. As her astral body came into the office, the doctor entered and sensed her presence, saying, "This will be a successful experiment. Now look at the objects on the table." As she did this, she described the objects to a secretary in New York, who took notes. Then the doctor said, "Make my apologies to the experimenter at your end. I have had an accident and cannot work as well as I had hoped." Mrs. Garrett noticed that his head was bandaged and at the same moment heard one of the experimenters in New York say, "This cannot possibly be true. I had a letter a few days ago, and the doctor was quite well then." Then the doctor took a book off the shelf and silently read a paragraph about Einstein and relativity, while Mrs. Garrett described the text in New York. The next day the doctor sent a telegram stating that he had had an accident just before the experiment, and a day later a letter arrived from Iceland verifying everything Mrs. Garrett had described on her OOB trip.

Are dreams of flying and falling related to astral projections?
Such dreams are interpreted in many ways by psychiatrists and dream researchers, but rarely as out-of-body experiences. Sylvan Muldoon claimed, however, that these sensations were actual OOBEs experienced as dreams.

Can a hypnotized person go out of his body?
Yes. The Swedish psychologist Dr. John Björkhem once hypnotized a girl and sent her home astrally to see her parents. Within an hour the mother called to report that she had seen the girl in the kitchen.

What is "bilocation"?
A form of astral travel in which a person is observed as though in the flesh simultaneously in two different places. In 1774 Saint Alphonsus Liguori, although in prison, was seen at the deathbed of Pope Clement XIV. Many saints, among them St. Anthony of Padua, have been seen in two places at the same time.

Has a "bilocator" ever been photographed?
In *The Unexplained* Allen Spraggett tells of a meeting in

British Columbia in 1865 when a photograph taken of the legislative council showed the face of Charles Good, a member of the council. At the time, however, Good was seriously ill in bed.

What are "delogs"?

In Tibet, where astral projection is common, this name is given to "those who return from the Beyond."

Was astral projection known in the ancient world?

It was a common experience in many ancient civilizations, among them China, India, Persia, Greece, and Egypt. In Greece the "double" was called *eidolon* and in Egypt *ka*. Plutarch writes about a soldier in Asia Minor in 79 A.D. who was knocked unconscious. When he was revived, he claimed he had seen and spoken with a dead relative. The "dead" man told him that his silver cord had reached the limit of its elasticity and that he must return to his physical body.

Do the Hindus believe in an astral body?

According to the Hindu religion, the physical body is accompanied by a duplicate subtle body of more delicate substance.

Do primitive tribes believe in astral projection?

Out-of-body experiences are common among the Zulus of South Africa, according to zoologist John Poynton. They call the physical body the *inyama* and the "shadow body" which is similar to the physical the *isithunzi*. The *isithunzi* is the vehicle of the person's spirit or *umoya*. Similar beliefs are held by the Maoris, the Tahitians, the Australian aborigines, and by many other primitive groups.

How many people go out of their bodies?

Probably many more than would admit it or even know about it. In 1952 parapsychologist Hornell Hart, an instructor at Duke University, asked 155 students this question: "Have you ever actually seen your physical body from a viewpoint completely outside that body, like standing beside the bed and looking at yourself lying in bed, or like floating in the air near your body?" Thirty per cent answered "Yes."

How can one consciously project his astral body?

Muldoon suggests constructing a dream before going to sleep in which the astral body can take an active part, then giving yourself a suggestion to wake up at a particular point in the dream when you will be in your astral body. Monroe recommends relaxing the body, concentrating mentally on a subject as you drift off, and trying to deepen your consciousness.

Is it safe to practice going out of the body?

It is not recommended for amateurs, particularly not for unstable persons. A parapsychologist or someone who has had a good deal of OOB experience should be consulted first. Do not subscribe to mail-order courses in astral projection.

What is the difference between ESP and astral projection?

In both OOBE and telepathy/clairvoyance, the psychic may bring back information not available to his physical senses. In astral projection, however, the subject is conscious of himself in another body and moving to another point in space. Sometimes, when there is uncertainty about the nature of the projection, the term "traveling clairvoyance" is used.

What is the consensus about the relationship between astral projection and immortality?

Perhaps it is best expressed in the words of Sylvan Muldoon, the busiest of all astral travelers: "For my part, had a book on immortality never been written, had a lecture on 'survival' never been uttered, had I never witnessed a séance or visited a medium; in fact, had no one else in the whole world ever suspected 'life after death,' I should still believe implicitly that I am immortal—for I have experienced the projection of the astral body." (See Chapter 17.)

15

What is a ghost?

In psychic phenomena a ghost is a manifestation of a dead
person that is seen, heard, felt, or sensed (sometimes even
smelled) by the living. Parapsychologists and others who investigate ghosts and spirits prefer the term "apparition" for
the visual aspect of a ghost, since they differ on whether the
experience is subjective or a ghost is actually present. The
terms "ghost," "apparition," "spirit," and "astral body" over-
lap: a "spirit" is the essence of a deceased person who has
survived bodily death; a "ghost" is the spirit's manifestation
to the senses of the living; the "astral body" is usually the second body of a living person; and "apparition" may be used
for any of these phenomena that are visual.

What do ghosts look like?

A ghost is a replica of a person who died, sometimes of
his appearance at an early stage of life. Often only the facial
features are clear, with the rest of the body made of a gauzy
substance. Sometimes the ghostly presence is merely a sta-
tionary or moving area of light. Only one part of the body
may appear, such as fingers and hands. A ghost thought to be
that of Anne Boleyn once manifested in the Tower of London
in the shape of a glass tube.

What do ghosts wear?

When ghosts are clearly seen, they generally appear in clothes they wore during their lifetime, which makes it easier to identify them. When the poet Horace Traubel lay dying, he saw the ghost of his friend Walt Whitman dressed in an old familiar tweed jacket. Sometimes the apparel worn is symbolic and meant to convey a message to the living.

Are ghosts solid?

Most of them seem to blend with the background, but sometimes they are quite solid and can even be touched. When the ghost of Grandpa Bull, a famous case in London, appeared to his family, he was a solid figure and could be heard walking in the house. Once his wife felt his hand on her forehead, and he spoke her name.

Do ghosts ever speak?

Grandpa Bull was one example of speaking ghosts, and there are many others, including some who hold long conversations with the living. Sometimes the ghost is heard but not seen. The ghostly voice speaks; there may be footsteps on the stairway, cries or sobs, tapping sounds on the window. The "clairaudients" among the living generally are attuned to sounds made by ghosts, while ghosts may be seen by those with an acute visual sense.

When do ghosts appear?

Ghosts, or apparitions, often appear to friends or relatives when the physical body dies. Ghosts of those already dead also appear at the bedside of the dying, according to reports from doctors and nurses (see Chapter 17). Otherwise, they may appear anywhere and at any time of day or night. One ghost was even observed in London in 1878 walking down the street in evening clothes.

Where are ghosts seen?

That depends on the ghost and his (or her) habits. Generally they attach themselves to houses, particularly those that hold memories of their lifetime experiences. Theatrical ghosts such as Joseph Grimaldi hang around theaters, while bookish ghosts are seen in libraries. Nathaniel Hawthorne saw one such ghost sitting each day in the old Athenaeum library in Boston, reading a newspaper.

Do children see ghosts?

Since children are more open than adults to the unknown, they respond to all kinds of psychic phenomena and have a special attachment to ghosts. Reference has been made to Eileen Garrett's childhood friendship with ghost children.

Do animals see ghosts?

They don't say so, but their actions often give them away. Dogs and cats circle the spot where the ghost may be present, they whine, arch their backs, growl, shiver, slink away, etc. When dogs howl at the moment their masters die in faraway places, they may be seeing the death clairvoyantly, or the ghosts of their masters may be manifesting to them.

Are there ghosts of animals?

Yes. Elliott O'Donnell, the ghost-hunter, wrote about a ghostly policeman and his horse who patrolled their beat each night in a Canadian city, then disappeared. In *Days of Our Years* Pierre van Paassen tells about the ghost of a large black dog that appeared in his house every evening, walking upstairs from the basement. His servant complained that the dog came into her room at night and woke her up. Finally van Paassen brought in two police dogs who did battle with the ghost dog until one of the live dogs fell dead and the other backed off, howling with pain. In addition to dog and cat ghosts, there have been elephant ghosts, horse ghosts, canary ghosts—practically the whole animal kingdom.

Is the same ghost ever seen by more than one person?

Yes. Some of the best evidence for the reality of ghosts comes from collective ghost-viewing. Grandpa Bull is one example. He was seen by each member of his family, separately and together. In some cases the ghost is seen by different persons at different times, and each may be unaware of the other's experience. A woman and her daughter in nineteenth-century England saw a male ghost who kept peeking at them from behind doors, although neither knew that the other had seen him.

Do ghosts ever appear in a group?

Yes—sometimes in pairs, often in large groups whose members shared a meaningful experience when alive. Many ghost groups have been seen in wartime, such as the dead soldiers who restaged many battles after the Civil War. In 1900 two Englishwomen vacationing in France found themselves in the court of Louis XVI at Versailles just as it was back in 1789, with Marie Antoinette, her attendants, and others attached to the court.

Did ghosts appear in ancient times?

Herodotus, the Greek historian, Pliny the Younger, and other ancients wrote about presumably true ghost incidents. The Greek philosopher Athenodorus rented a house in Athens where the ghost of an old man walked at night rattling chains. The ghost led the philosopher to the spot where his bones were buried and then disappeared. After the bones were given a decent burial, the ghost didn't appear any more.

Do the ghosts of famous persons ever come back?

If Abraham Lincoln, Buddha, Christ, and other famous figures of the past appeared to mediums as often as claimed, they would have little time left for their business in the spirit world. The ghost of Lincoln, however, has been seen many times in the White House. Anne Boleyn is often seen on the anniversary of her execution, carrying in her hand the pretty head that was cut off by order of Henry VIII.

Why do ghosts haunt houses?

It is questionable whether they "haunt" houses or merely return to old surroundings. When they have died violently in a house or had a traumatic emotional experience there, they are often drawn back as spirits. Sometimes they feel that the house belongs to them and not to the person living in it. And there are some ghosts who just come back for a friendly visit.

Is a ghost more likely to haunt an old house?

Yes, because it usually has an older history and was the scene of many emotional situations and perhaps violent deaths. Old castles in Europe are especially ghost-prone. Great Britain is estimated to have at least a hundred and fifty old mansions that are haunted. But newer houses, many of them in America, are also frequented by ghosts, so there is no absolute rule.

What was the famous Morton house-haunting?

This case is impressive because an observant young lady in the house, Miss R. C. Morton, observed the ghost closely and gave a detailed description of its appearance and behavior. The ghost appeared on and off in this English house for seven years, from 1882 to 1889, and was seen by Miss Morton and several other persons. The ghost was described as the solid figure of "a tall lady, dressed in black of a soft woolen material. . . . The face was hidden in a handkerchief held in the right hand. . . . I saw the upper part of the left side of the forehead, and a little of the hair above . . . the whole impression was that of a lady in widow's weeds." Footsteps could be heard when the ghost walked, and Miss Morton reported that the figure blocked off light.

Why do ghosts return?

There are as many reasons as there are ghosts. Often there is some unfinished business left over at the time of death, such as improper burial of their bodies. When they have died violently or in emotional circumstances, they are drawn back to the death scene. Some ghosts who had unhappy love affairs seem rooted to the scenes of their sorrows. This was the case with Evelyn Byrd, the gentle spirit who drifts etherially about the house and grounds of Westover mansion in Virginia. Sometimes ghosts return to warn of illness or approaching death to friends or relatives, or to help with the sick. Many ghosts do not reveal their motives for coming back, but seem to enjoy being with old friends and even strangers.

Are ghosts concerned about the living?

Most of them are. Grandpa Bull evidently wanted the British authorities to find another home for his poverty-stricken family. In many cases the ghost or spirit wants to direct members of his family to missing money or hidden wills. Camille Flammarion, the astronomer, reported many such cases. Ghosts are also concerned for those who are ill or about to die.

Can ghosts heal the sick?

A ghost named Eliza gave prescriptions for her dying sister, a case reported by the Society for Psychical Research. Some ghosts heal the sick by "laying on of astral hands," by giving medical advice to the living, or by performing psychic surgery. (See Chapter 5.)

Do ghosts have consciences?

Ghosts are no different from the persons they were in the flesh. One ghost, disturbed because she owed money at the time of death, asked a friend to pay it back for her.

Can ghosts predict the future?

Although most ghosts make no claim to seership, many do prophesy. Ghosts often appear as harbingers of death. The famous White Lady of the Hohenzollerns always showed up just before a tragedy occurred in the royal family. Once she appeared to Kaiser Wilhelm II, and he ran out of his castle. She was also seen by Napoleon before he invaded Russia.

Do ghosts eat and drink?

The famous Bell Witch of Tennessee was probably one of the heartiest imbibers in the spirit world, with a passion for corn whisky and—oddly enough—cream that she stole from the icebox. Ghosts not only drink liquor, they help to serve it at parties. As for food, in one case loaves of bread kept disappearing, and as soon as another batch was made, the ghosts would eat it.

Are ghosts good at finding lost objects?

Very good. A case in point is the wife of Periander, the tyrant of ancient Corinth. Periander lost a treasure he was keeping for a friend, and his ghost wife, Melissa, told him where it was. In modern times the Reverend Russell H. Conwell, at one time president of Temple University, was visited by his dead wife. To test her powers, he asked if she knew where his gold fountain pen was, and she promptly led him to its hiding place.

Do ghosts ever make telephone calls?

Ghosts have often called doctors and priests when a dying person needed help. Elliott O'Donnell tells about a doctor who got a call asking him to rush over to a friend's house. When he got there, the friend was in perfect health and knew nothing about the call. But just then he had a seizure, and the doctor was able to save his life by acting quickly.

Do ghosts have a sense of humor?

If they had one in life, they don't lose it as ghosts. The ghost of Cideville Parsonage in France, for example, entertained visitors by making tongs leap out of the fireplace and back and by lifting dogs into the air and letting them hang there.

Are there "domesticated" ghosts?

A young housemaid who died suddenly during the time of Frederick the Great came back to the rectory where she had worked and drove the priest to distraction with her frenzied cleaning. The Reverend Morell Theobald also wrote about ghosts who made breakfast and lighted the fire each morning.

Has a ghost ever appeared in a courtroom?

Ghosts have figured in court cases, and at least one appeared as a witness for the prosecution. Daniel Defoe in his *History and Reality of Apparitions* describes a ghost who materialized suddenly on the witness stand during the trial of a man accused of murdering him. The accused man was so unnerved that he immediately confessed. In another case the ghost of Thomas Harris, perturbed because his property did not go to his sons as intended, sought out a friend and told him the story. The friend appeared in court, and his testimony was accepted.

Do ghosts ever get lost?

Yes. Their sense of direction is not always perfect. One ghost zoomed from his home in England to a ship at sea to visit his son, who was the captain. The ghost looked in all the cabins but couldn't find his son. Ghosts who come often to the same house or apartment frequently get confused if the host moves to a new location.

Has a ghost ever written a book?

The ghosts of dead writers are anxious to let the world know that they are still active, and there is evidence that novelists such as Charles Dickens worked through psychics who did automatic writing. Oscar Wilde has ostensibly written new plays through the hand of Mrs. Travers-Smith. (See Chapter 9.) Since the authors were not seen, it may be questionable whether they could be called ghosts, but their personalities were felt by those present.

Has a ghost ever painted a picture?

Some examples were given in the chapter on automatic writing and drawing. In addition, a living artist claimed that the ghost of Renoir influence her painting style, which was remarkably like that of the French painter. Hereward Carrington, the parapsychologist, told of an artist friend who was visited by a young lady ghost (beautiful, of course) who gave him valuable art criticism.

Has a ghost ever composed music?

According to the English housewife Rosemary Brown, the ghosts of Franz Lizst, Frederic Chopin, and other famous composers appear to her regularly and instruct her in writing down their new compositions. Mrs. Brown has given concerts of the after-death works of these composers. The music itself sounds like a watered-down version of their authentic styles, but there is no doubt that something quite remarkable has been happening to Mrs. Brown.

Do ghosts ever play instruments?

A ghost played a trumpet at the time Caesar crossed the Rubicon. In nineteenth-century England a church organist died, then came back as a ghost and played the organ for the next seventy years. There have been violin-playing ghosts, ghostly pianists, and other ethereal musicians. The famous ghost of Cideville Parsonage in nineteenth-century France could beat time to any tune that was first hummed for him.

Are there theatrical ghosts?

Many British theaters have their house ghosts, mostly actors and directors from earlier periods. An invisible Joseph

Grimaldi from the eighteenth century gives encouraging pats to nervous young performers at the Drury Lane in London; Peg Woffington keeps returning to the site of the Smock Alley Theatre in Dublin; while the St. James has a ghost who helps ladies and gentlemen on with their coats. The old Metropolitan Opera House in New York had its ghostly visitors from an earlier era.

Are there sports-loving ghosts?

Elliott O'Donnell tells of a room in an English house where two ghosts meet nightly to have a boxing match. Some ghosts play billiards, and there are fencing ghosts. A story is current about the widow of a football coach who took over the high-school squad after her husband died, and he now directs the team through her.

Do ghosts play cards?

William Oliver Stevens writes about a woman ghost who appeared at a card game to make a fifth at bridge. It is questionable, however, whether woman ghosts play poker, but they often come back to break up the men's games, especially if their husbands are involved.

Are there eccentric ghosts?

Yes, just as there are offbeat people. Two ghosts in France, a priest and a dwarf, have been systematically tearing down a farmhouse for two hundred years—why, nobody knows. Another eccentric ghost was that of a snuff-loving curate who came back to the rectory each night to take his sniffs.

Are ghosts ever dangerous?

Only a small minority of them seem to be antisocial. Of these, many are only trying to get the attention of the living to help them with a problem. There is some evidence of "evil spirits" who cause trouble to the living and sometimes take possession of mediums.

Are there immoral ghosts?

Ghosts have no need to be immoral in the sexual sense, but there are a few cases of this kind reported by parapsychologists. Nandor Fodor tells about a young man who died, then came back and made improper contact with a former girl friend of his. Fodor wondered whether something in the psyche of the girl welcomed these advances.

How can a ghost be helped?

If a ghost has a problem, and the more restless ones seem to, a form of ghost-therapy is employed, often by clergymen. First communication is set up, mainly through séances, to find out what the trouble is. If his body has not been properly buried, a decent burial then quiets the ghost. Sometimes prayers, sprinkling the grave with holy water, etc., are helpful. If the ghost continues to be troublesome and obstreperous, the house he is haunting is sometimes torn down, thus erasing the associations and memories that may have brought him back. In the case of the ghost maid who made life miserable in the rectory by her frenzied housecleaning, Frederick the Great ordered the church torn down and rebuilt elsewhere, and she wasn't heard from again.

Are poltergeists the same as ghosts?

Ghosts and poltergeists may sometimes act alike but they are considered different phenomena. (See Chapter 4.) Ghosts often act like poltergeists when they throw objects around, pull the bedcovers off sleeping people, and otherwise behave mischievously. In such cases, however, it is apparent that a bona fide ghost is present, while in poltergeist cases the psychic energy is thought to come from a living person, generally a teen-ager. One of the most striking ghost/poltergeist cases was that of the Borley Rectory in England, where the ghost of a nun appeared on and off for a period of fifty-eight years, from 1885 to 1943. The late ghost-hunter Harry Price, who investigated the case, wrote of more than two thousand poltergeist happenings, including the ringing of bells, "showers of pebbles and keys coming from nowhere . . . raps, taps, and knockings" and "appearances, disappearances, and reappearances of strange articles." Whether the ghost nun who was seen through the years by seventeen persons was responsible for the physical phenomena or other factors were operating is not certain.

Have there been "live" ghosts?

Occasionally the ghost of a living person may manifest in a séance room or elsewhere. The person who is alive and well may not even know what is happening. In one case the ghost of a man on an icebound ship was seen on another ship, where he went for help. During this time he was asleep on the first ship and was not aware that his ghost had gone on a rescue mission. It is probably more accurate to call this manifestation the "astral body" rather than a "ghost," a term usually given to the spirit of one who has died.

How do ghosts prove they are real?

Their appearance is one form of identification, and the case is strengthened when they are seen by more than one living person. Another is to give details of their lives that are known only to their relatives and friends, or, if unknown to them, can be verified by an investigation. (See Chapter 17 for the evidence for survival.)

Are living persons ever "possessed" by ghosts?

In the rare cases of "possession," the original personality seems to disappear and is replaced by that of another entity. The most famous case is that of the "Watseka Wonder." (See Chapter 12.) When a medium goes into a trance, the discarnate entity may possess or at least share the physical body during the period of communication.

What is multiple personality? Is "possession" involved?

There are only a few cases of multiple personality on record, in which several entities seem to take over the same body at different times. The most famous case was that of Sally Beauchamp, whose body was controlled by five distinctive personalities, each insisting it had the prior right to possession. It was believed that each was a "secondary personality," split off from the main personality because of an emotional problem. When the different personalities were integrated into one healthy individual, the phenomenon ceased. This was also the case with "Eve," who had three personalities. Her cure did not last, however, as a fourth personality emerged later. Doris Fischer, studied by Dr. Walter Franklin

Prince, had five personalities which were given the names Real Doris, Margaret, Sleeping Margaret, Sick Doris, and Sleeping Doris. Some parapsychologists believe that one or more of the personalities in these cases may have been "possessing" spirits.

Is there a "natural" explanation for ghosts?

Skeptics claim that all ghosts are hallucinations. One theory that should be taken seriously, however, is that houses, objects, settings, etc., hold memories of all the events associated with them, particularly if accompanied by violence and the display of strong emotions. From time to time these events are replayed where they first occurred, usually in a haunted house, as though they were on a film projected by an invisible operator. A recent case in Brooklyn, New York, is an example: an old woman stands menacingly in a bedroom while the mutilated body of a young girl lies on the floor. Every observer, including well-known psychics, reports the same scene, which probably took place at one time in the house. In such cases actual ghosts may not be present, but when ghosts act intelligently and communicate directly with the living, they are probably real and not just psychometric memories.

Who is America's most famous ghost?

Probably the Bell Witch, who made life exciting and sometimes difficult for the Bell family of Tennessee in the early part of the nineteenth century. The witch cuffed John Bell in the mouth, brought Lucy Bell nuts and grapes when she was ill, and forced daughter Betsy Bell to marry her teacher rather than the young man who was her fiancé. The witch argued scripture with ministers, sang hymns, and once had a confrontation with Andrew Jackson.

16

YOUR QUESTIONS ANSWERED ABOUT
MEDIUMS OF THE NINETEENTH AND TWENTIETH
CENTURIES, THEIR SPIRIT "CONTROLS" AND THE
SPIRITS OF THE DEAD CONTACTED THROUGH THEM;
THE DIFFERENCE BETWEEN MENTAL AND PHYSICAL
MEDIUMS; TRANCE MEDIUMS, DIRECT-VOICE MEDIUMS,
LEVITATING MEDIUMS, ANIMAL MEDIUMS;
D. D. HOME, FLORENCE COOK, STAINTON MOSES,
EUSAPIA PALLADINO, LEONORA PIPER,
GLADYS OSBORNE LEONARD, MARGERY CRANDON,
EILEEN GARRETT, ARTHUR FORD, AND OTHER
OUTSTANDING MEDIUMS . . .

What is a medium?

A medium is a psychic or sensitive who ostensibly makes contact with someone or something in the spirit world and/or produces mysterious supernormal phenomena such as sounds without a source, objects that seem to move by themselves, levitation of persons and objects, and the materialization of spirit forms and objects.

What is a mental medium?

A mental medium is one who receives communications from the spirit world through purely mental transmissions. The medium may be completely conscious at the time, partly conscious, or in a completely unaware, trance state. Some mental mediums also use automatic writing or the ouija board for their contacts.

What is a trance medium?

A trance medium loses consciousness partly or altogether and is usually not aware of what is going on during a séance or reading. Often, while in this state, the medium's body is taken over, controlled, or possessed by a spirit entity who may speak or act through the medium's physical organism. The most famous trance medium was probably Mrs. Leonora Piper, who was investigated by William James and other parapsychologists of the early twentieth century. In modern times, two well-known trance mediums were Eileen Garrett and Arthur Ford.

What is a physical medium?

A physical medium, generally while in trance, produces physical phenomena such as raps and table-tilting, moving objects, voices and music, levitation of objects and living persons or animals, and materializations of spirit forms and objects.

How are spirits "materialized" by mediums?

Through ectoplasm, a substance that emanates from the body of the medium and gives shape to an object or to the alleged spirit who is present. Ectoplasm has been analyzed chemically as "colorless, slightly cloudy, fluid but thready, and with no smell."

Who were some outstanding physical mediums?

During the heyday of mediumship, about fifty to eighty years ago, there were quite a few, such as D. D. Home, Florence Cook, Eusapia Palladino, Eva C. (Marthe Béraud), and many more. The scarcity of physical mediums today may be due to the slackening of interest in mediumship since the era of laboratory experiments in ESP began. Parapsychologists who are skeptical of the reports about earlier physical mediums believe that the absence of modern scientific controls at the time allowed fraudulent practices to go unnoticed. However, careful investigators such as William Crookes and Cromwell Varley, the electrician who helped build the transatlantic cable, constructed ingenious mechanical devices that proved many of the phenomena to be genuine.

What is a direct-voice medium?

When a spirit takes possession of a trance medium's body, he may speak through the medium's voice box, but sometimes the spirit words come through "direct voice" in another part of the séance room, without an apparent source of energy.

What famous psychics were direct-voice mediums?

D. D. Home, David Duguid, George Valiantine, and Mrs. Gladys Osborne Leonard were a few. So was Margery Crandon, a controversial medium of the 1920s who was studied by many psychical researchers, including the skeptical Harry Houdini. Margery's dead brother Walter ostensibly spoke through a "voice box" that was later photographed as a white substance on her shoulder connected to her left ear and nostril. With some mediums the "voice" could not speak when the medium did, indicating that the medium was still providing the vocal energy. In other cases both the medium's voice and the disembodied voice were heard together.

What scientist was photographed with a medium and a spirit?

William Crookes, the outstanding physicist of his time, was a skeptic when he first investigated spiritualism in the 1870s, but he was converted to a belief in spirits after attending the séances of a fifteen-year-old girl, Florence Cook. Crookes noted the physical differences between Miss Cook and the materialized spirit, Katie King, and had himself photographed with the two girls, one living, the other presumably dead.

How many mediums have levitated?

Quite a few, if we believe some of the stories from an earlier day of mediumship. Many of these accounts have been well documented, particularly the "floating" ability of D. D. Home. (See Chapter 4.) Nandor Fodor, the psychiatrist/psychic investigator, tells of a medium whose body rose while he (Fodor) held the medium's hand, a feat confirmed by infrared photography.

Are there more male than female mediums?

The females seem to predominate. Some famous ones were Eileen Garrett, Eusapia Palladino, Florence Cook, Kathleen Goligher, Mme. d'Espérance—the list is almost endless. But there have also been outstanding male mediums—D. D. Home, Rudi and Willi Schneider, the Davenport brothers, Arthur Ford, etc.

Is puberty a fruitful time for mediumship?

Evidently. There is, for example, the frequent presence of poltergeists in the homes of adolescent boys and girls. According to psychical researcher Hereward Carrington and many other parapsychologists, it is possible that maturing sexual powers are diverted into psychic channels.

Who are the youngest mediums on record?

Automatic writing by the five-month-old son of Kate Fox was mentioned in Chapter 9. The seven-month-old child of another medium, Mrs. Margaret Cooper, gave communications through raps. One child was said to write automatically at the age of nine days.

Do mediums work only in the dark?

One of the charges against the genuineness of what happens in the séance room is that it is produced under cover of darkness. Aside from the fact that infrared photography has shown much of it to be genuine (and some of it fraudulent), many mediums have worked in broad daylight. Anna Rasmussen, who was carefully observed by a Danish professor for fifteen years, conducted her séances while the lights were on. Dr. Charles Richet, the French physiologist, witnessed physical mediumship in Paris in clear daylight. D. D. Home performed many of his astonishing feats during the day and in bright light.

What is a "control"?

The "control" is kind of master of ceremonies of the spirit world. He plays the role of intermediary between the medium and other spirits who wish to communicate but are unable to do so. The control interacts with the mind and body of the medium. Thus in many instances the medium and her control act as relay stations that boost the message between the living person and the spirit on "the other side."

Who were (or are) the controls of famous mediums?

Feda (Mrs. Leonard); Uvani (Eileen Garrett); Phinuit (Mrs. Piper); Fletcher (Arthur Ford); Yolande (Mme. d'Espérance); Walter (Margery). The control of British medium Douglas Johnson is Chiang, a philosophical Chinese spirit who claims he lived seven hundred years ago during the Han dynasty.

Do mediums ever have more than one control?

Yes. Along with Uvani, Eileen Garrett had a control named Abdul Latif. Mrs. Soule had two controls during her automatic-writing sessions who controlled her simultaneously. (See Chapter 9.) Mrs. Piper had a succession of controls, one of them George Pelham, who had died a short time before and was known to many psychic investigators. Sometimes there is a "group" control, such as the Imperator Group of medium Stainton Moses.

How do controls announce their presence?

Each seems to have an individual calling card. Sometimes the voice is heard either through direct speech or through the vocal apparatus of the entranced medium. Sometimes the style of handwriting in automatic writing identifies them. The way in which raps are made or tables tilted is another kind of signature.

Do all controls "possess" their mediums?

Not always. Sometimes the control takes over the organism of the medium while the latter is in trance. At other times the medium communicates mentally with the control.

What control says he manipulates his medium like a puppet?

Chiang, the centuries-old control of Douglas Johnson, explains that he does not take possession of Johnson's body but stands outside and works through the medium's aura, which Chiang calls "a field of force something like a magnetic field."

What does Chiang say about how a control communicates?

Many of Chiang's observations have been taped. In separate interviews with Johnson and his control (*Psychic* magazine, February 1971), Chiang said: "We have to be trained very carefully to communicate. It is not easy. We have to learn to adjust our wavelengths or vibrations . . . to that of the sensitive; readjust it to that of the sitter, and also to adjust it to ones who may wish to pass messages through. All this is a most complex process."

Which control worked with a medium for mutual therapy?

The late Arthur Ford, in an interview for *Psychic* magazine (October 1970,), said that the dead Fletcher, a French
Canadian whom the medium had known as a boy in Florida,
felt that the psychic relationship between them would be
helpful to both Ford and himself. At Fletcher's insistence,
Ford stopped drinking and smoking.

*Whose controls identified themselves through the medium's
pulse beats?*

Arthur Conan Doyle, the creator of Sherlock Holmes, was
visited by two spirit controls, Colonel Lee and Black Hawk.
Although his normal pulse beat was 82, when under control
of Colonel Lee it went to 100, and rose to 118 when Black
Hawk took over.

*What kind of spirit communications come through mediums
and their controls?*

All kinds—trivial comments, evidential messages proving the identity of the communicator, sometimes entertain-
ment such as songs, discourses, philosophical observations.
The quality of the message depends to a great extent on the
personality, temperament, and intelligence of the medium
and others present as well as the communicators. Perhaps the
most distinguished spirit communicators were the Imperator
Group, who had a serious philosophical purpose in the messages they sent through several mediums.

What was the purpose of the Betty communications?

Stewart Edward White was a travel writer who discovered that his wife, Betty, was a medium and could receive
messages from the spirit world. After Betty died, she became
a control through another medium and sent messages intended to prove the existence of another dimension and, with
the help of spirit entities who had been distinguished men of
letters, scientists, etc., to describe the nature and purpose of
the next world.

How do the controls get messages from other spirits?

Feda, Mrs. Leonard's control, said she might hear words
or sounds, see written words or symbolic pictures, or have

feelings of coldness, roughness, etc. It was easiest for her to get impressions through symbolic visual images.

How does ESP work between controls and other spirits?

Just as it operates between living persons. Sometimes the communicating spirits have said that the controls fished information out of their minds that they had no intention of conveying through the medium. This would account for garbled or inaccurate messages received.

Where do mediums go when controls possess their bodies?

Some mediums don't remember. They just seem to black out. Others wander in the spirit world while they are waiting to return to their bodies. A nineteenth-century medium, Mrs. Conant, went visiting, sometimes to other countries. During a séance in 1857, her control was asked to leave so that she could re-enter her body, but he said she was not present and he would have to wait for her return.

Do controls ever work with more than one medium?

Many of them like to move around. The Imperator Group once controlled Mrs. Piper. Uvani showed up once in the mind of British psychic Malcolm Bessent, although not during a trance state. Katie King was active with different mediums up to 1932. Once in the 1870s when she was the control of medium Charles Williams, she was able to teleport Mrs. Samuel Guppy, just about the largest woman in London, from her home three miles away to the séance room. At least that's what members of the circle said, and they all signed affidavits.

Can controls talk to each other through two or more mediums?

Yes. This happened during the Margery Crandon séances when another medium, Miss Scott, went into a trance. Walter, Margery's control, told the control of the other medium, her dead mother, how to accomplish this feat.

What are the nationalities of the controls?

The controls come from every culture and country and from different periods in history as far back as ancient Egypt.

There have been American Indian controls, East Indian, Egyptian, Chinese, French, English, Arabian, Kaffir, Senegalese, even Zulu (South African) controls.

Do controls always identify themselves?

Some freely give information about their life and times, others refuse to. Although Phinuit claimed he had been a French doctor, his French was suspect. George Pelham promptly gave his identity and was recognized by living friends. Many controls give themselves fictitious, even Biblical names. Members of the Imperator Group called themselves the Prophet, Malachias, Elijah, etc. D. D. Home's control spoke in the plural as "we." Some controls claim they never lived except as pure spirits.

What two controls were a colorful father-daughter team?

None other than Katie King and her father John King, who appeared separately and together at different times to different mediums. Katie claimed that in life she had been Annie Owen Morgan during the reign of Charles I and that she had committed many murders before dying at twenty-two. John King boasted that he had lived as the dashing buccaneer Henry Owen Morgan. John was also a control of Charles Williams, the Davenport brothers and, most notably, Eusapia Palladino.

Have there been child controls?

Many: Feda, Dewdrop (the control of medium Bessie Williams); Stasia (Mlle. Tomczyk); Yolande (Mme. d'Espérance); Harmony (Mrs. Susannah Harris); and many more. A modern child control is Sunbeam, a mischievous sprite who visits the Reverend Adrienne Coulter Meakin of Las Vegas, Nevada.

Do spirit controls have the same personality and temperament as their mediums?

Sometimes they are diametrically opposite, as was the case with Mrs. Curran and the brilliant Patience Worth. (See Chapter 9.) Eileen Garrett, who was always curious about the nature of her trance experiences, was the subject of many psychological tests that disclosed a marked difference between her controls and herself. Tests at Johns Hopkins University and the New York Psychiatric Institute showed that her controls functioned as independent entities.

Are controls generally courteous and respectful?

Generally, but there are some spectacular exceptions. Walter, Margery Crandon's control, often lost his temper and swore at those present, particularly Harry Houdini, who was trying to prove that the spirit was a fake. An Egyptian control swore in verse at a hypnotist who was trying to exorcize him from the medium's body. On the other hand, controls with a serious purpose are often saintly, such as the high-minded beings of the Imperator Group.

Do controls have a sense of humor?

There have been some delightful ones. Dewdrop, the control of Bessie Williams, would often take possession while Miss Williams was riding on a bus and would speak loudly in Indian to the amusement or terror of the passengers. "Little Stasia," the control of Polish medium Mlle. Stanislawa Tomczyk, performed tricks for the circle. Sunbeam, Adrienne Coulter Meakin's control, once told a minister that his breeches were going to split. Ten minutes later he stood up, and the fatal sound was heard.

What control sprayed her medium with perfume?

Starlight, the control of writer Shaw Desmond, evidently thought the scent improved his mediumistic powers. Friends noticed later that his clothes smelled heavily of perfume.

What control deserted her medium for his younger brother?

Olga was first the control of young Willi Schneider, who would go into a trance and insist that he was Lola Montez, the mistress of the blind king of Bavaria. One night, while Willi was performing and his eleven-year-old brother, Rudi, was asleep, Olga decided that Rudi would be her new medium. A few moments later Rudi left his bed and entered the room in a state of tance. From then on he displaced Willi in Olga's affections.

Who are the "sitters" in a séance?

They are the person or persons who seek information

through the medium, or they may be the combined circle at the séance.

How do the sitters help the medium?

They provide more physical and mental power. The Seeress of Prevorst claimed that she drew upon the vitality of her sitters, particularly if they were blood relatives. If any of the sitters are mediums, the power is increased. Eusapia Palladino was able to pick out those in her group who had mediumistic power, and she drained it from them in a hurry.

Why do spirits often communicate through table-tilting?

This may be the easiest way to harness the physical energy in a séance room. When the medium and sitters hold their hands over a table, a great amount of electrical force may be generated that the spirit can utilize. In such cases, of course, no spirit may be present and the phenomenon may be a case of mind—several minds—over matter. (See Chapter 4.)

Do mediums ever absorb the "physical" problems of spirits?

Yes. In one case a medium felt a horrible pain in the abdomen along with acute thirst when a spirit was communicating who had died of cancer of the liver. The medium Adele Maginot began to choke badly in trance as she described a man who had died by choking. In 1861 the medium Mrs. Conant was possessed by the spirit of a man who had died of hydrophobia. She foamed at the mouth and snapped at the sitters.

How can a medium distinguish ESP from spirit contact?

Mediums have different ways of recognizing that a spirit is present. Douglas Johnson says that when he is communicating with a spirit, he gets "an excited electrical feeling which is quite different from ordinary ESP."

What is mediumship by "induction"?

By this method mediums sometimes give others their power. Eusapia Palladino gave power to a sitter by holding her hand. Many persons acquire mediumistic powers by merely being in the presence of mediums. Psychical researchers Arthur Conan Doyle and Richard Hodgson developed mediumship during their investigations.

Have animals ever been mediums?

A professor in Venice, Italy, once published an article about a cat who wrote with his paw by scratching a paper blackened with smoke. The cat's master was also a medium, and through him a spirit was asked to make the cat write the word "Vittorio." The next morning the letters "Vitt" appeared on the paper. There was no room for the rest of the word.

Have animal spirits ever been materialized?

In his *Encyclopedia of Psychic Sciences* Nandor Fodor wrote about three Polish mediums in Warsaw who specialized in producing animal spirits. The dead pets of sitters are often materialized in the séance room—dogs, cats, monkeys, and in one case a pet robin.

Do mediums in trance ever speak in languages they never learned?

Yes. This is called xenoglossy. One medium, Laura Edmonds, could talk in Greek, Spanish, Indian dialects, and other tongues while in trance—whatever the sitter might request. Medium George Valiantine once spoke in the archaic tongue of Confucius in the presence of an Oriental scholar.

Are mediums ever guilty of fraud?

Sometimes a completely fraudulent medium will be caught in the act by astute researchers. In May 1960 the editor of a spiritualist magazine, the *Psychic Observer,* and Dr. Andrija Puharich, a parapsychologist, discovered trickery at a spiritualist meeting in Indiana through infrared photography. In other cases, genuine mediums sometimes practice fraud when their powers temporarily desert them and they don't want to make a poor showing before their followers or investigators.

Does an act of fraud prove the lack of mediumistic powers?

No. Psychic power comes and goes and cannot always be produced on demand. No medium was ever more thoroughly tested (over a period of twenty years) than Eusapia Palladino, both in Europe and in the United States, and by such well-known scientists as astronomer Camille Flammarion and physiologist Charles Richet. Although she undoubtedly practiced fraud at times, Richet and many others who studied her concluded that she had produced genuine phenomena.

Does mediumship have an adverse effect on the medium's personality?

It depends on the mental stability of the medium. Mrs. Osborne Leonard said that her mediumship made her more skillful in other areas. She became a better gardener and cook, and her nerves were under better control. An outstanding example of a great medium who was also a highly intelligent and stable person dynamically concerned with the world around her was Eileen Garrett.

17

YOUR QUESTIONS ANSWERED ABOUT
THE EVIDENCE FOR SURVIVAL OF THE SOUL:
DEATHBED VISIONS, SPIRIT COMMUNICATIONS, THE
CROSS-CORRESPONDENCES, BOOK TESTS, LINKAGE
EXPERIMENTS, THE COMBINATION-LOCK TEST, ETC.;
THE EVIDENCE FOR REINCARNATION FROM
IAN STEVENSON'S STUDIES THROUGHOUT THE WORLD;
OTHER REINCARNATION CASES; HOW TO PLAN FOR
YOUR NEXT INCARNATION BY PARTICIPATING IN THE
UNIVERSITY OF VIRGINIA'S EXPERIMENT IN
PROVING SURVIVAL . . .

What proof is there that the human personality survives bodily death?

If there is not absolute proof, there is impressive evidence: mediumistic phenomena; encounters with ghosts and spirits; "apparitions" of the dying seen by relatives and friends; celestial music and disembodied voices heard by the living when someone dies, along with falling pictures, stopped clocks, and other mysterious occurrences; deathbed visions; cases of photographing or seeing with the naked eye the departure of the "soul body"; out-of-body experiences; automatic writing with messages from the "dead"; cases of spirit possession; tests designed by the living and by those on "the other side"; and cases of apparent reincarnation. In addition, there are strong philosophical arguments for the survival of the human and animal souls.

How do deathbed visions give evidence for survival?

Many cases of this kind have been reported by medical personnel who attended dying patients. Dr. Karlis Osis, director of research for the American Society for Psychical Research, sent questionnaires to ten thousand doctors and nurses who stated that their patients reported seeing the spirits of dead persons at their bedsides, mostly relatives and friends. Many of the spirits seen were of persons who, unknown to the patients, had recently died.

Are deathbed visions hallucinations caused by coma or delirium?

The most remarkable aspect of the Osis survey was that those who had the visions were calm and clear-headed at the time and were better educated as a group than terminal patients not having this experience.

What was the deathbed-vision case of Edith and Jennie?

This was reported by the Reverend Minot Savage in the early 1900s. Two eight-year-old girls, inseparable friends, became ill during an epidemic. Jennie died, but this fact was kept from Edith. As Edith lay dying, her eyes suddenly brightened and she said, "Papa, why did you not tell me that Jennie had gone? Here is Jennie, come to meet me."

How did an "apparition" with a scratch on her face give proof of survival?

In 1867 a girl of eighteen died suddenly. Her older brother, a traveling salesman, was away from home at the time and unaware of her death. In the middle of the day, while he was in his hotel room, he saw his dead sister sitting with one arm on the table, a bright red line on her face. When he returned home, he was told of the girl's death, and he described the apparition and the scratch. His mother said that as she was touching up the body in the casket, she accidentally scratched the girl's face. She had carefully covered the mark with powder and told no one about it.

Is collective viewing of a ghost or spirit good evidence of survival?

When one person sees an "apparition," it may be put down to imagination. When two or more see the same spirit at the same time, it is more impressive but could still be a "collective hallucination." There have been innumerable cases, however, when the same spirit was seen at different times by different persons who were unaware of each other's experience. In most of these cases, each person gave the same description of the appearance and behavior of the spirit.

In general, how does a spirit "prove" he has survived?

According to Dr. Gardner Murphy, past president of the American Society for Psychical Research, when a spirit contacts friends or relatives directly or through a medium, he gives evidence of his identity by (1) remembering the events of his physical life; (2) revealing a familiar "personality style"; and (3) indicating that he has a serious purpose in communicating. A fourth kind of evidence, of great importance to the living, is the spirit's continuing affection for them.

How can the living best get this kind of survival evidence?

Dr. Murphy believes we should find "powerful mediums" such as Leonora Piper and others of past generations, through whom the evidence can be established.

How did the "personality style" of spirits manifesting through Mrs. Piper impress William James?

In his book *William James on Psychical Research*, Gardner Murphy quotes James as saying there is "something about the style of personality modulation that properly carries its own conviction, as in our recognizing a voice over the telephone or in recognizing the style of a master in the arts when sheer analysis of content or structure must fail."

What was the "one white crow" statement James made about Mrs. Piper's spirit communications?

Although James never fully committed himself on the survival question, he was so impressed with Mrs. Piper's mediumship that he said: "If you wish to upset the law that all crows are black, you must not seek to show that no crows are; it is enough if you prove one single crow to be white. My own white crow is Mrs. Piper."

What does J. B. Rhine say about "manifest purpose" as evidence of survival?

In *New World of the Mind* Rhine mentions the Duke University collection of more than three thousand cases of alleged survival, of which about a hundred point strongly to the spirit hypothesis. "The type of case that arrests attention is one in which the *manifest purpose* [italics mine] back of the effect produced is so peculiarly that of a deceased personality that it is not reasonable to attribute it to any other source."

How did the "cross-correspondence" cases give evidence for survival?

In the early twentieth century, several "powerful mediums" received fragmentary messages which were difficult to decipher alone but when put together were clear references to passages in classical literature. Each fragment came through a different medium—Mrs. Verrall, Mrs. Holland, Mrs. Willett, and Mrs. Slater. Many of these messages appeared to come from the spirit of the classical scholar Frederic Myers, and they fitted all three of Dr. Murphy's criteria —retention of memories, personality style, and continuity of aim or purpose. Also, since there were only unintelligible fragments in the mind of each medium, the completed message apparently could not have come from the subliminal mind of any one medium.

What were the "book tests" for proof of survival?

These tests originated with the medium Mrs. Osborne Leonard. While Mrs. Leonard was in trance, the spirit would visit the home of someone in her circle and find a passage in a book that had never been seen by those present. Later the passage would be verified.

What was the "five-finger exercise" test for survival designed by a famous physicist?

Several years before Oliver Lodge died in 1940, he gave a packet of sealed envelopes to the Society for Psychical Research containing music notes of a five-finger exercise Lodge had been in the habit of practicing on tables and chairs. From 1946 until the envelopes were opened in 1954, the Society did 130 tests with various mediums to see if the correct message would come from Lodge's spirit. One of the mediums got a "clear impression of music . . . now I seem to be sitting

at a piano, seem to be going through all the five-finger exer-
cises. . . ." Another medium thought of Lodge "playing a
tune silently with his fingers," and mentioned the scale of C
Major, in which the notes were actually written. A third medium sang a passage of ten notes in C Major, while a fourth
said, "I want to put up my hand with five fingers."

What are the "pacts" in which two persons agree to communicate over the barrier when one of them dies?

There have been many such pacts. In the eighteenth century Lord Brougham and a fellow student at the University of
Edinburgh made a pact written in their own blood. Years
later, when Brougham was lying in his bath one evening, he
saw the spirit of his friend sitting in a nearby chair. Later he
heard that the friend had recently died in India.

What was the after-death pact between magician Harry Houdini and his wife?

Although Houdini made it his business to expose fake mediums when he was alive, he also arranged an intricate code
with his wife that would establish his identity after death if it
came through a medium. The coded message, a complicated
system of ten words leading through letters of the alphabet to
the words "Rosabelle Believe!"—was received after Houdini's
death by medium Arthur Ford. Mrs. Houdini signed a statement that the code had been broken and confirmed it in a letter to Walter Winchell: "I have gotten the message I have
been waiting for from my beloved." Later she repudiated her
statement. Arthur Ford and others believed she did so under
pressure from skeptical friends.

Did Bishop Pike survive bodily death?

In an interview with *Psychic* magazine (see Chapter 3)
Pike's widow, Diane Kennedy, said that a medium had received this evidential message from Pike's spirit: "Tell Diane
that about three days before we went out into the wilderness,
I had a very unusual headache." This statement was verified
by Mrs. Pike. (See also Mrs. Pike's vision of Pike's spirit leaving his body in Chapter 14.)

Do dreams ever give evidence of survival?

Yes, particularly when information in the dream turns out to be true. In one case the spirit of James Chaffin appeared to his son in a dream four years after his death and told him where to find a hidden will. There are many dreams in which spirits give directions for finding sums of money and valuable articles that are lost.

In what dream did an apparent suicide set the record straight?

A young man named Robert Mackenzie came in a dream to his employer and said that the dreamer would hear of his death but that he had not committed suicide as would be reported. The next day the employer was told about the suicide, but it was established later that Mackenzie had mistakenly drunk a bottle of nitric acid.

Whose spirit "told" Eileen Garrett why the dirigible R-101 crashed in 1930?

The spirit of the R-101's captain appeared later to Mrs. Garrett and described in technical terms unfamiliar to the medium exactly what had caused the accident. These details were verified later in an investigation of the crash.

When was the human soul weighed at death?

In 1906 a Massachusetts physician, Dr. Duncan MacDougall, built scales around the beds of dying patients. At death one body lost three-quarters of an ounce. In other cases the loss varied from less than an ounce to slightly over an ounce.

What does psychic photography prove about spirit survival?

Many photographers who are mediumistic sometimes get extra faces on their pictures that could have come from spirits who are present. Some of these have been taken in the séance room. (See Chapter 4.) Pictures have also been taken of astral bodies departing at time of death. Dr. Baraduc, a nineteenth-century photographer, claimed he had snapped a picture of his wife's spirit leaving her body at death. The problem of evidence involving any still or moving picture is that trick effects are easy to produce.

What is the attitude of a newly dead person toward the body he has left behind?

Indifference, sometimes outright repugnance. In most cases reported by mediums and others, the released spirit feels a sense of freedom and is happy to leave his body. (See Chapter 14.)

How does the "other world" appear to those who have died?

Chiang, the Chinese control of psychic Douglas Johnson, says: "In our world everyone perceives each other as solid as you do on earth. However, our bodies vibrate at a faster rate than yours, and therefore we are invisible to you. . . . There are whole ranges of color that are not existent in your spectrum. We also have things that you have, such as music and all the arts. The range of interest is vast."

Are spirits "all-seeing" and "all-knowing"?

There is no reason, according to Chiang, why a spirit should suddenly acquire knowledge and powers he did not have while still in the flesh. "I have been asked to explain nuclear physics, of which I know nothing, nor could I explain anything about your earthly stocks and shares. . . . No, there is work to do in other directions."

Why is ESP a stumbling block in proving survival?

Generally, in mediumistic séances or direct communication between spirits and the living, information revealed by the spirit of his life on earth is already known to the surviving friend or relative and could be transmitted from the latter's mind to the mind of the medium. In other instances, such as the Lodge "five-finger exercise" and the book tests, clairvoyance could be involved. The cross-correspondences seemed to furnish the best evidence for survival by giving only fragmentary information to each medium and by indicating a serious purpose and personality style on the part of the alleged communicator.

Do "proxy sittings" counter the ESP hypothesis?

In "proxy sittings" someone unfamiliar with the spirit

takes the place of the relative or friend at a séance, and the information that comes through must be verified later by the relative. However, the medium could still pick up this information from the mind of the relative, even though he or she is not present. There is more impressive evidence when communications from the deceased reveal facts known to no living person that are later verified, as in the case of the Chaffin will, but clairvoyance could still be the answer.

How do "linkage" experiments counter the ESP hypothesis?

Dr. Karlis Osis, who designed these tests, says that the object is to "put more minds" between the mediums and "the living source of information." In one test thirteen mediums and several experimenters took part in four countries—America, England, Germany, and Switzerland. The mediums attempted to communicate with a dead biologist and ask him questions about events known only to his widow, who was the "living source of information" several minds removed from the mediums. One of the mediums said correctly that the biologist had been a teacher at Stanford University. Another, who asked the alleged spirit what was the last thing he was doing when he died, said that he had been painting a portrait. Actually, he had been sculpturing a head.

What is the combination-lock test to prove survival?

This is probably the best test devised since the cross-correspondences to rule out the ESP hypothesis. Here is the test, designed by Dr. Ian Stevenson: A living person buys a certain kind of padlock which allows the combination to be changed, so that he is the only living individual who knows the new combination. He then works out a key sentence, with the first letter of each word represented by a number in the combination. During his lifetime he conducts several tests with mediums to see if through telepathy or clairvoyance they can find out the key phrase or sentence and the combination that goes with it. If they are unable to do so while he is living but break the code after his death, it would be a strong argument that he had communicated the key phrase and combination from the spirit world.

204 : : 17

Is the survival hypothesis weakened by the fact that spirits of living persons sometimes come through mediums?

Not necessarily. If the "second bodies" of living persons, as shown in OOB cases, can travel apart from their physical bodies (or even if just their thought processes are traveling), this would add strength to the case for survival. One such communicator, Gordon Davis, was surprised later to hear that he had spoken through a medium. However, he may have been dozing at the time or in another altered state conducive to psychic travel. One surprising aspect of the Davis communications is that much of the information given was of events that occurred later.

How does William James's "brain-mind" theory support the survival hypothesis?

In his book *Human Immortality* James suggested that the brain might be a transmitter of mental processes rather than their generator.

How does "field theory" support the idea of survival?

According to this theory, everything—including people, objects, and events—is part of a total space-time continuum and only gives the illusion of existing separately. The view of classical physics is that biological death means annihilation of the individual, but field theory, in the words of parapsychologist Lawrence LeShan, "leads to a conclusion of conscious, self-aware survival of biological death."

Are there organizations devoted to a serious study of survival?

All groups that study psychic phenomena, such as the British and American Societies for Psychical Research, devote a certain amount of time to the survival question. An organization formed specifically for this purpose is the Psychical Research Foundation in Durham, North Carolina, under the direction of parapsychologist William Roll.

Who was James Kidd and what was his connection with the survival question?

Kidd, a Colorado miner, left a fortune to any organization that promised to use the money for survival research. In a court case, the judge awarded the bequest to the Barrows Neurological Institute of Phoenix, Arizona, which does research on the nervous system. On appeal, the Arizona Supreme Court reversed the decision and directed that the money be given to the American Society for Psychical Research. Another appeal is pending.

Did prehistoric man believe in survival?

There is much evidence that he did. The practice was common of burying the dead with articles they might need in the next world. Fifty thousand years ago Neanderthal Man, the forerunner of modern man, buried his dead this way.

What percentage of today's population believes in survival?

It seems to vary with different countries and cultures. An international poll taken in 1959 showed that in six of nine countries, more than half the population believed in life after death—more older than younger persons. In a Gallup Poll taken in the United States in 1968, 73 per cent said they believed in survival. A 1970 Gallup Poll showed that 50 per cent of the world's political leaders are believers.

Are there scientific investigations today of reincarnation—the doctrine that human beings live more than one life in physical bodies?

Yes. The most thoroughly researched cases are those of Dr. Ian Stevenson of the University of Virginia, who has traveled throughout the world, studying such cases in India, Alaska, Ceylon, Brazil, Lebanon, and other countries.

What kinds of evidence support the reincarnation hypothesis?

Sometimes a person, especially a child, can give information about a previous life which can be verified by other persons still alive who knew the former personality. He may have scars and other physical marks known to have been on the body of the previous personality. He may have tastes in food and other likes and dislikes that can be traced to the former personality. When the two lives are far removed in time, his knowledge of the earlier period and personality may be verified through investigations. He may in certain circumstances (in trance or dreams, under anesthesia, etc.) speak a language, in some cases an ancient tongue, he had no opportunity to learn in his present life. And he may have an unusual musical or other ability that blossoms at an early age, almost as if it were there at birth.

What was the classic reincarnation case of Shanti Devi?

In 1930 a four-year-old girl named Kumari Shanti Devi, living in India, claimed that she had lived her previous life in Muttra, a town a hundred miles away. She accurately described the town and the people in it, although she had never been there, and gave details of her former life, including her husband's name. The husband, Kedar Nath, visited the little girl, who recognized him and revealed knowledge known only to Kedar, telling him that in her other life she had buried 100 rupees in a room in Kedar's house. Later Shanti was taken to Muttra and recognized many landmarks and people living there.

How do scars and other physical marks suggest reincarnation?

Dr. Stevenson and other researchers have studied many cases in which a person had birthmarks that could be traced to a physical body in a previous life. A Tlingit fisherman in Alaska said before dying that two moles on his body would be duplicated in his next incarnation. Nine months after his death, his daughter-in-law had a baby with identical marks. A boy born with a gash in his right side claimed that he had been killed by a spear in his previous life. This was confirmed by relatives, who said the boy's uncle had been killed by a spear in the same area of the body.

How do tastes in food give evidence of reincarnation?

Dr. Jamuna Prasad, Deputy Director of Education for Uttar Pradesh, India's largest state, reported that a man whose case he had studied remembered dying in a previous life by choking on milk curd. It had been his favorite food then, but in this life he disliked milk curd intensely. Friends of the man who had died verified the manner of death.

How does unusual talent in small children give evidence for reincarnation?

Geniuses such as Mozart seem to know their art without being taught and require very few lessons before they outdistance their teachers. Proponents of the reincarnation theory believe that for such persons a course in music, painting, mathematics, whatever the area of excellence, is merely a "brush-up" course to revive memories and talent from earlier lives.

What was the "King David" reincarnation case?

In the 1960s a three-year-old boy, son of an Israeli man, began to speak in the Hebrew of Biblical days, exhorting his men to follow him into battle. The boy also played the harp, as King David had done. A Hebrew scholar said that the child spoke the ancient tongue more fluently than any adult he had ever met.

According to reincarnation theory, why are friends and lovers drawn to each other?

They may have had intimate relationships in former lives. In her book *Many Lives, Many Loves,* Gina Cerminara writes: "Souls who were closely related in one lifetime tend to meet in other lifetimes. If the relationship was one of love, the love persists; if one of enmity, the enmity must be overcome; if one of obligation, the obligation must be paid." The members of a family often were in the same family in previous lives.

Does each person have the same sex through all incarnations?

Cerminara and other researchers believe that sometimes men come back as women and vice versa. Many persons spontaneously recall living as members of the opposite sex. One young girl remembered another life as a soldier. Men with pronounced feminine qualities and women with masculine tendencies may be merely expressing what they were in a previous life. Transsexuals—those whose sex is changed through an operation—claim that they were born in the wrong body and really belong to the other gender. Previous lives may supply the answer.

Do dreams give evidence for reincarnation?

Many persons claim that they have dreamed of scenes in former lives, but this is difficult to prove. More impressive was the dream of Señora Adela Samona, who lived on the island of Sicily. On March 15, 1910, her five-year-old girl, Alexandrina, died. Three days later Señora Samona dreamed that the dead girl appeared to her and promised that she would return to her mother as another child. Later the girl's spirit came through a medium and said she would be born again as one of twin girls. On November 10, Señora Samona gave birth to twins as predicted. One of the girls was exactly like the dead girl in appearance and personality. When she was a few years old, she remembered events in the life of the dead girl.

Does regression under hypnosis give evidence for former lives?

It may, although hypnotic subjects as a rule try to fulfill the expectations of the hypnotist and may be play-acting while in trance. A controversial case of this kind was the Bridey Murphy regression. During the 1950s a Denver businessman, Morey Bernstein, hypnotized a young woman, Mrs. Virginia Tighe, and regressed her to a period before her birth. Under hypnosis she spoke with an Irish accent and claimed that her name was Bridey Murphy and that she had lived in Ireland in the nineteenth century. Although critics traced her "memories" to her childhood in Chicago, a newspaperman who conducted an investigation in Ireland found that about 50 per cent of what "Bridey" said under hypnosis was accurate, although she could have had no access to this information.

What is "group" reincarnation?

According to Edgar Cayce's trance readings, many persons share experiences in several incarnations, even living in the same geographical area from life to life and belonging to the same national or religious group. Cayce believed that many inhabitants of the prehistoric land of Atlantis have been reincarnating in America during this century.

What was the case of the reincarnated Cathar?

The Cathars were a fourteenth-century sect in France which broke away from the Catholic Church. An English psychiatrist, Arthur Guirdham, had a patient who from the time she was a small child had dreams and psychic impressions of a former life as a Cathar. Everything she said was later investigated and verified by scholars.

Why are there so few alleged cases of reincarnation in the Western democracies?

Actually, as interest in psychic phenomena grows, more of these cases are coming to light in America, although still few in comparison with countries such as India, Ceylon, and Burma, or with cultures such as the Tlingit Indians of Alaska, where reincarnation is an accepted fact. Belief in reincarnation, like a belief in ESP and other aspects of the paranormal, is discouraged or nurtured by cultural attitudes. If a small child in India says he lived in another village in a former life, most of the time his statement is taken seriously because the Hindus believe in reincarnation. An American child would be told not to lie and would soon find out that such talk only gets him in trouble.

How long is the "waiting period" between incarnations?

According to one theory, the soul when released from a dead body immediately enters another embryo or infant body. Many of Dr. Stevenson's cases in India, Alaska, and other countries suggest that there is little or no time between death and rebirth. The waiting period seems to vary, however, from culture to culture. Cases such as "the girl with the blue eyes" investigated in Canada by Jess Stearn, indicate that a generation or more may elapse. In such cases the subject may remember details of an earlier life that are verified by persons still alive who knew the former personality. If a longer period is involved, facts may be uncovered through consulting books, records, etc., that match those known to the living personality. Some spirits encountered through mediums or automatic writing, such as Patience Worth, seem to have gone for hundreds of years without entering another body. Assuming that reincarnation is a fact, there doesn't seem to be any set rule about the in-between period.

Are there cases where the new or reincarnated body is born before the previous one dies?

Strangely enough, Dr. Stevenson found a few confusing cases of this kind in India. In one, the astral body of a man who died apparently entered a new physical body three days after birth. In a very weird case, a three-year-old child named Jasbir "died" from smallpox, then came back to life and insisted he was a man from another village who had just been killed in an accident. Jasbir said that "he" had been poisoned before the accident by someone who owed him money. Perhaps this was an example of possession rather than reincarnation.

What contemporary psychic claims she is 40,000 years old?

Joan Grant says that her memories take her back that far, through thirty-one lives. She has written about her former lives in *Far Memory* and other books.

What did Plotinus say about the ancient belief in reincarnation?

The Egyptian philosopher from the third century A.D. called it "a dogma recognized throughout antiquity. . . . The soul expiates its sins in the darkness of the infernal regions and . . . afterwards passes into new bodies, there to undergo new trials."

What medium didn't believe in reincarnation, but her control did?

When Eileen Garrett was not in trance, she was a skeptic about reincarnation. However, when Abdul Latif, one of her controls, came through, he emphatically expressed his belief in the doctrine.

What is the Law of Karma?

Karma is based on the principle that every action creates a positive or negative effect and that in future lives a person has the opportunity to build on his positive actions or work through his negative ones. Thus someone who is born blind or who suffers from a physical weakness may have brought these problems on himself by thoughtless behavior in another life.

What is Dr. Ian Stevenson's "evidence for survival and reincarnation" experiment?

Dr. Stevenson sends on request a "Form for Participation in Planned Evidence for Survival after Death," which would include information about your present life (memorable events, identifying physical and psychological data, etc.); plans for your next incarnation (what traits you would like to develop, which sex you prefer, etc.); plans for your providing evidence of survival through mediums or in other ways; and information to be filled in by relatives and friends after your death. The forms will go into a permanent file, and it is hoped that some of the registrants will remember in their next lives and will compare their new bodies and personalities with those on record. For further information write to:

Dr. Ian Stevenson
Division of Parapsychology,
Department of Psychiatry
University of Virginia School of Medicine
Charlottesville, Virginia 22901

How can the average person recall his past lives?

Most persons can't, although there are startling exceptions such as Shanti Devi and Joan Grant. It may be best to let past lives "bury their dead," but if you are curious, here are a few suggestions. One way is through meditation, but this is difficult and requires many hours of practice and self-discipline. Another is regression under hypnosis, although you may find that a good deal of fancy is mixed with fact. A third is to go to a good psychic or possibly visit two or three and compare notes. (Going to psychics too often is not recommended, as it may lead to instability.) Also, watch your dreams for unusually vivid scenes that may point to a former life. Another method is to concentrate on your special skills in this life and try mentally to trace them back to their development in other lives.

18
YOUR QUESTIONS ANSWERED ABOUT
PSYCHICS AND PSYCHIC PHENOMENA IN ANCIENT
TIMES: OLD AND NEW TESTAMENT PROPHETS, GREEK
ORACLES, ROMAN AUGURS, SEERS, SOOTHSAYERS,
DIVINERS, DREAM INTERPRETERS, NECROMANCERS,
WIZARDS, MAGICIANS, FORTUNETELLERS, SCRYERS,
ASTROLOGERS . . .

What kind of psychics were there in the ancient world?

The modern occult explosion is quite mild compared with the situation in ancient times. Seers, soothsayers, diviners, necromancers, etc., were busier than psychiatrists are today. Magic, astrology, scrying, and fortunetelling were all in vogue. Countries such as Greece and Rome even had psychics on their payrolls, but they outlawed the private practice of magic and particularly necromancy (calling up the dead).

Who was the most famous medium in the Old Testament?

The Witch of Endor. When Israel was threatened by the Philistines, the distracted King Saul went to the witch in disguise and asked her to call up the spirit of the recently deceased prophet Samuel. So angered was Samuel that he predicted the death of Saul and his sons in battle. The following day they were killed.

How did Moses feel about occult practices?

Moses frowned upon divination, magic, necromancy, and other such practices of the pagan countries. He sanctioned only revelations through dreams and visions that had a high moral and ethical purpose in showing the will of God to Israel and her people. The Lord said to Moses: "A man or a woman who is a medium or a wizard shall be put to death; they shall be stoned with stones, their blood shall be upon them." King Saul committed the worst possible sin when he visited the Witch of Endor.

212

What Biblical figure saw his future land in a dream?

In the eighteenth century B.C. Jacob dreamed that the Lord came to him and promised that he and his descendants would live in Palestine and eventually spread throughout the world.

Which captive Hebrews used dream interpretation to gain favor with kings and pharaohs?

The most famous ones were Joseph (about 1700 B.C.) in Egypt and Daniel (about 550 B.C.) during the Babylonian captivity.

How did Joseph interpret the figure 3 in the dreams of two Egyptian prisoners?

The Pharaoh's baker and butler had been jailed for a minor offense. The butler dreamed of a vine with three branches producing clusters of ripe grapes. The King's cup was in his hand, and he pressed the grapes into the cup and gave it to the Pharaoh. Joseph said that the butler would be released in three days and restored to his post. The baker dreamed that on his head were three baskets of food, which the birds ate. Joseph predicted death for the baker in three days. Three days later the butler was set free, but the baker was hanged from a tree.

How did Joseph interpret the number 7 in the Pharaoh's two dreams?

In the first dream seven fat cows were coming out of the Nile, followed by seven thin ones. The thin cows ate the fat ones. In the second dream there were seven ears of plump grain growing on one stalk; after them sprouted seven thin and blighted ears that swallowed up the plump ones. Joseph predicted that Egypt would enjoy seven prosperous years followed by seven years of famine. The grateful Pharaoh stored up grain during the seven good years and rewarded Joseph with a high position in his court.

How did Daniel interpret the writing that appeared on a wall in Babylon?

King Belshazzar may have been drunk when he saw the writing on the wall of his palace, but the words were plain enough: MENE MENE TEKEL UPHARSIN. Here is Daniel's interpretation: MENE—God hath numbered thy kingdom and finished it; TEKEL—thou art weighed in the balance and found wanting; UPHARSIN—thy kingdom is divided and given to the Medes and Persians. That night the King was slain, and Darius the Mede became ruler of Babylon.

What was the golden age of prophecy in Israel?

The prophets flourished when Israel was an independent nation, a few hundred years after the death of Joseph and up to about the time of Daniel, roughly from 1000 to 500 B.C. They included Samuel, Isaiah, Amos, Micah, Jeremiah, Elijah, Ezekiel, and several others.

What was the principal motivation of the prophets?

During the periods of captivity it was necessary that the Hebrew psychics and dream-interpreters placate foreign kings and win favors for their people, but when Israel was independent, the chief concern of the prophets was the fate of the nation. Following the moral tone set by Moses during the Exodus from Egypt, their prophecies were in the form of exhortations to follow the precepts of the Lord.

What prophet predicted a great military victory in 701 B.C.?

Actually, the victory was a moral rather than a military one. The prophet Isaiah promised that the Assyrians, who had the city of Jerusalem under siege, would leave and the nation would be saved.

Which prophets foresaw the Assyrian and Babylonian captivity?

Jeremiah, Amos, and Isaiah were three of the best-known. Amos said that "Jeroboam shall die by the sword, and Israel shall be led away captive out of his land." Isaiah also promised, however, that Israel's downfall would not be permanent and that the day would come when the children of Israel would be a force for good in the world: ". . . for out of Zion shall go forth the Law and the word of the Lord from Jerusalem."

Which prophet predicted the death of one whom he called a "false prophet"?

Jeremiah denounced Hananiah and predicted that he would die within the year, because Hananiah had said he would "break the yoke of Jeremiah." The Bible says that "Hananiah the prophet died the same year in the seventh month."

What prophet vanished while a crowd was watching him?

Fifty Talmudic students were on the other side of the Jordan River when Elijah disappeared in a chariot of fire. Unless it was a collective hallucination, it is one of the most striking cases of psychic phenomena in the Bible.

How did the prophets put themselves into the prophetic mood?

One way was to listen to music. Samuel and his fellow prophets marched in groups and chanted to the accompaniment of instruments. The Bible says: "Thou shalt meet a band of prophets coming down from the high places with a . . . harp, tambourine, flute, and lyre before them; and they will be prophesying."

Which prophet had an assistant who played music?

Elisha worked with a minstrel whose melodies brought him "the power of the Lord." The visions that came to Elisha and the other prophets were thus partly induced by an altered state of consciousness brought on by music.

In what ways were the Biblical prophets like modern psychics?

They had psychic experiences during altered states of consciousness. They had visions and dreamed dreams. They heard voices. They went into trance, induced by music and in a measure by the mystery of the desert through which they often traveled.

Which Hebrew prophet knew where Christ would be born?

In 700 B.C. Micah predicted that the Messiah would be born in Bethlehem. Later the second Isaiah prophesied that "a virgin shall conceive and bear a son, and shall call him Immanuel (God Be with Us)."

Did the prophetic tradition continue into the New Testament?

Yes. Paul admonished the Christians to "desire earnestly spiritual gifts, but rather that ye may prophesy." Paul himself had visions and dreams in the prophetic tradition and three times referred to his vision on the road to Damascus.

Which New Testament prophet foresaw a famine?

Agabus, the Christian prophet, came down from Jerusalem to Antioch during the reign of the Roman Emperor Claudius and predicted the famine of 44–45 A.D. Agabus also told Paul that he would be arrested in Jerusalem and turned over to the gentiles.

Who was the outstanding psychic in the Bible?

Jesus. The miracles spoken of in the Bible certainly come under the heading of psychic phenomena, particularly the miracle healings. (See Chapter 5.)

Who were the Greek oracles?

The oracles were young girls who were kept at shrines in ancient Greece to reveal the divine will through prophecy and clairvoyance. Generally their utterances were rather obscure but were interpreted by priests. Not only Greek officials but monarchs throughout the ancient world came to Delphi and other shrines to consult the oracles.

What kind of questions did the oracles answer?

Most of the Greek dignitaries asked questions about legislation, colonization, religious ordinances, and the outcomes of battles and wars. Some of the oracles, however, gave answers to personal questions.

How did an oracle's reference to "houses of wood" save Greece from invasion?

When Xerxes, the Persian leader, threatened Greece by land and sea in 480 B.C., a group of Greek leaders asked the oracle at Delphi what they should do. The oracle replied that the Greeks would find their salvation in "houses of wood" and added this two-line prophecy:

"Divine Salamis, you will bring death to women's sons
When the corn is scattered or the harvest gathered in."

The professional interpreters thought this meant that the Greeks would be defeated in a naval battle at Salamis, a seaport. But one of the leaders, Themistocles, pointed out that "houses of wood" meant ships and that the Greeks would win at sea. If Greece was fated to lose, he added, "hateful Salamis" would be more appropriate than "divine Salamis." Themistocles' advice was followed, and the Greeks won a great victory at Salamis.

Why did the oracles usually speak in riddles?

Plutarch, the Roman writer, explained that this was a necessary subterfuge to confuse Greece's enemies: "When kings and heads of state consulted the oracles on important affairs it might be dangerous to divulge, the replies were enigmatical; but when private individuals came to consult the oracles on their own affairs, they obtained direct replies in the most explicit language."

What Greek oracle was consulted on marriage problems?

The seat of the oldest known oracle was at Dodona. Each questioner had his query engraved on a lead tablet. In addition to advice about getting married or how to handle a wife, other questions of a personal nature dealt with lost objects, whether to go on a voyage, etc. One Lysanias wanted to know if he was the father of his wife's child.

Who was told by the oracle that he would die "in the sight of a wolf fighting a bull"?

Pyrrhus, a descendant of Alexander the First of Epirus, was given this prophecy by the oracle at Dodona. Later he went into the town of Argo and walked past a group of statuary depicting the wolf-bull contest. At that moment an old woman, whose son Pyhrrus had executed, threw a tile at his head and killed him.

Which oracle clairvoyantly "saw" a king making soup in his palace?

King Croesus of Lydia devised a test of the Delphic oracle's ability by sending messengers to ask her what he was doing at the time. She said correctly that he was boiling a tortoise and a lamb in a bronze caldron with a bronze lid.

Which Roman emperor was told by the Delphic oracle to "beware of seventy-three"?

Nero. The emperor thought it meant he would reign until he was seventy-three years old, but the oracle was referring to the age of his successor, Galba.

How did the Delphic oracle prepare for prophecy?

First she bathed in the springs, then inhaled the fumes of burnt laurel and myrrh, and took several drinks of cold water —thus putting herself into an altered state of consciousness. It was believed also that hallucinogenic fumes issued from a cleft in the ground under her feet.

How did the oracles differ in their style of prophecy?

The oracle at Delphi spoke after getting mental impressions. The oracle at Dodona watched for signs—which way a dove flew, the movement of a waterfall, the pitch and timbre of sounds such as the rustling of a sacred oak or the clash of a cymbal. The oracles at Herakles and Lake Avernus were probably mediums who went into trance to bring up the spirits of the dead.

What was the fundamental difference in "psychic style" between the Hebrew prophets and the Greek oracles?

The Biblical prophets also went into something like a trance state in order to hear the voice of God, but they disdained the elaborate preparations and formal ceremonies of some of the oracles, and the reliance on signs and omens of the others.

How did the Biblical prophets and the Greek oracles differ on the question of "fate"?

When an oracle predicted the future, it was irrevocable. The Hebrew prophets, on the other hand, gave their people a choice. If they sinned, however, the punishment of Jehovah could not be averted, as Jeremiah insisted—but redemption was always possible. "For if ye thoroughly amend your ways and your doings, if ye thoroughly execute judgments between man and his neighbor; if ye oppress not the stranger, the fatherless and the widow, and shed not innocent blood . . . then will I cause you to dwell in this place."

What is divination?

This was the common practice in the ancient world, condemned by the Hebrew prophets, of getting psychic information through omens. Looking into a crystal (scrying), holding a seashell to the ear, casting lots, studying the way a chicken accepted its food—these were a few methods of divination, but the list is endless. Diviners almost always used "props" (see Chapter 8), such as knucklebones in Africa and coconuts in Polynesia. The Mayans studied the back of a peccary for signs of the future, while the Etruscans looked at the entrails of a dead animal. The Arabs interpreted impressions in the sand, and the Romans watched the flight patterns of birds. Astrologers were also called diviners.

What two kinds of divination were widely practiced in the ancient world?

Cicero, the Roman statesman and orator, referred to the interpretation of signs and omens as *ars* and extended the meaning of divination to "agitation of the mind," the purely mental practice of the oracle at Delphi and the Biblical prophets.

Who were the "augurs"?

The augurs were the Roman equivalents of the Greek oracles and Hebrew prophets. Distinguished citizens such as Pliny the Elder and Cicero were appointed to an official college of divination as augurs. They watched for omens in the behavior of birds, such as the flight patterns of eagles and vultures or the cries of ravens, owls, and crows. The augur would then report either that "the birds allow it" or that the proposed action must be postponed for another day.

How did the flight of an eagle save a Roman ruler from death?

Cicero writes that King Deiotarus set out one day on a journey but returned home because the flight pattern of an eagle warned of trouble ahead. The room he would have been staying in collapsed the next night.

How did a dead pig foretell the fate of a Roman marriage?

In the practice of hepatoscopy, a method of divination the Romans borrowed from the Etruscans, an animal's intestines would be studied for good or bad omens. At a Roman wedding, the *auspex* would examine the entrails of a pig and announce whether or not the marriage would succeed.

Did the Romans visit fortunetellers?

The people of all nations seemed to have done so, either openly or in secret when fortunetelling was officially discouraged. The Roman writer Juvenal speaks bitterly of the shameless exploitation practiced by these unworthies, who always told their clients what they wanted to hear. For a lonely woman the fortuneteller would promise a "youthful lover" or an equally welcome "large bequest from a rich and childless man."

Where and when did the practice of astrology begin?

It started over five thousand years ago in Mesopotamia, where it was the official means of forecasting events. From Babylon and Assyria it spread to Egypt and Persia, and throughout the ancient world as far as India. At one time astrology was a branch of astronomy.

In what country were hallucinogenic drugs used to induce dreams and visions?

Egyptian psychics fasted, took drugs, and practiced a form of sensory deprivation by sitting in the dark for long periods of time—techniques used today by psychologists, parapsychologists, and dream researchers. Then they would sleep in the temple and hope for divine communication in their dreams.

How did the ancient Greeks diagnose illness through dreams?

The Greeks practiced "incubation": sick persons slept inside the temple of Asclepius, the Greek god of medicine, and on the following morning the priests would suggest cures based on the content of their dreams.

Who was the Edgar Cayce of the ancient world?

Claudius Galen, a Greek physician of about 200 A.D. There are similarities between Cayce and Galen and also differences. Cayce, ignorant of medicine and medical terms when conscious, while in trance could "see" a diseased organ in someone miles away and give bona fide prescriptions. Galen dreamed of remedies for disease that helped him cure his patients. Galen became a doctor after Asclepius appeared in a dream to his father with a message for him.

What Greek rebel dreamed of his imminent assassination?

Alcibiades, the dashing tyrant of fifth-century Greece (B.C.), dreamed that his enemies had cut off his head and burned his body. A few days later his house was set on fire, and as he ran out a swarm of arrows hit and killed him.

What was the dream of a beautiful woman that portended death for Socrates?

The Greek philosopher, while in jail, dreamed that the woman came to him and recited a verse from Homer: "Gladly on Phthia's shore the third day's dawn shall behold thee." Socrates knew from the dream that he would die in three days.

What dream told Cyrus how long he would rule Persia?

Cyrus dreamed that the sun was at his feet. Three times he tried to grasp it, and each time it turned away and finally disappeared. The Magi, wise men of Persia, explained that he would rule for three times ten, or thirty years. Cyrus was king of Persia from the age of forty to seventy.

Who dreamed that she would give birth to a lion?

Agariste, mother of Pericles, had this dream a few days

before he was born. Pericles later ruled during the golden age of Greece in the fifth century B.C. According to Plutarch, when Cicero was born, his nurse had a vision that foretold his deeds in later years.

What did Philip of Macedon dream just before the birth of Alexander the Great?

He dreamed he had sealed up his wife's womb. The soothsayer Aristander of Telmessus predicted that the child would have exceptional courage and determination.

How did Alexander the Great's dream of a satyr foreshadow a military victory?

After the city of Tyre in Persia had kept Alexander at bay for seven months, he dreamed that a satyr was playing near him but kept eluding his grasp. After circling the satyr many times in the dream, Alexander persuaded him to surrender. His dream-interpreters divided satyr into two words—*Sa Tyros*—which meant "Tyre is yours." Alexander then attacked the stubborn city with great fury and conquered it.

What kind of psychics were attached to the court of Alexander the Great?

Plutarch says there were "sacrificers, purifiers, and prognosticators" along with dream interpreters and soothsayers, who kept him keyed up and in an optimistic mood. Alexander's psychics knew all the tricks of their trade that were part of divination practice in the ancient world.

19 YOUR QUESTIONS ANSWERED ABOUT
WITCHES PAST AND PRESENT AND THEIR
CEREMONIALS; THE HISTORY AND PRACTICE OF
WITCHCRAFT; SATAN-WORSHIP, THE DEVIL'S MARK,
THE EVIL EYE, THE "FAMILIAR"; THE SABBAT AND
ESBAT, BLACK AND WHITE MAGIC, THE COVEN,
THE MAGIC CIRCLE; OTHER CUSTOMS OF WITCHES
AND WARLOCKS . . .

What is a witch?

A witch (from the Anglo-Saxon *wicca*) was traditionally a female who practiced magic and sorcery and was in league with the Devil. According to popular belief, she was an old, ugly woman who used her unnatural powers to help her friends and hurt her enemies, met with other witches in secret to practice magic rituals, and carried on an unholy alliance with Satan and his demons. The concept of a witch has changed somewhat today. Those who join witch cults come from all classes of society and all age groups, consider themselves members of a religion, and are for the most part out in the open.

How did witchcraft begin?

Its origins are lost in antiquity, but it has common roots with religion in the practice of magic extending back to prehistoric times. Its proponents claim that it is the oldest religion, beginning with fertility rites and the worship of nature gods in agricultural societies. With the rise of early Christianity and other religions, witchcraft became associated with devil-worship and demonology.

How widespread is the practice of witchcraft?

Witchcraft in its "magic" aspect has been practiced in every country and every culture. Sorcerers, wizards, medicine men, temple priestesses, members of mystery cults in ancient Greece and other countries—all have been closely related to witches and their craft. Voodoo in Africa and kahuna in the Pacific islands are allied to witchcraft. Witches and sorcerers were tolerated up to a point in most societies but severely dealt with in Palestine and banished from ancient Rome. When heresy, or devil-worship, was added to the sin of wizardry, the frenzy against witches reached a peak during the Middle Ages in Europe, and thousands were hanged or burned to death.

What is a warlock?

In the United States and England a warlock is the male equivalent of a witch, but in many other countries, such as Nigeria, a witch can be male or female.

Why are most witches women?

The battle of the sexes may be responsible. Primitive man had a deep-seated fear and awe of women based on the mystery of their menstrual period and ability to have babies. The earliest myth is that of the Great Mother and her influence on the growth of crops. Women in certain African tribes reinforced this fear by forming secret societies from which men were excluded. The belief that women were in league with the dark powers found expression in the early Christian attitude that they were lustful, carnal creatures. So if women didn't first have the idea of becoming witches, men may have forced them into witchcraft. Women enjoy power as witches that is denied them in other religions.

Must a witch always be old and ugly?

Not always. During the most intense witch-hunting period in history, many young girls in Germany were burned or hanged as witches. The term "witch" has been extended to include beautiful girls, since they are sent by the Devil to torment men. Visitors to modern covens report that witches are getting younger and prettier all the time.

According to legend, who was the first witch?

Lilith, Adam's first wife, and she was a mean one, too. Before Adam came to his senses and took the more gentle Eve

as his second wife, the ferocious Lilith mothered hosts of demons. Later she was known as the "night visitor" and a saying arose that it was "indiscreet" for one to sleep in a house
as the sole occupant, for "Lilith will seize him." Other famous
witches or sorceresses were Circe and Medea of Greek
mythology.

What is a witches' coven?

It is the basic unit of witch cults. According to tradition,
it was composed of twelve witches and a leader who took the
name of Satan.

What are "esbats" and "sabbats"?

Traditionally the local covens met once a week for an
"esbat," but four times a year the members of the covens of a
district met for a special "sabbat." There was also a Great
Sabbat every seven years. Some authorities believe that the
esbat and sabbat were not adopted by the witches until the
sixteenth century, after the concept was dreamed up by their
persecutors.

What happened (and may still happen) at the sabbat?

When the witches had gathered, they paid homage to
their presiding "devil" and novices were initiated with the
"devil's mark." After a banquet, there was wild dancing that
ended in sexual orgies. The "Devil," often disguised as a goat,
took a leading part in the ceremonies with his "demons."
Many of today's witches claim that this is a distorted version
of their ceremonies that has come down from the Middle
Ages.

What was the "devil's mark"?

The presiding "devil" at an esbat or sabbat put his special
brand on the body of a novice witch. During the witch-hunting hysteria of the Middle Ages, any blemish on the skin—a
mole, wen, scar, bunion, etc.—was regarded by the authorities as a devil's mark, and the alleged witch was put to death.
Sometimes, when there was no visible mark, the inquisitors
would find an "invisible" one by jabbing their victim with
needles.

What was a "familiar"?

When a witch was initiated, the devil gave her an inferior demon who assisted her in her malevolent acts. The demon took the form of a domestic animal such as a cat or dog. Sometimes the "familiar" was a rabbit, hare, even a toad, bee, or mouse.

What is lycanthropy?

The ability to change into a wolf and back again. Many witches, believing that the Devil gave them this power, got down on all fours and howled. More serious were gruesome murders attributed to witches or warlocks who thought they were wolves. One such werewolf confessed in 1573 that he had torn a young girl to pieces and eaten her flesh.

Why did (or do) witches meet at night?

Secret societies, such as the ancient mystery cults, usually chose the night as a propitious time for their ceremonies. The witches were also "night people," ostensibly meeting in dark places and "riding" on their brooms in the light of the moon.

Did witches actually fly on broomsticks?

There were many ways for a witch to convince herself that she was flying. One was to rub a special ointment over her body, made of such ingredients as poplar leaves and hemlock mixed with soot. Drugs also helped give the illusion of flying. A forerunner of this belief may have been an early European fertility rite of "riding a broom." Many fear-ridden accusers of witches also must have had hallucinations.

What is the "magic circle"?

The circle, nine feet in diameter, is a symbolic device to protect those who enter it and to give more power to the rituals that take place in it. The circle also is a connecting symbol between this world and the next and enables the witch to commune with spirits. In ancient Assyria the circle warded off evil spirits. In India the circle was drawn to ease childbirth. It is an integral part of modern witch ceremonials.

What was a "grimoire"?

It was a magician's manual, with detailed instructions in the magician's and witch's art, including chants and rituals.

What are black and white magic?

The nice witch practices white magic, the bad witch, black. The evil witch uses charms, amulets, effigies, etc., to harm her neighbors and other innocent persons. White witches use their powers for good—to cure disease, make crops grow, reunite lovers, etc.

Have government and church authorities favored white witches over black?

No. Any kind of magic that seemed to derive from occult powers, such as the necromancy practiced by the Witch of Endor in the Old Testament, was discouraged and often severely punished, even if the purpose was a good one. In some countries, one of them Rome, official magic or divination in the service of the state was approved, but magicians who practiced in private were suspect.

In English law, what was the "maleficium"?

This was the essential element in black witchcraft—"the working of harm to bodies and goods of one's neighbors by means of evil spirits and of strange powers derived from intercourse with such spirits."

How did (or do) witches "hex" their enemies?

The "hex" has been used in nearly all cultures, primitive or sophisticated, as a form of black magic. An image of the enemy is molded in wax or other pliable substances; his name is scratched on it; then it is pricked with a sharp point or melted over heat while an incantation is uttered. The old-style witch claimed she could ruin crops, cause lightning and thunder, even poison children this way. "Murder by effigy" was forbidden in Anglo-Saxon law. The reader is urged to refrain from this practice, as the "hex" may turn back on him.

What is the difference between a spell and a charm?

A spell is written or spoken; a charm is an object or mixture of ingredients. Both are used in black and white magic. A spell often sounds like gibberish, but it apparently has a mystic meaning for modern witches.

What is the "evil eye"?

Throughout history this has been one of the most formidable weapons of witches and others in league with the powers of darkness. If one was born with an evil eye, he could bewitch others, kill with a baleful glance, control demons, cause disease and madness, etc. One of the most potent pair of evil eyes in history belonged to Grigori Rasputin, who fascinated the Czar and Czarina of Russia and almost everyone else who caught his glance.

What was a witch midwife?

She was an actual midwife who assisted in the birth of children to witches. As they were born, she dedicated them to Satan.

When did Satan-worship actually begin?

There is a difference of opinion. The witches claim that they have worshiped him since prehistoric times and point out that in caves dating back 30,000 years there are paintings and carvings of horned creatures. In Greek mythology there are also horned creatures such as the satyrs, and the early Christians had visions of a devil with horns. Satan as the adversary of Jehovah is mentioned in the Book of Job. Some authorities contend that Satan worship didn't enter the picture until the Christians first began to persecute witches for heresy, with the first official recognition of the Devil by the Council of Toledo in 447 A.D. The polarity of good and evil, however, has always been with us. In ancient Persia the Manichean cult was based on the belief that there are two such opposing forces in perpetual conflict. Gnostics in ancient times also believed in the "evil principle" and often were drawn more to the power of Satan than to God. The Church had to fight the fascination of many priests and even popes with the idea of Satan.

Are Satan and the Anti-Christ related?

If not the same, they are bosom companions. The concept

of the Anti-Christ arose in the Bible, which predicted that he would arrive one day to undo the good works of the Lord. For two thousand years religionists have been watching for the Anti-Christ and thought many times that he had finally been born. According to Anglo-Saxon belief, the Anti-Christ would bring wizards and sorcerers with him. Insofar as witches were working with Satan and therefore with the Anti-Christ, they were considered the enemies of God and the Church.

How long have demons been with us?

They are probably as old as Satan himself. There were demons in ancient Assyria and Greece and a cult of demonology in the Old Testament that was taken over by the Christians. The Hebrew Talmud paid its respects to demonology and at one point computed the probable number of demons in existence—7,405,926.

How did St. Augustine (354–430 A.D.) fight demons?

He outlawed them. The following is from his *De Doctrina Christiana:* "St. Augustine condemns consultations and certain pacts arranged with demons—operations of the magic arts."

What Christian bishop was put to death for practicing magic?

In 385 A.D. Priscillian was executed at Treves. Priscillian denied Christ and favored the "evil principle." It was the first time such severe punishment had been meted out for heresy.

What was the Black Mass?

The Church alleged that witches mocked the Christian ceremony in their rituals. The crucifix was placed upside down, the Lord's Prayer chanted backwards, the sign of the cross made in the wrong direction, black candles were burned, etc. Some researchers claim that the Black Mass was invented by witch-hunters, but there is evidence that Catherine de Medici, wife of King Henry II of France, practiced the Black Mass and that a Black Mass was performed during the reign of Louis XIV. Many priests were executed for performing this sacrilegious act, and several were implicated in a Satanic conspiracy in seventeenth-century France. The Black Mass is part of the ritual in many American and British witch cults today, but it may be a "put-on."

When did the infamous witch-hunting period begin?

When the Church thought that witchcraft was a deliberate attempt to worship Satan and downgrade God, a frenzy of witch-hunting started in Great Britain and continental Europe in the fifteenth century and continued into the sixteenth and seventeenth centuries. The hysteria spread to Puritan New England and resulted in the Salem, Massachusetts, witch trials.

Which pope launched the witch-hunts?

In 1484 Pope Innocent VIII issued a papal bull denouncing witchcraft as heresy and accusing men and women in northern Germany of consorting with "devils, incubi and succubi, and by their incantations spells, conjurations, and other accursed charms and crafts, enormities and horrid offenses, have slain infants yet in their mother's womb as also the offspring of cattle. . . ." Further bulls were issued in the fifteenth and sixteenth centuries, calling for severe punishment for alleged witches.

What was the "bible" of the witch-hunters?

In 1486 two Dominican monks, Jacobus Sprenger and Heinrich Kramer, published the *Malleus Maleficarum*, describing in detail the pact with the Devil, the sabbat, and other witch practices, and giving the procedure for catching witches and bringing them to trial. The authors described eighteen techniques used by witches and spoke of a powerful class of witches who "raise hailstorms and hurtful tempests and lightnings; cause sterility in men and animals; offer to devils, or otherwise kill, the children whom they do not devour." One of the chapter headings is "How, as it were, they deprive man of his virile member."

What was a "witch-finder"?

Matthew Hopkins created this job for himself during the seventeenth-century witch-hunts in England. Together with other witch-finders, he was responsible for the trial and execution of hundreds of alleged witches.

Who was tried for spoiling a glass of beer?

Almost any accusation of "witch" made during the hysteria in Great Britain and the continent would result in trial and death. In one case a woman was accused of making a man's beer turn sour when she stood in an open window and stroked her cat.

Did many witches "confess" during the trials?

Yes, but in most cases they did so only after being tortured. The Scots exacted confessions by flogging, making the accused sleep naked on cold stones, crushing her fingers in a vise, pulling out her fingernails with pincers, and other such practices.

Did many witches confess who were not accused?

Yes, and we may find the explanation in depth psychology. Many self-confessed witches were motivated by masochism or guilt feelings, perhaps wanting to be punished for real or fancied sins. In one case a woman dreamed that she had murdered a child and when she found that the child had actually died during the night, she gave herself up. Other "witches" also dreamed that they had performed evil acts and promptly turned themselves in.

Were all the witches innocent of wrong-doing?

Probably not, although this is the contention of many researchers. Many women (and men) probably did think they were practicing black or white magic, and it may have worked, particularly if their victims also believed in it. The history of both psychology and psychic phenomena indicates that the power to influence mind and matter is a very real one. However, there is little doubt that the hysteria of the times resulted in death and torture to thousands of both practicing witches and others who were unjustly accused.

Was religious zeal the only reason for the witch trials?

No. Money was the motive in at least one case. In the fourteenth century King Philip of France coveted the wealth of an order of warrior monks, the Knights Templar. He had members of the order arrested in 1307 and forced them to confess that they had worshiped the Devil in the form of a black cat. The order was dissolved and its money went into the King's treasury. The fact that a witch's property could be confiscated was the motive for many accusations.

What part did children play in the Salem trials?

When the witch-hunting hysteria spread from England to the United States, the trials in Massachusetts were marked by the same fanaticism, cruelty, and wholesale "confessions." In the Salem trials most of the accusers were young children and teen-agers, whose fantasies were accepted without question by the courts.

Who was the dog condemned as a witch?

The identity of the animal is unknown. The dog was tried in a Salem courtroom and hanged for its sins.

How did ghosts and spirits influence the Salem trials?

In the modern era, many persons who had readings from Edgar Cayce were told that they had lived in Salem in a previous incarnation during the witch-hunting era. Cayce said that the accused witches were in communication with spirits, an offense as serious in Puritan days as it was when Saul sneaked off to see the Witch of Endor. There are many accounts of ghost visitations written by such seventeenth-century writers as Cotton Mather and Richard Baxter.

When did witch-hunting officially end in England?

In 1736 witchcraft was removed from the list of felonies.

How many alleged witches were killed during the sixteenth and seventeenth centuries?

From 200,000 to 1 million were brought to trial, condemned, and burned or hanged. It has been estimated that the total number of witches put to death in Europe during the last 2000 years is 9 million.

When did the modern witchcraft movement begin?

After a rather quiescent eighteenth and nineteenth century, there has been a strong upsurge since the founding of the Golden Dawn in 1888. A member of this order, Aleister Crowley, was probably the leading practitioner of black magic in the twentieth century. It was said that the Black Mass was performed at his funeral in 1947.

What is the status of witchcraft today?

In the 1960s and 1970s witchcraft has resurfaced as a religion or psuedo-religion in America and England and in various forms throughout the world. According to a recent estimate, there are close to 2000 members of witch cults in England and 60,000 in the United States.

Is devil-worship practiced today?

Yes. The "pact with Satan" aspect of witchcraft seems to be a vital element in modern covens, although most witches claim that, as a religion in its own right, it does not conflict with Christianity and other sects. In San Francisco the First Satanic Church of the United States sings the praises of the Devil and performs the Black Mass. Some witch cults show the influence of Women's Lib. Our Lady of Endor Coven claims Lilith as its spiritual mother. An organization called W.I.T.C.H.—Woman's International Terrorist Corps from Hell—is presided over by a female deity.

Do the Satanists practice black or white magic?

Although many of the organized groups follow the alleged medieval custom of burlesquing the Christian religion, they claim that their ritual magic is of the helpful "white" variety —bringing lovers together, improving one's financial position, etc. However, there has been evidence of "black magic" in England, where graves have been opened and desecrated, churches robbed of holy water and sacramental wines, etc. Black magic of a milder variety was practiced by three women students at the University of Chicago, who put the hex on their sociology professor by chanting "Fie on thee, Morris Janowitz! A hex on thy strategy!" There is no evidence that the professor was adversely affected by this incantation.

Are most witches today from the younger-generation drug culture?

No. Witchcraft attracts members of every social and economic group—college students, professional men and women, housewives, the wealthy, and the poor. Students are flocking to courses in witchcraft offered in high schools and universities. One coven of witches was found on the campus of a Catholic university. There are also many privately taught courses on how to become a witch. Shelves in bookstores are lined with books on witchcraft, and stores do a big business in witch toys for children.

Why has there been a revival of witchcraft?

The "evil principle" in man, recognized from prehistoric times and dramatized in the Bible, is never far away. The rise of science and rationality, particularly in Western countries, pushed the dark side of man out of sight for a time, but it has now surfaced with a vengeance, and witchcraft is one expression of it. For the most part, the rituals in modern witch covens—nudity, chanting, etc.—may act as a safety valve for what Jung called the "shadow side." But ritual murders, such as those by members of the Manson cult, as well as other acts of violence here and in England, suggest that the dark forces of the unconscious, whether stirred up in witchcraft or other occult practices, may spill over into criminal acts.

20

YOUR QUESTIONS ANSWERED ABOUT
WELL-KNOWN MEN AND WOMEN THROUGHOUT HISTORY
WHO HAVE ACCEPTED THE PARANORMAL OR WHO
HAVE INVESTIGATED OR WERE SYMPATHETIC TO
THE INVESTIGATION OF TELEPATHY, CLAIRVOYANCE,
PRECOGNITION, ASTRAL PROJECTION, SURVIVAL,
REINCARNATION AND OTHER ASPECTS OF
THE PSYCHIC . . .

Which kings and emperors employed court prophets?

From ancient times through the Middle Ages and close to the present day, professional seers have been attached to royal courts. One example is Alexander the Great (see Chapter 18). Another is Ivan the Terrible of Russia, who once asked his court prophet when he would die. The clever seer replied that both he and the King would die on the same day, thus insuring his own safety while the king lived. Nostradamus was called in many times by Catherine de Medici and her husband, King Henry II of France, to make predictions. When Catherine asked him what the fate of her three sons would be, he thought to himself, "Two will die but one will rule." But he told Catherine truthfully that each would occupy a throne. Her oldest son, Francis II, died soon after inheriting the crown from his father. The next son, Charles IX, ruled for only a short time, dying at the age of twenty-four. The third son, King Henry III, ruled for fifteen years.

What Roman emperor was told he would die "in the fifth hour"?

Domitian, who was Emperor of Rome in the first century A.D., had been warned since he was a young man that he would die "in the fifth hour" of September 18, 96 A.D. As the day approached, Domitian took every precaution, even having his secretary executed to prevent a possible plot against

235

his life. When September 18 arrived, the Emperor posted guards around his bedchamber and refused to leave until he was told that the "fifth hour" had come and gone. But when he went into the bathroom to bathe, a conspirator entered and stabbed him to death. Actually, the conspirators had lied to him—it was still the "fifth hour" when he was killed.

Which king started a war because of a dream?

Xerxes' invasion of Greece in 480 B.C. was inspired by a dream (see Chapter 18). The Persian leader had been debating whether to go to war, but his uncle, Artabanus, had persuaded him to abandon the idea. One night he dreamed that a tall man appeared at his bedside and told him that he should go through with his plans. When Xerxes woke up, he put the dream out of his mind, but the next night the same figure returned, reminding him that he was the son of the great Darius, and warned that he would lose his power if he did not undertake the war. The worried Xerxes asked Artabanus to sleep in the royal bed and see if the same dream figure would return with the same message. The ghostly figure appeared to Artabanus and threatened to burn out his eyes with hot irons. The terrified Artabanus awoke with a yell and ran to Xerxes, telling him that the war must be undertaken. Whatever the source of the dream was, Xerxes went to war and was eventually routed by the Greeks.

Did Napoleon believe in psychic phenomena?

There is impressive evidence that he believed in ghosts and spirits. While in exile on St. Helena, he once told General de Montholon, who was also in captivity, that the ghost of Josephine had visited him and that they would be together again after his death. Napoleon's mother, Madame Bonaparte, was visited by a strange man on the day of her son's death, and she was convinced that it was the spirit of Napoleon himself.

Which three kings saw the same ghosts in Sweden?

King Haakon of Norway, King Frederick of Denmark, and King Gustav of Sweden all saw the ghosts said to haunt the royal palace at Stockholm.

What famous queen saw her own astral body?

Catherine the Great of Russia was proceeding into the throne room of her palace one day when, to her amazement, she saw a ghostly queen, her exact counterpart, being seated by ghostly attendants who looked exactly like the members of her retinue. She ordered her guards to fire upon the astral queen, who disappeared along with the other shadowy figures.

What twentieth-century Russian dictator had an astrologer on his payroll?

Surprisingly, there were at least two Soviet leaders with a superstitious bent. Stalin had his own astrologer, Yuri Yamakhin, who was later put into an official suite by Khrushchev. Another psychic, Wolf Messing, was used by Stalin as an entertainer (see Chapter 11). In 1943 Messing predicted before a theater audience that World War II would end in May 1945, probably in the first week. Actually, Hitler committed suicide on April 30, 1945, and the Russian army marched into Berlin as predicted. (See Chapter 3.)

What twentieth-century German dictator had a stable of prophets?

None other than Adolf Hitler. The job of his astrologers was to predict a Nazi victory in World War II, and when they saw otherwise, they were sent to concentration camps. Hitler himself went to a palm-reader in 1932, Dr. Joseph Renald, who predicted a violent end for him.

What famous American statesman of revolutionary days believed in reincarnation?

Benjamin Franklin. When he was a very young man Franklin wrote his own epitaph:

THE BODY OF B. FRANKLIN,

PRINTER,

LIKE THE COVER OF AN OLD BOOK,

ITS CONTENTS TORN OUT

AND

STRIPPED OF ITS LETTERING AND GILDING,

LIES HERE

FOOD FOR WORMS
BUT THE WORK SHALL NOT BE LOST
FOR IT WILL AS HE BELIEVED
APPEAR ONCE MORE
IN A NEW AND MORE ELEGANT EDITION
REVISED AND CORRECTED
BY THE AUTHOR.

Franklin added this passage: "Finding myself to exist in the world, I believe I shall, in some shape or other, always exist; and, with all the inconveniences human life is liable to, I shall not object to a new edition of mine, hoping, however, that the *errata* of the last may be corrected."

Did Abraham Lincoln believe in survival?

There is good evidence that he did. Although he joked quite a bit during the séances that were held in the White House, he seemed to believe that the phenomena were genuine. More to the point is that he once told an aide that he was certain he would see his dead son Willie again.

Which First Ladies saw the ghost of Abraham Lincoln?

Mrs. Coolidge was one. Another was Eleanor Roosevelt, who said she often sensed the presence of Lincoln in her White House sitting room, which had been his bedroom when he was President.

Did Franklin Roosevelt believe in psychic phenomena?

He evidently believed in psychics. Six months before his death, he sent for Jeane Dixon and asked her to read his future. She correctly told him that he had six months to live.

Did President Truman believe in ghosts?

It is not certain whether he believed in them, but in his book *Mr. President* he wrote that the White House maids and butlers claimed they saw the ghost of Lincoln many times.

Did President Kennedy have a premonition of his own death?

Yes. His White House physician, Dr. Janet Travell, tells in her book *Office Hours: Day and Night* of many occasions when Kennedy sensed he would be killed. He seemed concerned about the twenty-year cycle of Presidential deaths:

every President elected in a year ending in "0"—starting with William Henry Harrison in 1840—died while serving his term.

What is the official attitude of Congress toward psychic phenomena?

There is no official attitude, but many members of both the Senate and the House of Representatives make off-the-record visits to psychics and mediums. The late Mendel Rivers had readings with the trance-medium Arthur Ford, while Senator McClellan of Arkansas was present at a séance in 1962 when Ford had a vision of Kennedy's assassination. Even the *Congressional Record,* however, accepted an article in its November 17, 1971, issue inserted by Representative Claude Pepper of Florida and written by Stanley R. Dean, asking for a task force of psychiatrists to investigate the paranormal.

Which British Prime Minister was president of the Society for Psychical Research?

Lord Balfour. An even more famous Prime Minister, William Gladstone, not only was an honorary member of the SPR but had sittings with the English medium William Eglinton. Gladstone once stated: "Psychical research is the most important work that is being done in the world—by far the most important."

Did writer Ralph Waldo Emerson believe in survival of the soul?

Emerson wrote: "Nothing is dead; men feign themselves dead, and endure mock funerals and mournful obituaries, and there they stand, looking out of the window, sound and well, in some strange new disguise . . ."

What contemporary of Emerson's believed in reincarnation?

The writer of *Walden,* Henry David Thoreau, was closely attuned to nature but also admired Hindu philosophy and suggested strongly in his writings that he believed in survival and reincarnation: "In the Hindu scripture the idea of man is quite illimitable and sublime. There is nowhere a loftier conception of his destiny. . . . It is impossible to tell when the divine agency and its composition ceased, and the human began. . . ." Thoreau also wrote: "It is unavoidable, the idea of transmigration; not merely a fancy of the poets, but an instinct of the race."

What famous American writer saw a ghost in the library?

Nathaniel Hawthorne spent part of each day in the reading room of the Athenaeum, a library in Boston. A Unitarian minister, the Reverend Dr. Harris, also came to the Athenaeum each day to read. One day Hawthorne heard that the Reverend Dr. Harris had died, but the next morning the minister was sitting in his favorite chair, reading the Boston *Post* —at least Hawthorne saw him there. Although presumably dead and buried, each day for quite a while thereafter Dr. Harris would be in his accustomed place. One day he pushed back his spectacles and stared at Hawthorne, who wondered whether he should speak to the ghost but decided not to. After that he never saw the ghost of Dr. Harris again.

What famous German writer saw his friend's astral body?

Goethe once saw the "second body" of his friend Frederick, who was asleep at the time. Goethe also had a precognitive experience: he saw himself on horseback, wearing a strange garment, a vision that came true eight years later.

What famous Greek philosopher called divination "an innate faculty of the soul"?

Surprisingly, it was Aristotle, who was usually very hardheaded about the occult practices of his time and skeptical of dream interpretation.

What Greek philosopher had a "guardian spirit"?

Socrates had a "daemon" who kept advising him what to do and also could predict the future. Socrates described his daemon as "a divine and spiritual influence. . . . This began with me from childhood, being a kind of voice, which, when present, always diverts me from what I am about to do. . . ."

What did Plato think of psychic phenomena?

Plato, one of history's great minds and a philosopher who has profoundly influenced our thinking, was a firm believer in all aspects of the psychic, particularly precognition in dreams and visions. He accepted survival and reincarnation and thought that a newborn baby's mind was full of scenes from his past lives. Plato was a mystic in the sense of believing that everything in the physical universe is the reflection of an enduring idea.

Did the philosopher Kant believe in survival?

Kant said that "if we should see things and ourselves as they are, we should see ourselves in a world of spiritual natures, with which our entire real relation neither began at birth nor ends with the body's death."

What German philosopher known for his pessimism admitted seeing ghosts?

Schopenhauer. Once, on a visit to Frankfort-am-Main, he had "a very clear vision of some spirits. They were, so I think, my ancestors: they announced that I would survive my mother, who was still alive then. My father, who was dead, was carrying a candle." Another comment of Schopenhauer's suggested a belief in reincarnation: "When we die, we throw off our personality like a worn-out garment, and rejoice because we are about to receive a new and better one. . . ."

What seventeenth-century scientist investigated poltergeists?

Robert Boyle, who formulated Boyle's Law and had a strong influence on modern chemistry. Boyle concluded that the poltergeists were genuine spirit phenomena. Father Herbert Thurston, a Jesuit priest, did extensive research into Boyle's investigations.

What famous seventeenth-century scientist wrote about the Biblical prophets?

Sir Isaac Newton. Newton's interest in prophecy and predictions extended to a belief in astrology. He is best known for his discovery of the law of gravitation. When he saw the apple drop, Newton wrote, a "mysterious voice" whispered in his ear: "The apple and the moon are doing the same thing."

What famous nineteenth-century naturalist was also a spiritualist?

Alfred Russel Wallace, co-discoverer with Darwin of the principles of evolution. Wallace, who believed in survival of the soul, often went to court as a witness for mediums accused of fraud.

What early twentieth-century physiologist investigated mediums?

There were more than one, but the best known is Charles Richet, a Nobel Prize winner. (See Chapter 16.) Richet, who studied and wrote on all aspects of the psychic, once stated: "There are some puzzling cases [of mediums] that tend to make one admit the survival of human personality."

What did Julian Huxley say about psychic phenomena?

The grandson of Thomas Huxley, and one of the world's leading biologists, said: "We must follow up all clues to the existence of untapped possibilities like extrasensory perception. This may prove to be as important as the once unsuspected electrical possibilities of matter."

What distinguished marine biologist was president of the British Society for Psychical Research?

Sir Alister Hardy, who is now making a serious study of religious attitudes in his "Religious Experience Research Unit" at Oxford University. Hardy is quoted as saying that "if only one per cent of the money spent upon the physical and biological sciences could be spent upon the investigation of religious experience and psychical research, it might not be long before a new age of faith dawned upon the world."

What astronomers of the early twentieth century investigated psychic phenomena?

Camille Flammarion, who collected hundreds of cases of ghosts and spirits, was one. Another was Schiaparelli, who attended the séances of Eusapia Palladino and believed she was a genuine medium. Simon Newcomb was president of the American Society for Psychical Research.

What British physicist believed he had communicated with the spirit of his dead son?

Sir Oliver Lodge, whose son Raymond died in World War I, claimed contact through several mediums, particularly Gladys Osborne Leonard. (See Chapter 17.) Lodge's belief in survival antedated the death of his son, however, and he was a lifelong student of the psychic. Lodge was one of the earliest parapsychologists and did ESP tests with drawings in the 1880s.

What physicist investigated dowsing and crystal-gazing?

Sir William Barrett, one of the outstanding early members of the British Society for Psychical Research, did extensive research in dowsing, crystal-gazing, automatic writing, and other psychic phenomena, and wrote several books on these subjects. (See Chapter 9.)

Did Einstein believe in extrasensory perception?

He didn't actually make investigations or conduct experiments as many of his fellow physicists did, but he was very sympathetic to the possibility of ESP. Einstein wrote an introduction to Upton Sinclair's book *Mental Radio* (see Chapter 2) in which he asked science to take the subject seriously.

What statement by Sir Arthur Eddington has profound implications for the reality of psychokinesis?

Eddington, one of the twentieth century's outstanding physicists, said: "I believe that the mind has the power to affect groups of atoms and even tamper with the odds of atomic behavior, and that even the course of the world is not predetermined by physical laws but may be altered by the uncaused volition of human beings."

What did a distinguished Yale University physicist say about laboratory experiments in ESP?

Dr. Henry Margenau, who has lectured for the American Society for Psychical Research, believes that parapsychologists as a group are as careful and objective in their experiments as those in any scientific discipline.

What Russian astrophysicist believes in precognition?

Nikolai Kozyrev has formulated a theory about the nature of time that would have implications for both telepathy and the ability to see the future. He believes that time is a form of energy that is "thin" near the sender of psychic messages and more "dense" around the receiver.

What famous inventor belonged to the Theosophical Society?

Thomas Alva Edison, inventor of the phonograph, motion-picture camera, electric light and numerous other boons to mankind. At the time of his death Edison had been building a machine for possible communication with spirits of the departed. Dr. Miller Hutchinson, Edison's assistant, wrote: "Edison and I are convinced that in the fields of psychic research will yet be discovered facts that will prove of greater significance to the thinking of the human race than all the inventions we have ever made in the field of electricity."

Did Sigmund Freud believe in ESP?

Freud, who was a member of the British Society for Psychical Research, said in the twilight of his career: "If I had my life to live over again, I should devote myself to psychical research rather than psychoanalysis." Freud, who took note of several examples of extrasensory perception in his practice, theorized that the psychic sense was acute in primitive animals before the physical senses were well developed.

Do business executives believe in ESP?

They are probably the most ESP-prone of all groups. (See Chapter 3 for a discussion of Douglas Dean's computer tests for precognition in executives.) Henry Clews, who turned down an offer to be United States Secretary of the Treasury, said that his success on Wall Street was due to "inspiration" and "mysterious forebodings." J. P. Morgan, the banker, consulted astrologers. The famous speculator Jesse Livermore relied on hunches. One day in 1906 he went to Wall Street to buy a block of Union Pacific stock, which had been shooting up, but something told him to sell rather than buy. He kept selling for the next few days. Then word came of the San Francisco earthquake, and the stock plummeted.

Do astronauts believe in psychic phenomena?

Many astronauts and NASA technicians belong to Spiritual Frontiers Fellowship, a nationwide church-oriented group that studies the paranormal. Wernher von Braun, a rocket expert and a major figure in the space program, has said, "Everything science has taught me strengthens my belief in the continuity of our spiritual existence after death." The astronaut with the keenest interest in parapsychology is Captain Edgar Mitchell, who conducted ESP tests during the space flight of Apollo 14. Just before the launching of Apollo 14, a *New York Times* news item (February 1, 1971) said of Mitchell: "It is . . . his nature to wonder and ponder over things that he, and other men, cannot understand. Commander Mitchell is fascinated . . . by the phenomenon of extrasensory perception."

Are government attitudes toward ESP research changing?

It appears that they are. The Russian government seems to support the work of its scientists in parapsychology, and Bulgaria has an official seer. Dr. Rhine disclosed recently that some time ago he received grants from the United States government to test the possibility that dogs use ESP to locate land mines. The results were positive and the findings, after being classified for twenty years, were published in the *Journal of Parapsychology*. Ten years ago an Army medical research unit studied other Rhine experiments at Duke University. Although the government doesn't advertise its interest in ESP, it appears that such investigations have been quietly going on for a long time.

What outstanding woman anthropologist helped an organization of parapsychologists to achieve status in the scientific community?

In December 1969, as a result of Margaret Mead's speech to the American Association for the Advancement of Science, membership was granted to the Parapsychological Association, an international group of professional parapsychologists.

Bibliography

BOOKS

Aymar, Gordon C. *Bird Flight*. New York: Dodd, Mead, 1935.

Baring-Gould, Sabine. *Curious Myths of the Middle Ages*. 1884. Reprint. New York: Gordon Press.

Bernstein, Morey. *The Search for Bridey Murphy*. Rev. ed. New York: Doubleday, 1965.

Besterman, Theodore. *Crystal Gazing*. London: Rider, 1924.

Bird, James Malcolm. *"Margery" the Medium*. Boston: Small, Maynard, 1925.

Bond, Frederick Bligh. *The Hill of Vision*. London: Marshall Jones, 1919.

Boss, Medard. *The Analysis of Dreams*. London: Rider, 1957.

Brown, Raymond Lamont. *A Book of Witchcraft*. New York: Taplinger, 1971.

Buttrick, George A., ed. *The Interpreter's Dictionary of the Bible*. 4 vols. Nashville: Abingdon, 1962.

Cameron, Verne L. *Aquavideo: Locating Underground Water, A Complete Dowsing Method by the World Renowned Master*. Elsinor, Calif.: El Cariso Publications, 1970.

Carcopino, Jerome. *Daily Life in Ancient Rome: The People and the City at the Height of the Empire*. Edited by Henry T. Rowell. Translated by E. O. Lorimer. New Haven: Yale University Press, 1940.

Cerminara. Gina. *Many Lives, Many Loves*. New York: Morrow, 1963.

———. *Many Mansions*. New York: Morrow, 1963.

Conan Doyle, Arthur. *Edge of the Unknown*. 1930. Reprint. New York: Berkeley Publishers, 1968.

Cottrell, John. *Anatomy of an Assassination: The Murder of Abraham Lincoln*. New York: Funk and Wagnalls, 1966.

Craig, Thurlow. *Animal Affinities with Man*. London: Country Life Limited, 1966.

Cranston, Ruth. *The Miracle of Lourdes*. New York: McGraw-Hill, 1955.

Crookall, Robert. *More Astral Projections*. Hackensack, N.J.: Wehman, 1961.

———. *The Study and Practice of Astral Projection*. Hackensack, N.J.: Wehman, 1961.

Crookall, Robert. *The Techniques of Astral Projection.* Hackensack, N.J.: Wehman, 1964.

Crow, W. B. *History of Magic, Witchcraft, and Occultism.* Hackensack, N.J.: Wehman.

Defoe, Daniel. *History and Reality of Apparitions.* London: J. Roberts, 1727.

De Vesme, Caesar. *Peoples of Antiquity.* London: Rider, 1931.

Douglas, Mary, ed. *Witchcraft, Confessions and Accusations.* New York: Barnes and Noble, 1970.

Dunne, J. W. *An Experiment with Time.* 1927. Reprint. New York: Hillary House, 1958.

Ebon, Martin, ed. *The Psychic Reader.* 1969. Reprint. New York: New American Library, 1970.

———. *Witchcraft Today.* New York: New American Library, 1963.

Eddy, Sherwood. *You Will Survive After Death.* New York: Holt, Rinehart and Winston, 1950.

Eisenbud, Jule. *The World of Ted Serios.* 1967. Reprint. New York: Pocket Books, 1969.

Eliade, Mircea. *Myths, Dreams, and Mysteries: The Encounter between Contemporary Faiths and Arabic Realities.* Harper Torchbooks. New York: Harper & Row, 1957.

Flaceliere, Robert. *Greek Oracles.* New York: Norton, 1965.

Flammarion, Camille. *Death and Its Mystery.* New York: The Century Company, 1921–23.

Fodor, Nandor. *Encyclopedia of Psychic Science.* New Hyde Park, N.Y.: University Books, 1966.

Ford, Arthur A. (with Marguerite Harmon Bro). *Nothing So Strange.* 1958. Reprint. New York: Paperback Library, 1971.

Forman, Henry James. *The Story of Prophecy.* New York: Tudor Publishing Company, 1940.

Fuller, John G. *The Great Soul Trial.* New York: Macmillan, 1969.

Gaddis, Margaret and Vincent. *The Strange World of Animals and Pets.* 1970. Reprint. New York: Pocket Books, 1971.

Gardner, Jeanne, and Moore, Beatrice. *A Grain of Mustard.* New York: Trident, 1969.

Garrett, Eileen. *Adventures in the Supernormal.* New York: Garrett-Helix, 1949.

Greenhouse, Herbert B. *In Defense of Ghosts.* Essandess Special Editions. New York: Simon and Schuster, 1970.

———. *Premonitions: A Leap into the Future.* New York: Geis, 1971.

Griffen, Donald R. *Bird Migration.* New York: Doubleday, 1964.

Guirdham, Arthur. *The Cathars and Reincarnation.* London: Neville Spearman, 1970.

Gurney, Edmund. *Phantasms of the Living.* 2 vols. 1886. Reprint. Gainesville, Fla.: Scholar's Facsimiles & Reprints, 1970.

Hardy, Alister. *The Living Stream: Evolution and Man.* New York: Harper & Row, 1965.

Haynes, Renee. *The Hidden Springs*. Old Greenwich, Conn.: Devin-Adair, 1961.

Head, Joseph, and Cranston, S. L. *Reincarnation in World Thought*. New York: Julian, 1968.

Heywood, Rosalind. *The Infinite Hive*. London: Pan Books, 1964.

Hill, Brian, ed. *Such Stuff as Dreams*. London: Rupert Hart-Davis, 1967.

Hill, J. Arthur. *Man Is a Spirit*. London: Cassell, 1918.

Hillman, William. *Mr. President*. New York: Farrar, Straus, 1952.

Holms, A. C. *The Facts of Psychic Science*. London: Kegan Paul, Trench, Trubner and Company, 1925.

Hutton, J. Bernard. *Healing Hands*. New York: McKay, 1967.

James, William. *Human Immortality*. Boston: Houghton Mifflin, 1898.

Johnson, R. C. *The Imprisoned Splendour*. New York: Harper & Bros., 1953.

———. *Psychical Research*. London: The English Universities Press, 1955.

Jung, Carl G., and Pauli, W. *The Interpretation of Nature and the Psyche*. Bollingen Series, vol. 51. Princeton: Princeton University Press, 1955.

King, Francis. *Ritual Magic in England*. Hackensack, N.J.: Wehman, 1970.

Kittredge, George Lyman. *Witchcraft in Old and New England*. 1929. Reprint. New York: Atheneum, 1972.

Knight, David C., ed. *The ESP Reader*. New York: Grosset and Dunlap, 1970.

Litvag, Irving. *Singer in the Shadows*. New York: Macmillan, 1972.

Loehr, Franklin. *Power of Prayer over Plants*. New York: New American Library, 1969.

Logan, Daniel. *The Reluctant Prophet*. New York: Doubleday, 1968.

Medhurst, R. G., ed. *Crookes and the Spirit World: A Collection of Writings by or Concerning the Work of Sir William Crookes, O.M., F.R.S., in the Field of Psychical Research*. New York: Taplinger, 1972.

Moberly, Anne, and Jourdain, Eleanor. *An Adventure*. London: Macmillan, 1911.

Monroe, Robert A. *Journeys Out of the Body*. New York: Doubleday, 1971.

Muldoon, Sylvan J., and Carrington, Hereward. *Projection of the Astral Body*. New York: Weiser, 1970.

Murphy, Gardner. *Challenge of Psychical Research: A Primer of Parapsychology*. New York: Harper & Bros., 1961.

———, and Ballou, Robert, eds. *William James on Psychical Research*. 1960. Reprint. Clifton, N.J.: Augustus Kelley, 1970.

Myers, F. W. H. *Essays Classical and Modern*. London: Macmillan, 1921.

———. *Human Personality and Its Survival of Bodily Death*. London: Longmans, Green, 1903.

Nichols, Beverley. *Powers That Be*. New York: St. Martin's, 1966.

O'Donnell, Elliott. *Animal Ghosts: or, Animal Hauntings and the Hereafter*. 1913. Reprint. Ann Arbor: Finch Press.

Ostrander, Sheila, and Schroeder, Lynn. *Psychic Discoveries Behind the Iron Curtain*. Englewood Cliffs, N.J.: Prentice-Hall, 1970.

Owen, Robert Dale. *Footfalls on the Boundary of Time*. Philadelphia: Lippincott, 1860.

Parke, H. W. *The Oracles of Zeus: Dodona, Olympia, Ammon*. Cambridge, Mass.: Harvard University Press, 1967.

Peck, Harry T., ed. *Harper's Dictionary of Classical Literature and Antiquities*. New York: Cooper Square, 1965.

Pollack, Jack Harrison. *Croiset the Clairvoyant*. New York: Doubleday, 1964.

Prince, Walter F. *The Case of Patience Worth*. Boston: Boston Society for Psychical Research, 1927.

———. *Noted Witnesses for Psychic Occurrences*. 1928. Reprint. New York: Olympia, 1972.

Rhine, J. B., ed. *Progress in Parapsychology*. Durham, N.C.: Parapsychology Press, 1971.

Rhine, Louisa E. *Hidden Channels of the Mind*. New York: Apollo Editions, 1966.

———. *Mind over Matter: The Story of PK*. New York: Macmillan, 1970.

———. *New Frontiers of the Mind: The Story of the Duke Experiments*. 1937. Reprint. Westport, Conn.: Greenwood Press.

Richet, Charles. *Thirty Years of Psychical Research*. New York: Macmillan, 1923.

Robbins, Russell Hope. *Encyclopedia of Witchcraft and Demonology*. New York: Crown, 1959.

Robertson, Morgan. *The Wreck of the Titan, or Futility*. 1912. Reprint. Freeport, N.Y.: Books for Libraries, 1970.

Schmeidler, G. R., and McConnell, R. A. *ESP and Personality Patterns*. New Haven: Yale University Press, 1958.

Schwarz, Berthold Eric. *Parent-Child Telepathy: A Study of the Telepathy of Everyday Life*. New York: Garrett Publications, 1971.

Selous, Edmund. *Thought Transference (or What?) in Birds*. London: Richard R. Smith, 1931.

Seith, Ronald. *Witches and Their Craft*. New York: Taplinger, 1967.

Sinclair, Upton. *Mental Radio*. 2d rev. ed. Springfield, Ill.: Charles C. Thomas, 1962.

Smith, Susy. *Enigma of Out-of-Body Travel*. New York: Garrett-Helix, 1965.

———. *Today's Witches*. Englewood Cliffs, N.J.: Prentice-Hall, 1970.

Spragett, Allen. *The Unexplained*. New York: New American Library, 1967.

Stearn, Jess. *The Search for the Girl with the Blue Eyes*. New York: Doubleday, 1968.

Stevens, William Oliver. *Unbidden Guests.* New York: Dodd, Mead, 1945.

Stevenson, Ian. *Twenty Cases Suggestive of Reincarnation.* New York: American Society for Psychical Research, 1966.

Sugrue, Thomas. *There Is a River.* New York: Henry Holt, 1942.

Thurston, Herbert, S. J. *Ghosts and Poltergeists.* Chicago: Regnery, 1954.

Travell, Janet. *Office Hours: Day and Night.* 1968. Reprint. New York: New American Library, 1971.

Van Paassen, Pierre. *Days of Our Years.* New York: Dial, 1940.

Vetter, George B. *Magic and Religion.* New York: Philosophical Library, 1958.

Wedeck, Harry E. *A Treasury of Witchcraft.* New York: Citadel, 1966.

Westwood, Horace. *There Is a Psychic World.* New York: Crown, 1949.

White, Stewart Edward. *The Betty Book: Excursions into the World of Other Consciousness.* New York: Dutton, 1937.

———. *The Unobstructed Universe.* New York: Dutton, 1940.

Wickwar, J. W. *Witchcraft and the Black Art: A Book Dealing with the Psychology and Folklore of the Witches.* 1925. Reprint. Detroit: Gale, 1971.

Woods, Ralph L., ed. *The World of Dreams.* New York: Random House, 1947.

Yost, Caspar S. *Patience Worth: A Psychic Mystery.* New York: Henry Holt, 1916.

Zotos, Stephanos. *Greeks: The Dilemma of Past and Present.* New York: Funk and Wagnalls, 1964.

JOURNALS AND PERIODICALS

Key to Abbreviations

JASPR—*Journal of the American Society for Psychical Research*
PFN—*Parapsychology Foundation Newsletter*
PR—*Parapsychology Review*

Anderson, Margaret. "The Use of Testing for Extrasensory Perception." JASPR 60 (April, 1966): 150–163.

"Case for Post-Mortem Survival, The." PR 1 (May–June, 1970): 14.

Cerminara, Gina. "The Soul-Searching Trial in Phoenix." *Psychic* 3 (August, 1971): 40–44.

Congressional Record 117, no. 176 (November 17, 1971), p. 1.

Dommeyer, Frederick C., and White, Rhea. "Psychical Research in Colleges and Universities." Reprinted from the JASPR January, April, and July 1963 and April 1964.

"Dowsing Televised." PFN 15 (May–June, 1968): 5.

Eisenbud, Jule. "Mental Suggestion at a Distance." *Psychic* 4 (February, 1971): 18–21.

"Evidence of Underlying Perception Found in Organic Life." PFN 16 (January–February, 1969): 5.

"Faith, Hands." *Time,* October 16, 1972, p. 73.

Grad, Bernard. "The 'Laying on of Hands': Implications for Psychotherapy, Gentling, and the Placebo Effect." JASPR 61 (October, 1967): 286–302.

"Hypnosis, Psi and the Dream Lab." PFN 16 (July–August, 1969): 11.

"Interview: Diane Kennedy (Pike)." *Psychic* 3 (August, 1971): 4.

"Interview: Douglas Johnson." *Psychic* 2 (February, 1971): 5.

"Interview: Thelma S. Moss." *Psychic* 2 (August, 1970): 4.

Kamiya, Joseph. "Conscious Control of Brain Waves." *Psychology Today,* April 1968, pp. 57–61.

Krippner, Stanley. "Experimentally-Induced Telepathic Effects in Hypnosis and Non-Hypnosis Groups." JASPR 62 (October, 1968): 387–397.

———, Ullman, Montague, and Honorton, Charles. "A Precognitive Dream Study with a Single Subject." JASPR 65 (April, 1971): 192–203.

LeShan, Lawrence L. "The Vanished Man: A Psychometry Experiment with Mrs. Eileen J. Garrett." JASPR 62 (January, 1968): 46–62.

Murphy, Gardner. "Body-Mind Theory as a Factor Guiding Survival Research." JASPR 59 (1965): 148–155.

———. "Trends in the Study of Extrasensory Perception." *American Psychologist* 13 (1958): 69–76.

"OOBE in South Africa." PFN 16 (July–August, 1969): 20.

Osis, Karlis. "Linkage Experiments with Mediums." JASPR 60 (April, 1966): 91–120.

Ostrander, Sheila, and Schroeder, Lynn. "Psychic Enigmas and Energies in the U.S.S.R." *Psychic* 2 (June, 1971): 9.

"Padlock Test Conducted: Clairvoyance or Survival?" PFN 16 (July–August, 1969): 18.

Pahnke, Walter N. "The Use of Psychedelic Drugs in Parapsychological Research." PR 2 (July–August, 1971): 5.

"Participation in Planned Evidence of Survival after Death." *American Society for Psychical Research Newsletter,* Summer 1971, p. 3.

Rhine, J. B., and L. E. "Investigation of a 'Mind-Reading' Horse." *Journal of Abnormal and Social Psychology* 23 (1929): 449–466.

———. "Second Report on Lady, the 'Mind-Reading' Horse." *Journal of Abnormal and Social Psychology* 24 (1929–30): 287–292.

Richmond, Nigel. "Two Series of PK Tests on Paramecia (Single-Celled Organisms)." *Journal of the (British) Society for Psychical Research* no. 669 (March–April, 1952), p. 577.

Roberts, Gilda H. "Water Witching—Responsible?" *Product Engineering,* February 15, 1971, p. 72.

Roll, W. G. "The Newark Disturbances." JASPR 63 (October, 1968): 123–174.

———. "Pagenstecher's Contribution to Parapsychology." JASPR 61 (October, 1967): 219–239.

Roll, W. G., and Pratt, J. G. "An ESP Test with Aluminum Targets."
JASPR 62 (October, 1968): 381–386.

St. Clair, David. "Spiritism in Brazil." *Psychic* 2 (December, 1970):
8–14.

Schmidt, Helmut. "PK Experiments with Animals as Subjects." *Journal
of Parapsychology* 34 (1970): 255–261.

Sidgwick's Committee, Professor H. "Report on the Census of Hallucinations." *Proceedings of the Society for Psychical Research* 10
(1894): 25–422.

"Significant Results in Enzyme Activity from Healer's Hands." PFN 16
(January–February, 1969): 5.

Tart, Charles T. "A Psychophysiological Study of Out-of-the-Body Experiences in a Selected Subject." JASPR 62 (January, 1968): 3–23.

"Those Vital Enzymes." PR 2 (July–August, 1971): 12.

Tietze, Thomas R. "Science Officially Meets Psi." *Psychic* 2 (June,
1971): 18.

———. "Some Perspectives on Survival." *Psychic* 3 (August, 1971):
40–44.

Vaughan, Alan. "Development of the Psychic." *Psychic* 2 (August,
1970): 40–46.

Von Klinckowstroem, Count Carl. "The Problem of the Divining Rod."
Scientific American, November 1933, pp. 218–219.

Walther, Gerda. "Hitler's Black Magicians." *Tomorrow* 4 (1956): 7–23.